PRAISE FOR
STRATEGIC SUPPLY CHAIN MANAGEMENT

"Following on from their groundbreaking first edition, the authors provide further evidence of the critical role of supply chain management in creating competitive advantage. Managers facing the challenge of coping with increasing levels of complexity in global supply chains will find valuable guidance in this revised work."
—Martin Christopher, Emeritus Professor of Marketing and Logistics, Cranfield School of Business, Cranfield University

"Offering practical insights relevant to all members of the management team, this book illustrates how companies can use their demand chains to become market leaders. I recommend it highly."
—Takafumi Asano, Senior Vice President, and President, Eisai Demand Chain Systems, Eisai Co. Ltd.

"This is not another one of those books that are heavy on theory but light on practical advice. Filled with examples of companies from a wide range of industries and geographical regions, it provides guidance that is clear and easy to understand."
—Greg Clapp, SVP, Operations, Fujitsu

"*Strategic Supply Chain Management, Second Edition,* is a great refresher for senior executives seeking to update their knowledge of modern supply chain management. It's equally useful for those new to the subject, who need to understand how top global supply chains work."
—Bill Black, Group SVP for Quality and Operational Excellence, ABB

"This book has it all—innovative content, compelling data, and accounts of top global companies that have made their supply chains potent strategic assets. It should be on all senior executives' reading lists."
—Robert Keels, Director of Manufacturer Services
Development, Alliance Healthcare

"Theory can take you only so far. This book goes the distance, with practice, advice, and concrete examples that illustrate how top companies use their supply chains for a competitive edge—not only what makes for a robust supply chain strategy, but also how to put that strategy into practice."
—Abe Eshkenazi, CEO, APICS,
The Association for Operations Management

"This essential read presents a practical account of how to get the most out of your supply chain. It should be required reading for the senior management team."
—Bill Muir, Chief Operating Officer, Jabil

"Concise and cogent, *Strategic Supply Chain Management, Second Edition,* lays out the key components for top supply chain performance and backs up these insights with new benchmarking research. Managers across the organization will find answers to their supply chain questions here."
—Paul Bischler, Vice President and Controller,
Burlington Northern Santa Fe Railway

STRATEGIC SUPPLY CHAIN MANAGEMENT

STRATEGIC SUPPLY CHAIN MANAGEMENT

SECOND EDITION

THE FIVE DISCIPLINES FOR TOP PERFORMANCE

SHOSHANAH COHEN &
JOSEPH ROUSSEL

Mc
Graw
Hill
Education

New York   Chicago   San Francisco   Lisbon   London
Madrid   Mexico City   New Delhi   San Juan
Seoul   Singapore   Sydney   Toronto

1 2 3 4 5 6 7 8 9 0   DOC/DOC   1 9 8 7 6 5 4 3

ISBN   978-1-265-79862-8
MHID   1-26-579862-1

e-ISBN   978-0-07-181309-8
e-MHID   0-07-181309-9

Library of Congress Cataloging-in-Publication Data

Cohen, Shoshanah.
  Strategic supply chain management / by Shoshanah Cohen and Joseph Roussel. —Second Edition.
    pages cm
  Includes bibliographical references.
  ISBN-13: 978-1-265-79862-8
  ISBN-10: 1-26-579862-1
  1. Business logistics.   I. Roussel, Joseph, 1962-   II. Title.
  HD38.5.C64   2013
  658.7—dc23   2013006373

Shoshanah Cohen:

To Collin for his unfailing support,
and to Meredie and Riley for their unbounded spirit.

Joseph Roussel:

To Jana, Robert, and Claire, for their encouragement,
and to my mother, Alma, for her inspiration.

CONTENTS

CHAPTER THREE

SUPPLY CHAIN MANAGEMENT PROFILE

CHAPTER FOUR

SUPPLY CHAIN MANAGEMENT PROFILE

CHAPTER FIVE

SUPPLY CHAIN MANAGEMENT PROFILE

CHAPTER SIX

PREFACE

When the first edition of *Strategic Supply Chain Management* was published, in 2005, we were convinced that the supply chain provides a vital source of competitive differentiation. Although it goes without saying that the goods and services that people want are prerequisites to a company's success, a well-managed supply chain is a major contributor to profitable growth. Research conducted by PwC's Performance Measurement Group (PMG) for the second edition backs up this premise, demonstrating that superior supply chain performance is directly correlated with superior financial performance.

The supply chain's strategic value has only grown since we published the first edition, as the business landscape has become more challenging. Economic instability, marked by decreased access to working capital and volatile energy prices, has become a constant. Competition for natural resources has intensified. The playing field has gotten more crowded with the entry on the global scene of companies from less-developed economies. The rise in labor costs has forced companies to rethink long-held assumptions concerning their global footprint. Natural disasters are occurring more frequently. A stronger focus on sustainability and corporate social responsibility has posed other challenges. These trends have conspired to make global supply chains more critical to success but also more vulnerable to disruption.

As a result, companies worldwide have changed their thinking about the supply chain. Not only have they increasingly made the supply chain a management priority, they've changed the way they use it to drive business success. These developments have made familiarity with the supply chain critical for people who work in the supply chain organization as well as for executives across the enterprise.

Which brings us to a much-discussed question: What exactly is a supply chain? We define it as a core enterprise process that encompasses all the activities—that is, all the physical, informational, and financial flows—required to produce and deliver goods and services. It also involves interactions with consumers, trade customers, and multiple tiers of suppliers.

The second edition provides the reader with an overview of the basic principles of supply chain management as well as the innovative practices that supply chain managers are following today. Each of the first five chapters addresses one of five core disciplines: supply chain strategy, process architecture, organization, collaboration, and performance measurement and management.

1. View your supply chain as a strategic asset

5. Use metrics to drive supply chain performance

2. Develop an end-to-end process architecture

4. Build the right collaborative model

3. Design your organization for performance

Chapter Six summarizes cross-industry benchmarking analysis by PMG and provides insight into the practices that characterize companies with top-performing supply chains. This includes the key Plan, Source, Make, and Deliver practices they have honed as well as the ways they manage supply chain complexity to their advantage.

Chapter Seven addresses the challenge of how to marshal the core disciplines to make the supply chain a greater strategic asset. The discussion offers new thinking on successful supply chain transformation, with a focus on today's large, geographically distributed organizations. Like the chapters on the disciplines, it is grounded in real-life company examples.

There is probably no better way to demonstrate superior supply chain management than with an in-depth profile of a company. We are privileged to include profiles of six companies that are all leaders in their industries: BASF, Essilor, Haier, Kaiser Permanente, Lenovo, and Schlumberger. These profiles illustrate how each company uses its supply chain strategy, and the supporting core disciplines, to execute its business strategy.

We wrote the second edition with various kinds of readers in mind: supply chain operations professionals who are looking for insights into practices that can make a difference, managers in functions outside of the supply chain who are interested in getting a better view of how these functions affect supply chain performance, senior executives who are seeking a better understanding of the importance of the supply chain for the management agenda, and students of business who are eager to supplement their knowledge of how companies operate. Whichever category you fit into, we hope you will find the book useful and thought-provoking.

So, step back from the daily grind and start reading. Maybe you will gain a new perspective. Perhaps you will find inspiration in other companies' successes. You may even want to chart a whole new course. Whatever the outcome, you'll have a better understanding of your supply chain's strategic potential.

ACKNOWLEDGMENTS

From start to finish, the work—research, writing, editing, and design—that transformed the first edition of *Strategic Supply Chain Management* into this second edition took less than a year. This time frame and the fact that a considerable amount of the content is new attest to the intensity of the effort, not only by the core development team but also by the many individuals and organizations that provided unflagging support worldwide.

The book in its entirety would not have been possible without the guiding hand of executive editor Julia Heskel, who managed all aspects of content development and ensured adherence to exacting standards. Julia oversaw a team of writers, copy editors, and graphic designers. Moreover, she conducted many of the interviews for the company profiles and wrote much of the profile content. Based in Boston, she worked on a daily basis with both authors, one based in California and the other in France—no small feat!

One of the key strengths of the book is the quantitative analysis and benchmarking provided by PwC's Performance Measurement Group (PMG). Kara Kardon led this effort. She developed the content for Chapter 6, providing critical thought leadership in the form of quantitative research on supply chain performance, practices, and complexity. PMG analyst Alma Arrayales worked many hours to glean insights from raw data; her effort helped us throughout the book.

Special thanks are due to Susan Campbell from PwC's graphic-design department for her superb work in transforming our scribbles into the book's insightful illustrations. She was an example of patience and professionalism through the many revisions and refinements we requested.

Our project manager, Marcia Carvalho, and our project support manager, Mark Harrison, kept us on schedule and on budget, coordinating hundreds of tasks between McGraw-Hill, the research team, the authors, and the executive editor. Marcia and Mark diligently managed the budget, kept hundreds of files organized, ran weekly calls, planned our major face-to-face working sessions, and executed many other tasks, including the arduous process of ensuring that examples and quotations were properly vetted and approved. They were ably supported by Marie Le Corre, who scheduled and set up numerous calls and meetings, and Neha Krishna, who provided research support.

We are also grateful to the companies that agreed to share their stories: BASF, Essilor, Haier, Kaiser Permanente, Lenovo, and Schlumberger. Their challenges and successes in using their supply chains to achieve strategic advantage are inspiring. We'd especially like to thank Andreas Backhaus (BASF), Eric Javellaud (Essilor), Lim Chin Chye (Haier), Laurel Junk and Laurie Spoon (Kaiser Permanente), Mark Stanton (Lenovo), and Stéphane Biguet and Phil Teijeira (Schlumberger) for mobilizing their organizations behind the project.

Thanks are also owed to a number of individuals who, because of their relationships with these companies, helped secure the companies' participation: Volker Fitzner, Harald Geimer, and Mark Lustig for BASF; Etienne Boris and Christine Bouvry for Essilor; Craig Kerr and Lillian Wang for Haier; Vitaly Glozman and Rick Judy for Kaiser Permanente; Kevin Keegan for Lenovo; and Marc Waco for Schlumberger.

We are also indebted to a talented team of freelance writers and editors—Jennifer Baljko, Catherine Cuddihee, Elyse Friedman, Bronwyn Fryer, Jeff Garigliano, Lauren Keller Johnson, and Neil Shister—who helped write and edit the content.

It's fair to say that the second edition would not have come into existence without the support of PwC. We are grateful to the PwC network for the many resources it provided. Thanks are owed to Tony Poulter, who championed the book project, and to Mark Strom and Joe Ipolitto, who provided guidance. We are also indebted to a number of individuals who volunteered their nights and weekends to review the book from cover to cover: Gordon Colborn (United Kingdom), Mike Giguere (United States), Brad Householder (United States), Craig Kerr (China), Johnathon Marshall (United Kingdom), and Yorozu Tabata (Japan). Their objective feedback proved immensely helpful. We also thank Stanford University professor Hau Lee, who provided advice and counsel throughout the writing process.

We would be remiss if we failed to mention the enthusiastic support of Knox Huston, our editor at McGraw-Hill Education. Respectful of our knowledge and professional experience, Knox has graciously allowed us to write the kind of book we thought was needed. Moreover, he made it possible for us to accelerate the publishing cycle.

Ultimately, a book of this scope would not have been possible without years of experience in making change happen. It's that experience that has shaped our view of what's happening today and what's emerging in the practice of supply chain management. We thank all the organizations and talented professionals with whom it has been our privilege to work.

CHAPTER ONE

DISCIPLINE 1: ALIGN YOUR SUPPLY CHAIN WITH YOUR BUSINESS STRATEGY

Management teams are under intense pressure from their boards and shareholders to develop business strategies that can be executed in the real world. Key to any actionable business strategy is a supply chain strategy that is robust enough to support all aspects of operations, yet nimble enough to address today's rapidly changing market conditions. This is a tall order, but the right approach can make your company's supply chain a true source of competitive differentiation.

Few would dispute that we are in a world of slower economic growth, unpredictable swings in demand, and volatility in the prices of key inputs such as commodities. Many prominent economists refer to this period of ongoing economic uncertainty as the "new normal."[1] While broader macroeconomic adjustments are needed to return to sustained growth, it is also necessary for every company to take action, on multiple fronts.

In this new normal, the supply chain has become a critical asset for any company pursuing global growth and profitability. Yet many companies think about their supply chains only when something is broken—high inventory levels, dissatisfied customers, or supplier problems, for example.

Or perhaps a benchmarking analysis showed supply chain performance lagging behind that of others in the industry. The best-performing companies are harnessing their supply chains for competitive advantage. They constantly search for new ways for their supply chains to add value and push the boundaries of performance. Moreover, they keep making refinements so that their supply chains—and their overall business performance—stay one step ahead of the competition.

Of the various disciplines needed for strategic supply chain management, the most important is supply chain strategy. Companies with high-performing supply chains understand that their supply chain strategy should be closely aligned with their overall business strategy. They know that their supply chain strategy decisions will, to a large degree, determine decisions regarding all the other core disciplines: process, organization, collaboration, and performance measurement and management.

Developing a good supply chain strategy requires addressing a fundamental paradox. Although it can take years to fully implement a supply chain strategy, companies must be able to respond quickly to changes in the business environment. This balance of long-term and short-term considerations can be extremely difficult to achieve. But by thoughtfully laying out the elements central to the strategy, companies can navigate issues whenever they arise, while building a supply chain that will support differentiation over the long term.

THE CORE STRATEGIC VISION

An effective business strategy begins with a core strategic vision that establishes the boundary conditions for your business: what you are, what you'll do, and—just as important—what you are not and what you won't do (Figure 1.1).

The core strategic vision answers three key questions: What are your company's overall strategic objectives? What value does it deliver

Figure 1.1 Boundary Conditions of the Core Strategic Vision

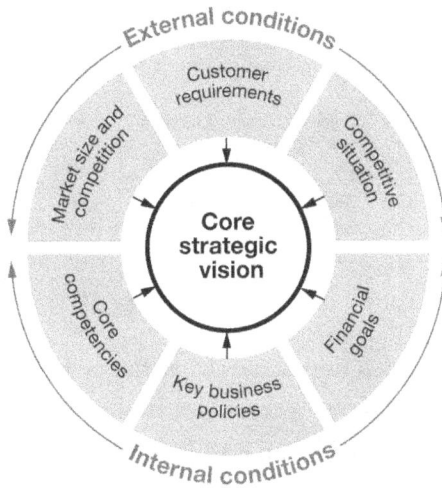

to customers? How does your company differentiate itself in the market-place? The answers must inform your supply chain strategy decisions, or your supply chain will be operating in a vacuum.

HOW COMPANIES USE THEIR SUPPLY CHAIN TO COMPETE

Companies compete on the basis of innovation, customer experience, quality, and cost (Table 1.1). While all four factors are important, leading companies choose one to be their primary basis of competition in a chosen market and use the others to support that competitive positioning. The key is to excel at the basis of competition that really matters for the customer and that provides a strong means of differentiation versus the competition. A supply chain can play a major role in this endeavor, provided the company's basis of competition informs the supply chain strategy and the supporting disciplines of process architecture, organization, collaboration, and performance measurement and management.

Table 1.1 Using the Supply Chain As a Strategic Asset

Primary basis of competition	Product and service attributes	Key supply chain contributions
Innovation	Cutting-edge, must-have	Time to market and time to volume
Customer experience	Tailored to meet customers' specific needs	Supply chain interactions designed from the customer's perspective
Quality	Reliable performance	Procurement and production excellence and quality control
Cost	Lowest priced	Efficient, low-cost configuration and processes

The best companies understand that they can't be all things to all people. Make sure that your company's supply chain strategy supports the company's primary basis of competition, but remember that strategy is a balancing act. No cost leader can afford to ignore customer experience, nor can an innovator ignore the price ceiling of a market. Companies with top-performing supply chains understand the trade-offs among service levels, lead times, working capital, and costs, and they make decisions that best fit their overall strategic mission. The key is to choose where to focus and then to achieve best-in-class supply chain performance in those areas.

COMPETING ON INNOVATION

Companies that compete on innovation develop the must-have products and services in their industry. Innovation leaders like Apple, BMW, and Alstom have a finger on the pulse of their customers and consistently launch products that outsell those of the competition.

How does the supply chain support a company that competes on innovation? Time to market is critical because the window of opportunity before fast followers start taking market share can be small. Success depends on integrating the supply chain with the design chain—that is, integrating all of the activities inside and outside the enterprise that are involved in the design of a new product or service. This degree of integration entails coordinated management of processes, physical assets, and information.[2]

Time to volume is also important. For an innovation-driven company, creating strong demand for a new product and then being unable to produce enough volume to meet that demand is one of the worst things that can happen. Close collaboration between the design chain and the supply chain helps to ensure that when demand cranks up, the whole supply chain is ready.

Consider Zara, a Spanish clothing retailer that competes on innovation while keeping a close eye on costs.

Many apparel manufacturers keep costs down by outsourcing production to Asia. Contract manufacturers' use of fixed production schedules, however, can limit retailers' ability to change, on short notice, the types and volumes of the products they order. This is especially problematic in a sector like fashion, where consumer preferences shift rapidly. With too many of the wrong garments on hand, retailers can end up with marked-down inventory and eroded margins.

Zara uses a very different model. The retailer, owned by global giant Inditex, positions itself as the purveyor of "fast fashion"—trendy clothes for the price-conscious consumer. To deliver on that strategy, Zara manufactures almost 50 percent of its garments nearby, in Spain, Portugal, and Morocco. Although production costs are 15 percent to 20 percent higher than those of the competition, Zara more than makes up for the cost differential by taking steps to ensure that the products that customers want are available when they want them. Point-of-sale information from stores worldwide makes it possible to identify best-selling items and get them produced and delivered to stores quickly. The result: more full-priced sales and fewer markdowns. From 2005 through 2011, Inditex's annual revenue doubled; in 2011, Zara's profit margins were 19.3 percent, substantially higher than competitors'.[3]

COMPETING ON CUSTOMER EXPERIENCE

Companies that compete on this factor provide an experience that meets their customers' specific needs. They use a deep understanding of customer preferences to tailor the associated supply chains. Research conducted by

PwC's Performance Measurement Group (PMG) indicates that companies that provide exceptional customer experience average almost 5 percent higher earnings before interest, taxes, depreciation, and amortization (EBITDA) than the competition. They also average a compound annual growth rate of sales that is more than 8 percent higher.[4]

Why does superior customer experience lead to such striking financial gains? Companies that excel in customer experience understand the relationship between cost to serve and profitability, and can assess the cost of offering customized services. They know not only when to offer lots of choices to customers but also when not to. By getting products and services to customers when and where customers want them, they avoid the costs related to both expedited production and customer churn. That's why companies that compete on customer experience report lower account turnover, reduced customer-retention costs, and a stronger bottom line.[5]

The Internet has made it easier for business-to-consumer companies to enhance the customer experience. Take, for example, the apparel industry, where a number of online start-ups now offer custom-made clothes for a fraction of what bespoke clothing once cost. One U.S.-based company, J. Hilburn, took a different tack, developing a buying process that is part online, part offline. First, the customer places an order online; then, a sales consultant goes to the customer's home to take measurements and share fabric swatches. After the order has been delivered, the consultant returns to make sure the clothes fit correctly. J. Hilburn keeps the customer measurements in a file online so that the customer can easily log on and place new orders. This innovative supply chain—custom orders placed in the United States, fabrics designed and woven in Italy, and clothing produced in China—has allowed J. Hilburn to offer custom-fitted clothes for the cost of off-the-shelf garments.[6]

Customer experience is an important source of competitive advantage in the business-to-business arena as well. In many industries, companies have created customized services that are invoiced according to their contribution to the customer's ability to generate revenue. Take the mining industry, for example, where 24-7 operations require tools to be constantly available, and where reliability and safety are paramount. A drill needs to run for years in extreme conditions as deep as 10,000 feet underground, drilling up to 100 miles every year.

Sandvik Mining, a part of the Sandvik Group, is a leading supplier to the mining industry and is known for its reliability and leading-edge technology. Its offerings include rock drilling, exploration drilling, cutting, and crushing, as well as materials handling for surface and underground mining. "Service has become the key differentiator in the rapidly changing global mining business," explains Sandvik's president of drilling, exploration, and rock cutting, Gerald Elliott. "More and more mining companies are now more focused on productivity, as opposed to upfront equipment and spare-parts costs."

In Sandvik's case, this means charging for the number of hours worked, the number of feet drilled, or, in some cases, the tons of product produced. In return, the company keeps the equipment up and running for its entire life cycle, with the help of service experts deployed at the customer site. This approach allows Sandvik to provide its customers with what matters most: greater output at a lower total cost.

COMPETING ON QUALITY

Companies that compete on quality are best known for their premium products and services, offerings that are consistent and reliable. Lexus automobiles, Louis Vuitton leather goods, and Tropicana juices are three examples that immediately come to mind. Product development is critical to quality, and so are key supply chain processes such as production, sourcing, quality assurance, and return. If a product is fragile or perishable, transportation and storage also play integral roles.

Consider Tropicana, the world's leading producer of branded fruit juices. As the largest single buyer of Florida fruit, Tropicana developed what it calls the "grow to glass" approach, a proprietary system to ensure that fruit is harvested at its peak. The company also uses specially engineered carton and plastic packaging to keep the juice fresh, while state-of-the-art refrigerator trucks and specially designed railcars deliver juice to distribution centers throughout North America.[7]

For many companies competing on quality, the ability to trace a product back to its point of origin, known as *traceability*, has become a source of differentiation (although for some industries it is a response to regulatory mandates). In industries in which counterfeiting has become a serious threat, such as pharmaceuticals, the integrity of the end-to-end supply chain is essential. To ensure traceability, manufacturers closely control product flows to consumers. Moreover, they use markings and track-and-trace technologies to guarantee that what customers purchase is the "genuine article."

COMPETING ON COST

To be sure, all companies need to keep an eye on costs. But that's not the same thing as competing on cost. Companies that compete on cost offer prices to attract cost-sensitive buyers or to maintain share in a commodity market. This basis of competition demands highly efficient operations. Standardization of products and processes is fundamental, as are supplier and production quality and inventory control. Supply chain performance is measured with efficiency-related metrics such as asset utilization, inventory days of supply, product costs, and total supply chain management costs.

Consider India's number one pharmaceutical company, Dr. Reddy's Laboratories, a vertically integrated maker of proprietary and generic drugs. Dr. Reddy's generics business aims to make pharmaceuticals affordable to people worldwide by offering lower-cost alternatives to high-priced products. The company produces both branded and unbranded generics in its plant in India, while its supply chain manages distribution from its plant in India to customers in more than 100 countries across the globe. The company has honed its supply chain costs so well that it is able to provide products that match those of local competitors on both quality and price.[8]

KEY ELEMENTS OF SUPPLY CHAIN STRATEGY

A supply chain strategy involves many interlocking activities and decisions, large and small. According to Michael Porter, strategy guru and author of *Competitive Advantage*, successful business strategy relies on the concept of "fit"—that is, a group of activities that support a chosen competitive strategy. Although any single activity can be copied, the activities taken together form a system that is virtually impossible to duplicate.[9]

Porter's concept of fitness holds equally true for supply chain strategy. Five elements of your business—and the choices you make regarding these elements—are fundamental:

- *Customer service.* What are your objectives in terms of delivery speed, accuracy, and flexibility?
- *Sales channels.* How will your customers order and receive your goods and services?
- *Value system.* Which supply chain activities will be performed by your organization and which by your partners?
- *Operating model.* How will you organize the planning, ordering, production, and delivery processes to provide customer service while still meeting your working capital and cost objectives?
- *Asset footprint.* Where will you locate your supply chain resources, and what is their scope of action?

Companies often make decisions about each of these elements in isolation, without considering the others. It's possible, for example, to develop a manufacturing footprint that reduces costs, only to fall short of required customer-service levels. To get the full strategic benefit a supply chain can offer, however, it's critical to treat each element as part of an integrated whole (Figure 1.2).

Figure 1.2 Elements of Supply Chain Strategy

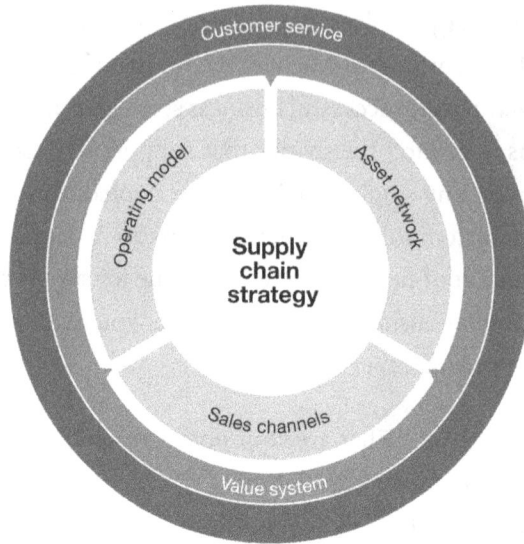

CUSTOMER SERVICE

The first step in developing a supply chain strategy is to define customer service objectives. Offering various levels of delivery speed, accuracy, and flexibility for different types of customers can help distinguish the overall customer experience. Should, for example, deliveries reach all customers in the same amount of time, or should customers who are more valuable receive deliveries faster? Should the ordering process be the same for all customers? Answers to questions like these will be dictated by your company's business strategy and target audience—that is, whether you are addressing B2C or B2B segments.

Business to Consumer

In the B2C world, off-the-shelf product availability is often the key service criterion. Customers are willing to wait for hot products from a leading brand—but only up to a point. Retailer Nordstrom introduced an innovation in online retailing when it made the inventory of its 115 brick-and-mortar stores visible to consumers shopping on its online store. Previously, customers saw only what was available in the web warehouse and sometimes found that the product they wanted was not available. The retailer's change in practice led to higher product availability, increased sales, and lower inventories.[10] Approaches such as this one help Nordstrom maintain its reputation for outstanding customer service and overall customer experience.

Business to Business

In the B2B world, customer service is often synonymous with meeting committed delivery dates, because the customer uses the product or service in revenue-generating activities. But lead-time performance can also be critical.

Consider, for example, a supplier of mining equipment that sells machinery to two very different customer types: companies that own their mines, and contractors that conduct mine development and other activities for those mining companies. Because mining companies have capital investment plans and a fleet to maintain, they typically order equipment far in advance of when they need it, on a predictable timeline. So mining-equipment suppliers typically have six months or more to deliver equipment to mining companies. Contractors, by contrast, typically operate on a very compressed calendar: they wait until they have a contract in hand from a mining company before placing equipment orders, and they need the machines delivered in three months or less.

SALES CHANNELS

Companies have multiple options for getting products and services to buyers. They can use indirect channels—distributors or retailers—or they can sell directly to customers via the Internet or a sales force. The market segments and geographies being targeted will drive these decisions. Since profit margins vary depending on which channels are used, you have to decide on the optimal channel mix, and who gets the goods in times of product shortages or high demand.

Consider the multibillion-dollar bottled-water industry. The industry uses three different distribution channels to serve its three major consumer segments. Traditional retail distributors serve retail customers, vending machines serve the individual consumer market, and service agents provide on-site water units for home and office users. Each segment requires different supply chain processes, assets, suppliers, and performance metrics.

If you are a new player in the bottled-water industry, should you sell your product through distributors that already have relationships with key retailers or distribute directly to those retailers? If you choose the distributor channel, should you integrate your order-management and inventory-management systems with the distributors' systems? If so, to what extent, and who should pay for it? Should you maintain dedicated inventory for all distributors or only those distributors that you consider to be strategic partners? These decisions will drive your company's asset and cost performance and so must be a part of your overall channel strategy—along with decisions on pricing, vendor-financing policies, promotions, and so on.

VALUE SYSTEM

An effective supply chain strategy requires a solid understanding of the company's value system, which according to Porter, encompasses the value-adding activities of the enterprise as well as those of suppliers, customers, suppliers' suppliers, and customers' customers.[11] This understanding will help determine which supply chain activities will be performed by the company in question and which by its partners.

In this context, companies must consider two types of activities: those related to decision making and those related to execution. Often companies choose to outsource execution-related activities while retaining control over decision making. For example, many consumer packaged goods (CPG) companies that produce a high volume of goods in their own plants outsource the last stage of production to contract manufacturers (CMs). The CPG companies maintain responsibility for purchasing raw materials, while the CMs have full responsibility for quality and lead time. That way, the CPG companies use their economies of scale to get lower materials prices while also benefiting from the CMs' lower manufacturing costs.

Benefits and Risks of Outsourcing

Generally speaking, companies outsource supply chain activities to gain access to other companies' scale, scope, technology expertise, or resources:

- *Scale.* Third-party providers can often offer services such as manufacturing or logistics with less expense because they have a large customer base, which keeps utilization rates high and unit costs low. External partners can also help companies scale up quickly without having to invest in new capacity.

- *Scope.* In cases where a company wants to expand into new markets or geographical areas, partners can provide access to operations in new locations that would not be economical for the company to replicate internally at current business volumes.

- *Technology expertise.* Partners may have expertise in a product or process technology that would require a sizable capital investment to develop internally.

- *Resources.* External partners in the value chain can offer rapid access to materials, talent, or financing.

Outsourcing also poses significant risks. A supply chain that's been lengthened by the addition of numerous external partners can result in longer lead times and higher working capital. Risk is also an issue if production depends on a single supplier for a critical component and that supplier suddenly halts production for financial or other reasons. Therefore, value systems need processes and information systems that create transparency and enable proactive decision making, so that companies can adapt quickly to unanticipated changes in demand or supply.[12]

Making the Decision to Outsource

Executives often treat outsourcing as a decision of "core versus noncore," arguing that core competencies, as things a company is good at, should be kept in-house, whereas noncore competencies should be outsourced. That reasoning, however, is overly simplistic. An activity or process that a company excels at isn't necessarily a core competency and, conversely, areas of less-than-optimal performance may in fact be core to the company's success. Most important is maintaining control of activities that are critical to competitive differentiation, business growth, customer experience, or superior offerings.

Vertical integration can be a core means to achieving that control. Consider Manufacture des Montres Rolex SA, known around the world for its Rolex brand. The company produces not only the components for its watches but also the machines, tools, and supplies needed to manufacture those components.[13] Maintaining control of production is integral to ensuring the quality that sets Rolex apart as a premium watchmaker.

OPERATING MODELS

Taken together, the decisions about how a company produces goods and services constitute its operating model. These decisions affect more than manufacturing. They shape how planning, order management, procurement, and physical delivery are handled as well.

There are four types of operating models (Table 1.2):

- *Make to stock.* This is the most broadly used approach for standardized products that sell in high volume. A plant produces goods in advance of receiving customer orders; finished products are stored to await a customer order. The larger production batches keep production costs down, and the readily available inventory means customer demand can be met quickly.
- *Make to order.* This is the preferred model for customized products or products that are in infrequent demand. Companies

Table 1.2 Types of Operating Models

Operating model	When to choose this model	Benefits
Make to stock	• Standardized offerings selling in high volume	• Low production costs • Meeting customer demands quickly
Make to order	• Customized offerings • Offerings with infrequent demand	• Low inventory levels • Wide range of product options • Simplified planning
Configure to order	• Offerings requiring many variations	• Customization • Reduced inventory • Shorter delivery times
Engineer to order	• Complex offerings that meet unique customer needs	• Responding to specific customer requirements

produce the service or product only when they have a customer order in hand. This approach keeps inventory levels low while allowing for a wide range of product options.

- *Configure to order.* This is a hybrid model in which a product is partially completed, to a generic level, and then finished when an order is received. This is the preferred model when there are many variations of the end product and it's important to have a shorter customer lead time than is possible with the make-to-order model. A variant of the configure-to-order model is assemble to order; companies using an assemble-to-order model produce component parts in response to sales forecasts and then finalize assembly upon receipt of a customer order.

- *Engineer to order.* This model shares many of the characteristics of the make-to-order model. It is used in industries that create complex products and services with specifications that are unique to a particular customer. In the final step of the customer's ordering process, the manufacturer's engineering function defines the specifications and develops a list of needed materials unique to that customer's order.

The operating model can provide a key source of performance advantage. Consider a consumer software company that made to stock, shipping products directly to inventory sites in various countries. Because of the small size of the packaged product and the need for many language variants, items were customized for a particular market very early in the production process. This approach, however, created unnecessary inventory and obsolescence as product definitions evolved.

To improve service levels while reducing inventory, the company shifted from a make-to-stock model to a configure-to-order model. Under the new model, generic products were shipped from the plant floor to a central distribution center. As orders came in from each market, products were customized and shipped accordingly. A configure-to-order model posed some important advantages. Under the old operating model, multiple stock locations required separate forecasting and inventory-management functions for each site, raising the likelihood that supply and demand would be out of sync. In a centralized distribution center, by contrast, it became much easier to ensure that the right amount of inventory was on hand to meet demand. At the same time, the new approach simplified supply chain planning, allowing focus on a relatively small number of different generic products instead of hundreds of language-based variants. Not surprisingly, product availability shot up and inventory declined.

It may be advantageous to deploy different operating models for different products or market segments. The automotive industry offers a good example. While most automakers have long preferred the make-to-stock model, manufacturers of high-end vehicles have pursued make-to-order and configure-to-order strategies.

But make to order is challenging: given the millions of potential end configurations, it's difficult to offer passenger cars on a make-to-order basis while maintaining a competitive lead time. Unless suppliers can be fully integrated into the make-to-order supply chain, automakers run unnecessarily high inventory risks, meaning they could be stuck with obsolete or unsellable inventory. In addition, changing the production process to allow each car to match a unique set of characteristics is a very costly undertaking.

Not surprisingly, only 2 percent of Lexus passenger cars sold in 2011 in the United States were made to order. The rest were made to stock and sold from dealer lots. The percentage of made-to-order vehicles in Europe was greater. In the German domestic market, for instance, about 60 percent of the high-end cars made by BMW, Audi, Porsche, and Mercedes were made to order. In Japan, approximately 50 percent of Nissan sales were configured to order.[14]

These numbers tell only part of the story. A significant part of customization now takes place at retail car dealerships. This customization is basically a make-to-order or configure-to-order activity based on the vehicle provided by the manufacturer. In North America, dealers offer two types of customization activities. One type involves making major changes to the vehicle, such as modifying the engine, raising the suspension, or repainting. The other type of customization doesn't touch the vehicle itself; it ranges from nonstandard tires and rims to frills like mud flaps.

As is the case with the other elements that make up a company's supply chain strategy, the operating model needs to be responsive to changes in demand throughout the product life cycle, from launch to exit. During this progression, a company may start with a make-to-stock model to ensure maximum product availability; it may then move to make-to-order to reduce inventory risk while still ensuring availability at a competitive price (Figure 1.3).

Figure 1.3 Change in Operating Models over Product Life Cycle

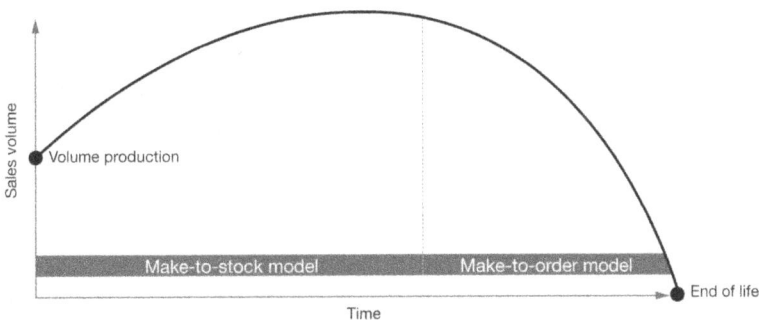

New technologies are altering production processes, and operating models along with them. The most familiar examples are digital print-to-order and digital distribution, which have revolutionized publishing. And in industries ranging from healthcare to industrial products, new 3D printing technology—also known as "additive manufacturing"—allows single-unit production of very complex designs, such as artificial limbs. This technology, in which the printer creates an object by layering different materials such as plastics or metals on top of each other, is ideally suited for make-to-order production strategies. Eventually, it may be used for many product categories that are currently made to stock.[15]

ASSET FOOTPRINT

The final element to be considered in defining a supply chain strategy is the asset footprint. This includes not only hard assets (like plants, warehouses, equipment, order desks, and service centers) but also soft assets (like the people, processes, information systems, and access to capital). The location, size, and purpose of these assets have a major impact on supply chain performance. The asset footprint may differ for production, sourcing, planning, order management, and warehousing and distribution.

Production Assets

For production assets, most companies choose one of three network models, taking into account factors like business size, customer service requirements, tax advantages, existence of a supplier base, local content rules, and labor costs. The network models are:

- *Global model.* In this model, production of a given product line takes place in one location for the entire global market. This model is suited for companies that wish to control unit production costs for very capital intensive products or that need access to highly specialized production skills.

- *Regional model.* Production takes place primarily in the region where the products are sold. In some cases, however, the production center in the given region is dedicated to one type of product, and plants from other regions produce other types of products. Companies often opt for the regional model when products need to meet specific regional requirements, when delivery times can't be achieved by the global model, or when total costs (duties, transportation, and so on) make it preferable to produce goods close to the customer.

- *Country model.* Production takes place primarily in the country where the market is located. This is the model of choice for goods that are prohibitively expensive to transport, such as newsprint. Other factors include duties and tariffs, and market access that is conditional on in-country production.

Many production-asset-footprint decisions are driven by the product life cycle. In rapidly evolving industries such as consumer electronics, companies may start with a global model while ramping up production of a new product to test the manufacturing process, and then transition to a regional model to improve customer service. At the end of the product life cycle, the global model may once again be a better choice as a way to fulfill demand with the lowest product cost and inventory investment.

Planning and Sourcing Assets

It's important to organize planning and sourcing assets in a way that is consistent with the decisions made on production assets. Just because you're using regional and country production-asset models doesn't mean it's necessary to use regional and country planning and sourcing. The key is locating these assets in places that will ensure effective operational performance.

Tax optimization is an additional consideration for some companies when it comes to locating sourcing and planning assets. Locating resources that make decisions on supply levels and purchasing volumes in a lower-tax jurisdiction can have a significant impact on the effective tax rate. The more that decision making and decision control are centralized, the greater the potential tax savings. For companies that have used a decentralized decision-making model for sourcing or planning, centralizing such decision making in a tax-efficient location can be a major undertaking. It's important that nontax benefits such as customer service and working-capital performance are sufficient to justify the move.

MULTIPLE SUPPLY CHAIN CONFIGURATIONS

For some companies, one supply chain with a single set of physical assets, processes, and information systems may be insufficient if a company has customers with widely varying needs. In such situations, multiple supply chains are advantageous because they make it easier to meet the specific needs of each customer without compromising the needs of the rest.

One example is Michelin. The company's passenger-car tire business serves two market categories: automakers and aftermarket customers such as distributors and retailers that sell tires to individual consumers. The same Michelin factories produce tires for both automakers and the aftermarket, an approach that allows the company to use a single production-planning process and maximize capacity utilization.

The paths that automaker and aftermarket tires take after production, however, are quite different (Figure 1.4). For automakers, which depend on precisely timed deliveries to keep production on schedule, Michelin delivers tires to mounting centers; the mounting centers then move the tires directly to the automotive assembly line, observing very tight delivery deadlines. Tires for the aftermarket, by contrast, go to distribution centers that supply a vast network of distributors and retailers.

Research shows that even within an individual channel, industry leaders tailor their supply chains to meet the needs of different customer segments.[16] Leading companies recognize that the requirements along the supply chain

Figure 1.4 Example of Multiple Configurations to Meet Needs of Different Market Segments

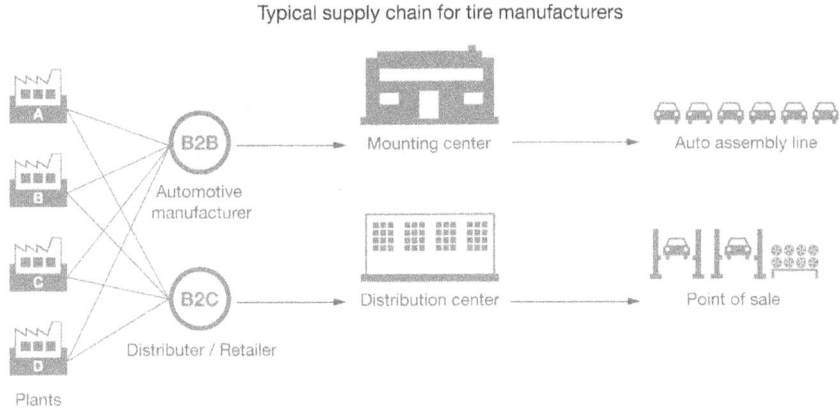

Typical supply chain for tire manufacturers

have more to do with the specific channel and customer needs than with the products or services being sold. The goal of each configuration is to meet those needs by providing the best balance of delivery performance, cost to serve, and flexibility.

TESTS OF A GOOD SUPPLY CHAIN STRATEGY

Each of the five elements of a supply chain strategy—customer service, sales channels, value system, operating model, and asset footprint—needs to meet a number of criteria if your company's supply chain is going to provide a real competitive edge. As Figure 1.5 demonstrates, your supply chain strategy must be:

- *Aligned with the power position.* This is the way to match supply chain objectives with market influence.
- *Tailored to the right level of complexity.* This ensures that the supply chain can deliver the product or service offering without becoming unwieldy.

Figure 1.5 Tests of Supply Chain Strategy

- *Resilient.* Resilience is the way to manage and mitigate risks.
- *Responsible.* Responsibility promotes social and environmental well being.
- *Adaptable.* Adaptability is the readiness to respond to a changing business environment.

ALIGNED WITH THE POWER POSITION

A good supply chain strategy requires an understanding of your company's influence relative to that of customers and suppliers. That's because a company's relative power determines to a large degree its ability to reconfigure the supply chain to meet strategic objectives.

Many of the supply chain innovators you read about are in an enviable position: they're large, and they have enormous market clout. These companies can leverage their volume of output to buy inputs more cheaply, boost asset utilization, and reduce the cost of everything from information systems to transportation. Just as importantly, they can impose their own processes and rules on suppliers and customers. In the auto industry, for example, a supplier that fails to deliver on time—thereby forcing an automaker to stop production—can be subject to a penalty as high as the equivalent of the revenue lost while the line is down. Of course, not every company can dictate such terms. It requires power of scale.

But scale is relative. Companies often underestimate their own power because they're thinking about power in broad, global terms, instead of country or market-segment terms. Even relatively small companies can find ways to work with select suppliers or customers to gain a competitive edge. The key is to segment, focus, and consolidate.

To fully assess your company's power position, determine if your supply chain is brand-led, channel-led, or supplier-led. Do you need your channels more than they need you? How about your suppliers? A supplier in an industry that's fragmented on the supply side but concentrated on the demand side, as is the case in the auto industry, may have limited power. The opposite would hold true in the electronics industry, in which there are relatively few contract manufacturers able to provide the specialty components that are in great demand by original equipment manufacturers (OEMs).

Although supply chain *control* is a possibility, supply chain *collaboration* is a better bet for most companies. (See Chapter 4.)

TAILORED TO THE RIGHT LEVEL OF COMPLEXITY

Complex supply chains cost more to operate, tie up greater working capital, and are slower to adapt to changes in demand. Decisions regarding the allocation of work to partners have a tremendous bearing on complexity, as do asset footprint decisions regarding the number of locations needed for production, order management, and distribution. Operating-model choices are another source of complexity, especially if multiple models are used.

While the key elements of supply chain strategy are important, product/ service strategy—the number and variety of products/services, the level of customization, and the number of options available to customers—is often an even bigger driver of supply chain complexity.[17] Research conducted by PMG shows that companies that have demonstrated best-in-class supply chain performance don't differ much from other organizations in terms of the number of manufacturing sites, distribution centers, orders, and customers. Best-in-class supply chain companies do, however, have a more limited product and service offering. They maintain almost 50 percent fewer distinct saleable items. (See Chapter 6.)

But complexity is not all bad. The same decisions that drive "bad" or unnecessary complexity are also responsible for "good" complexity—that is, the specifics that can prove a powerful source of advantage. For example, a decision to create many different product or service options can boost sales, or it can simply contribute to higher inventory. The goal is not to eliminate complexity but rather to determine the right level of complexity and manage performance. More than half of the best-in-class companies measure complexity drivers on an ongoing basis and integrate these measures into their management's key performance indicators, while only 15 percent of companies that are not best in class have adopted this practice.[18]

While consideration of complexity management starts with decisions on the five elements of supply chain strategy, it's also critical to consider complexity when designing supply chain processes, organization roles and responsibilities, and performance measurements. (See Chapters 2, 3, and 5.)

RESILIENT

Resilience is a key characteristic of a robust supply chain strategy. Global networks that are built solely to optimize costs and inventory during ideal conditions may be unable to deliver in times of natural disasters, political turmoil, or financial stress. But supply chain resilience isn't just about managing risk and devising a plan to deal with catastrophes. It's about taking steps to be ready for potential disruptions in a way that can create competitive advantage.[19]

Strategies for building supply chain resilience typically feature a combination of redundancy and flexibility.

Redundancy strategies such as dual sourcing, multiple production facilities, and additional inventories ensure that backup resources are available when needed. Each of these strategies incurs additional costs that must be justifiable. Companies with strong pricing power can simply pass these costs along to customers. But most companies need to determine where redundancy is critical and where lean makes better sense.

Flexibility strategies focus on making the most of the existing asset footprint to meet changes in demand and supply. The key is to have visibility on where resources are in abundance and where they're in short supply. In the case of a shortage, such visibility makes it possible to reallocate scarce materials to the production of the goods or services of greatest strategic importance. Visibility also makes it possible to shift activities such as production or transportation to meet demand spikes.[20]

RESPONSIBLE

Responsible companies ensure that activities across the value system meet sustainability, labor, and ethical standards.

Sustainability has become a key concern in supply chains, as companies continue to reduce their use of materials for production and packaging, procure those materials from sustainable sources, and ensure that what is used can be recycled. Companies that succeed in these efforts not only cut their supply chain costs—they're often able to differentiate themselves to customers who are increasingly attuned to environmental issues. These companies have their eye on what is called the "triple bottom line."

Also known as the three Ps—profit, people, and planet—the triple
bottom line measures social and environmental performance in addition to financial performance. Similarly, transparency with regard to
supply chain practices has become a requirement in today's business
environment. Some companies have addressed the issue of illegal,
abusive, or forced labor in overseas contract factories. The rise of the
Fair Labor Association and similar organizations requires that companies
control and verify working conditions in their facilities and those of
their partners across the value chain, regardless of where those facilities are located.

Companies with multiple outsourced production facilities worldwide are taking note. Take Nike, for example. Viewed as a leader in
supplier responsibility, Nike ranked twenty-fifth on Interbrand's 2011 list
of "Best Global Brands." And it ranked tenth on *Corporate Responsibility
Magazine*'s "100 Best Corporate Citizens" list for 2011. That's because
Nike established monitoring and enforcement systems to identify
factories with subpar labor conditions and then published the names
and addresses of supplier factories. This strategy not only helped Nike
ensure compliant labor conditions but also prompted Puma, Adidas,
and Reebok to follow suit.[21]

ADAPTABLE

Since change is constant, remaining adaptable is key. An unwatched
supply chain strategy can soon fall out of sync with market needs. Both
internal and external factors can trigger a need to adjust the supply chain
strategy. These factors include:

- *A change in market conditions.* When customers have to tighten
  their belts, companies can still meet their needs without
  sacrificing margins. Rethinking one or more of the supply chain
  elements can lead to new approaches that drive down the cost
  of meeting customer requirements without affecting quality.

- *A technology that transforms the dynamics of your industry.* Disruptive technologies have the potential to introduce new players and dislocate existing ones, thereby changing the fundamentals of the value system. New technologies such as electronic delivery can make possible more frequent product launches, higher levels of customization, and less costly delivery of smaller orders, requiring changes in customer service, asset footprint, and operating models.

- *A change in offerings or markets.* If a company is offering new products or services, targeting new markets, or expanding geographically, it may need to expand production capacity, add new distribution capabilities, develop new channels, find new suppliers, or perhaps rethink the supply chain strategy overall.

- *A change in the basis of competition.* Perhaps a new competitor has emerged with a stronger value proposition, or your company wants to enter a market that requires faster delivery, greater flexibility, or higher quality. Any major change to your company's basis of competition should drive a reexamination of the supply chain strategy.

- *The need to assimilate a new acquisition.* Mergers and acquisitions can create a need to reconfigure the supply chain. You'll have to see where it makes sense to eliminate redundancies, where to keep operations separate, and where to integrate. The desire to accelerate delivery of the targeted value will need to be balanced with an understanding of which supply chain activities can be changed quickly without jeopardizing customer-facing performance.

A company's growth trajectory can have major implications, too. Is the volume of sales rising or falling? Is the industry expanding or contracting? A supply chain strategy designed to support growth may no longer be appropriate during retrenchment, when the focus is on cost control.

Although change is a given, the frequency of significant change will differ by industry. Consumer electronics moves more quickly than does, say, aerospace. But the pace of change can also vary within a given industry. In the PC category, for instance, the principal option for consumers throughout much of the 1990s and 2000s was PCs. Since that time, the pace of change has greatly accelerated, as computer technology has leapt from one platform to another: laptops, netbooks, tablets, and ultrabooks.

Change can provide a powerful incentive for companies to adapt. Danone, the global food conglomerate, felt the effects of the global recession of 2008 as much as any other large company. However, rather than hunkering down and waiting for demand to return, Danone took concerted steps to drive sales volume by lowering the price of products in its Fresh Dairy Products unit, which represented roughly 60 percent of total sales. Implementing a program called "Reset," Danone decided to wring out supply chain inefficiencies so that it could reduce prices without sacrificing margins. Some of these leaning efforts allowed Danone to reduce prices by as much as 15 percent. The resulting increase in sales volume more than justified the price reductions.[22]

Finally, companies periodically review their overall business strategy and how well they are executing. A 2012 PwC survey of corporate directors found that more than one-third (36 percent) of companies review their strategy every six months.[23] Boards of directors are increasingly pressuring management teams to develop strategies that the company can execute without any surprises or missteps. These periodic reviews are a good time to review your supply chain strategy as well. After all, any changes in the business strategy—even minor adjustments—will require corresponding changes in the supply chain strategy. This balancing act is difficult, but as top-performing companies know, it's crucial to success.

KEY TAKEAWAYS

- Your supply chain strategy should be aligned with and support your company's overall business strategy.
- To ensure this alignment, design your supply chain strategy around several key elements—the customer-service proposition, sales channels, value system, operating model, and asset footprint.
- Test the supply chain strategy frequently against several criteria. Is it aligned with your company's power position? Is it tailored to the right level of complexity? Is it resilient, responsible, and adaptable?
- Evaluate and update the supply chain strategy regularly—top-flight performance demands it.

BASF:
INCREASING FARM YIELDS THROUGH INNOVATIONS IN CHEMISTRY

A few weeks before harvest time, unusually heavy rains have drenched wheat fields all over Germany, making a devastating fungal infestation likely. A protective fungicide is needed right away. The best solution is Adexar®, BASF's innovative control agent. However, the timing is extremely tight. Farmers, who can't keep a supply of the agent on hand because they lack adequate storage facilities for housing this kind of material, need to be able to get Adexar from the nearby dealer with little advance notice. Moreover, they have little time to administer the fungicide before harvest.

Meanwhile, in Brazil, millions of acres are now being prepared for soybean planting. Farmers there can count on Opera®, another protective fungicide in BASF's portfolio. After inspecting the fields, locally stationed BASF representatives provide guidance on how to use this high-tech product to ensure that it's applied correctly and efficiently.

In both scenarios, BASF, the world's largest chemical company, must make sure that the product is delivered from the warehouse to the distributor in the next 24 hours, and there's no margin for delay. Complicating matters, the total lead time required to produce these fungicides is well over a year.

MASTERING A MULTI-INDUSTRY CHAIN

The timing of Adexar's and Opera's production and delivery would pose a challenge for any supply chain. It's even more daunting in this case because these are just two of thousands of products that BASF sells. The company's portfolio covers a wide range of areas, including chemicals, plastics, performance products, crop protection, and oil and gas. Products include chemicals for semiconductors, polyurethanes for packaging and car parts, pigments for inks, technology for the production of liquefied natural gas, thermal insulation used in construction, super-plasticizers to improve the flow of wet concrete, coating for automobiles, super-absorber for baby diapers, and made-to-measure molecules for pharmaceuticals. Not to mention several crop-protection agents.

THE VALUE OF *VERBUND*

Producing and delivering so many different kinds of products requires an unusually versatile supply chain. For decades, BASF's secret recipe for success has been a novel production approach called *Verbund*, or "linked to the ultimate degree." At each Verbund site—there are six in all, located around the globe—the Verbund system creates efficient value chains that extend from basic chemicals right through to high value-added products such as coatings and crop protection agents. In addition, the by-products of one plant can be used as the starting materials of another.

In the Verbund system, chemical processes consume less in the way of raw materials and energy while producing higher product yields. As a result, Verbund helps conserve resources, minimize emissions, and reduce transport distances. For these reasons, Verbund provides benefits that are ecological as well as economical.

The Verbund model continues to provide a substantial source of competitive advantage. Recent changes in the business environment, however, have required BASF to take additional steps to maintain its edge. As the number of competitors increased worldwide and offerings that once commanded a premium became commodities, several BASF business units recalibrated their overall strategies. In an effort to focus more strongly on the customer, they expanded the proportion of specialized higher-value products in the portfolio.

The new offerings included higher-technology products, such as Adexar. They also included solutions—that is, products with services wrapped around them. For example, instead of selling just paint to the automotive industry, BASF's coatings experts work on the original equipment manuafucturer's (OEM's) production line, providing support during the car-body-painting process. Both products and solutions create greater value for the customer while generating higher margins and return on capital for BASF.

These offerings, however, posed a new challenge for the supply chain. Since the customer segments across the different business units had widely varying needs, the higher service levels spawned an enormous variety of planning and sourcing processes, as well as IT systems. The supply chain of BASF's Crop Protection Division, for example, had to be able to meet demands for fungicide within a day's notice in different parts of the world without creating unacceptable levels of inventory.

HARMONIZED PROCESSES

Clearly, a one-size-fits-all approach was infeasible. BASF experts looked instead to streamline supply chain processes without sacrificing responsiveness. To get the best of both worlds, they established a central supply chain organization whose mission was to integrate supply chain operations enough to allow each business unit to execute its own business strategy without sacrificing the economies that were possible with BASF's global scale. This meant providing the business units with sufficient flexibility to maximize revenues while at the same time managing costs across the enterprise.

The solution was harmonization, which BASF defined as a standardization of processes with some room left for variations. Key to the effort were "global process experts," who were tasked with formulating a number of standard supply chain processes, each of which featured a menu of options.

The idea is for each business unit to use the basic process as it was defined, with a choice of various options for the parts of the process that involve direct interaction with the customer.

"We have a backbone of the order-to-cash process, which is more or less the same for everybody," explains Andreas Backhaus, senior vice president of global supply chain and process innovation. "You get an order in, you allocate it and you transport it to the customer." The order, however, could be received in a variety of ways—telephone, fax, or e-commerce channels. Correspondingly, there might be several different ways of providing order dates and managing the scheduling of deliveries, thus allowing each unit to deploy the process that is best suited to its business.

As a result of these changes, processes taking place on the back end are highly standardized, with filling, warehousing, and logistics carried out for all the business units. By contrast, the parts of the supply on the front end—that is, the processes where BASF directly interacts with the customer—are more customized. Those are the processes in which BASF invests the most because they help differentiate BASF's offerings from those of competitors.

"The supply chain is critical to our goal of moving closer to our customers," says Robert Blackburn, president of BASF Group's information services and supply chain. "We are developing differentiated supply chain models that will allow BASF to leverage our economies of scale and extensive knowledge of our customers' industries."

DEALING WITH UNPREDICTABLE DEMAND A YEAR IN ADVANCE

BASF's harmonized supply chain processes provide a starting point for the Crop Protection Division supply chain in its effort to produce and deliver its fungicides to farmers. The unit uses the same processes for filling, warehousing, and logistics as other business units, while tailoring distribution and the supporting planning processes to meet the needs of its distinctive business model.

The crop protection business is unique among BASF businesses in a number of respects. For one thing, it produces goods for the end customer, in this case the professional farmer. These products have to earn the money to cover very high R&D investments, much like pharmaceuticals. Additionally, in most cases BASF does not sell its products directly to farmers. Rather, it sells to distributors, which store the fungicides in warehouses and sell them to farmers on a per-need basis.

PLANNING CHALLENGES

These factors in combination present some unique planning challenges. Basically, the agricultural supply chain organization needs to predict demand for its many products accurately enough that distributors have sufficient quantities on hand to meet farmers' last-minute orders without building up excess inventory. Owing to unpredictable factors like disease and weather, however, that's not easy to do. The average accuracy of demand forecasting for agricultural products rarely surpasses 70 percent.

What makes planning so important—but also so difficult—is the lead time involved. It takes a long time to produce the high-tech chemicals that go into the fungicides—in some cases as long as 18 months. That needs to be balanced with the customer's need to receive delivery within a day of placing an order. Products are formulated with an eye to always having sufficient levels of active ingredients in stock, but those ingredients are expensive and perishable. Moreover, some products can become obsolete if laws or registration requirements change. As a result, keeping extra stock on hand is not an option.

In addition, fungicides must be registered in the country where they are to be sold. A fungicide that's registered in one country cannot just be sold in another without having a registration there. Product formulations also vary according to the regulations of the particular market. So both product formulations and labels must be customized. This means BASF generates a great many end products that are produced in relatively small batches, each with a different formulation and label. To take one example:

BASF has some 1,500 agricultural-product references for the region of Europe, Africa, and the Middle East, which encompasses several thousand customers. When all the customized formulations and labels are tallied, there are more than 10,000 unique saleable items to deal with.

Taken together, these different issues make demand planning an arduous task, requiring the Crop Protection Division supply chain organization to continuously weigh working-capital costs against lost sales. And it's not just a matter of the current year's sales that are at stake: lost revenue can lead to long-term loss of customers to competitors as well.

The Agrochemical Supply Chain

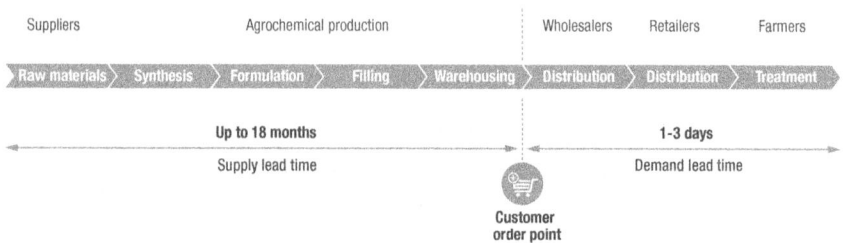

Suppliers	Agrochemical production			Wholesalers	Retailers	Farmers
Raw materials ⟩ Synthesis ⟩	Formulation ⟩	Filling ⟩	Warehousing ⟩	Distribution ⟩	Distribution ⟩	Treatment ⟩

Up to 18 months — Supply lead time

1-3 days — Demand lead time

Customer order point

Source: BASF

DEMAND PLANNING AT WORK

The typical agricultural-products consumer is a farmer who contacts the local wholesaler or distributor to place an order. The wholesaler places an order with the distributor, who ships the fungicide to the wholesaler or directly to the farm. Thanks to real-time visibility on these inventory levels, BASF can replenish inventory within 48 hours.

BASF's demand-planning process ensures the fungicide is available for replenishment. For most products (that is, those for which demand is fairly stable), the agricultural supply chain has a process for aligning demand and supply that occurs twice per year, six months or so before the beginning of the spring and autumn growing seasons. In this process, demand by country is aligned with supply, and volumes of supply are allocated to each country. The final plan is then used to develop a production plan for the formulation plants. On the eve of the growing season, as farmers prepare to plant their first seeds, BASF conducts price negotiations with its distributor customers. The supply chain organization uses this information to further refine the plan for the products in the case of short supply.

In addition to this basic process, the agricultural supply chain organization has a sales and operations planning process that focuses on high-margin products with a significant degree of demand volatility. Regional teams meet once a month with the global team to update the demand forecast and to determine the needed quantity of supply.

The real test of supply chain excellence is reliability. "Our daily work is about fulfilling our customer's expectations on what they get by when," notes Henry Comolet, head of sales excellence for Europe, Africa, and the Middle East. "This is our daily mission." The goal of the overall planning process is to ensure BASF can keep those commitments.

PRODUCTS IN THE FIELD

Although BASF's agricultural supply chain focuses much attention on getting demand planning right, it also goes to great effort to ensure the correct and most efficient use of its products in the field. Several years ago, some BASF agronomists deployed an initiative with farmers in India called *Samruddhi*, Sanskrit for prosperity. Through town hall education, on-field trials, and visits to individual farms, sales representatives provide advice on crop yields, price setting, and profitability. The initiative has proved quite successful, resulting in higher yields and net income for the farmers. Since that time, the strategy has been rolled out to other countries in Asia as well as a number in Africa.

MEASURES OF SUCCESS

BASF has a strong focus on business performance management and is known for constantly evaluating and optimizing its portfolio. From a supply chain perspective, performance measurement and management are priorities. The central supply chain performance measurement team produces monthly reports for senior management and for supply chain operations; the team also helps managers across the company in understanding supply chain performance data. These reports are provided to each of BASF's global businesses and cover key supply chain measures such as inventory figures, logistics costs, and customer delivery performance.

Managers across the company use these data to create real value for BASF. They use logistics costs and customer service data to optimize the physical network as well as to negotiate with service providers. Inventory data are a key input in product portfolio decisions as well as in the monthly planning process.

Data are particularly important for understanding customer delivery performance. For agriculture, this means collecting data from more than 400 shipping points around the globe. "BASF looks at customer delivery from both perspectives—whether deliveries reach the customer on the date requested by the customer as well as the date BASF committed to," explains Senior Manager for Supply Chain Performance Measurement Traci May. "Because customer service is a top priority, performance data are updated on a daily basis and made available online to people across the business."

The supply chain performance measurement team works closely with what BASF calls a "community network." Consisting of representatives from each of the businesses, the community network sees to it that measurement standards are applied across the company. It also ensures the ongoing evolution of the system by defining solutions that meet the specific requirements of each business.

Once again, harmonization, not standardization, is the rule. The supply chain performance team works with the community to take into account business-specific measurement needs so that each unit can monitor its supply chain operationally, while maintaining globally consistent key performance indicators for management reporting and benchmarking purposes. By measures both objective and subjective, BASF's supply chain transformation is achieving success and contributing value to the enterprise.

But responsive agricultural supply chains are more than just a business objective at BASF—they are a social imperative. It's estimated that without crop protection products, nearly half of the worldwide harvest would be lost each year.[1] As the world population continues to grow, the need for greater agricultural yields will grow as well.

BASF's global supply chains will need to keep evolving to meet this need. Since getting innovative products from the lab to the fields isn't likely to get easier anytime soon, mastering this challenge will be essential to ensuring that the world's food supply keeps pace with demand.

CHAPTER TWO

DISCIPLINE 2: DEVELOP AN END-TO-END PROCESS ARCHITECTURE

The first step in executing a supply chain strategy involves designing a process architecture that maps out the activities of the entire supply chain. Companies with high-performing supply chains design an integrated architecture, in which Plan, Source, Make, Deliver, Return, and Enable processes work together in a highly coordinated fashion to provide an important source of competitive advantage. Although a daunting undertaking, it's critical to getting the most out of your supply chain.

Once the supply chain strategy is in place, the next step is to assemble the supply chain processes that will allow the company to realize that strategy. Fundamentally, at the heart of every supply chain are six main processes—planning, procurement, production, order fulfillment, returns, and enablers. Each of these processes comprises a set of subprocesses and activities—the thousands of steps required to produce a product or service and deliver it to customers. And the steps must be integrated and coordinated into a coherent workflow.

Getting the different pieces to fit together seamlessly is no easy task. For this reason, it is critical to develop a *supply chain process architecture*—that is, a blueprint of the six main supply chain processes. This blueprint also provides the basis for selecting and operating supporting information systems, which are fundamental for supply chains to function.

The architecture must map out how the entire supply chain will operate, not only during normal conditions but also in the event of an unanticipated disruption. The best process architectures are flexible, reliable, and adaptable to changes in the business environment.

Most important, the best process architectures support a company's basis of competition. For example, Amazon competes on customer experience. As a result, while it excels at many aspects of supply chain management, it's particularly good at the order fulfillment process. Lexus, by contrast, competes on quality and excels at production. To be sure, a company can't focus exclusively on one process and ignore the rest. But it's important to place special emphasis on the processes that can differentiate the product or service in the marketplace.

There is no single ideal process architecture for a given industry segment or even for a given product. What works for one company could fail for another. What's key is that the process architecture should support the basis of competition.

DESIGNING AN INTEGRATED SUPPLY CHAIN PROCESS ARCHITECTURE

The supply chain process architecture details all of the processes and information needed for the supply chain to function well. Above all, it ensures that the processes are *integrated*. The six major processes—planning, procurement, production, order fulfillment, returns, and enablers—are all interdependent processes, each with its own inputs and outputs.

Each process also involves interactions on two other levels: with other functions in the enterprise and with the supply chains of suppliers and customers. Ideally, each process is designed with special attention to these interactions and to the timing of the inputs and outputs. An integrated

Figure 2.1 Internal Supply Chain Process Architecture

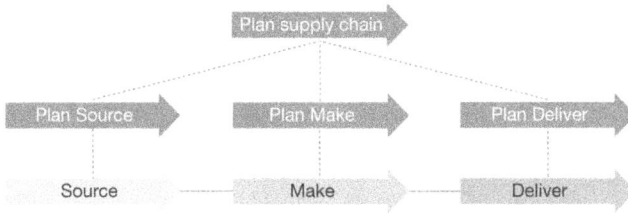

supply chain consists of such interlocking of processes across the supply chain, functions, and customers and suppliers. Figure 2.1 provides a simplified depiction of interactions within one company; a real-life supply chain architecture, however, comprises interactions across the end-to-end supply chain, including with suppliers and customers.

Extensive integration is key to supply chain functionality; without it, cycle times lengthen, and working-capital requirements and operational costs increase. For example, the sourcing process provides information on which materials will be received from suppliers and when. If this procurement information is incorrect, equipment time and labor will be allocated to production orders that can't be started because of missing materials, and valuable production time will be lost.

INTEGRATION WITH OTHER FUNCTIONAL PROCESSES

The supply chain has a high number of critical interactions with other core processes, including marketing and sales; product, service, and technology development; and customer service and support (Figure 2.2). Consequently, even a supply chain process architecture that's integrated with suppliers and customers won't be effective unless it's also integrated with your other internal processes.

Research conducted by PwC's Performance Measurement Group (PMG) backs this up. Best-in-class companies—the top 20 percent as measured by customer service, working capital, and operating costs—are more

Figure 2.2 Enterprise Process Model

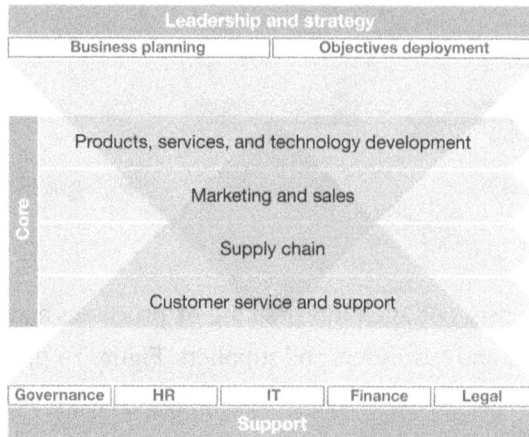

likely to have a process architecture in which all six major processes are closely integrated and that links closely to the processes of other functions, such as product development and sales.[1]

Cross-enterprise process integration requires that the scope of each process be clearly delineated. Moreover, the inputs and outputs between the supply chain and other enterprise processes must be well defined and synchronized. Integration of processes across the enterprise is fundamental, but it's only one part of the equation. Companies must set *partner integration rules* that dictate which processes to integrate with suppliers and customers. The level of integration with external parties will depend on where each customer and supplier is on the collaboration spectrum. (See Chapter 4.)

Product, Service, and Technology Development

For organizations in an engineer-to-order environment—for example, providers of turnkey power plants or makers of custom furniture—integrating the supply chain and the technology, product, and service development processes is a part of customer order execution. For other companies, integrating these processes is key to the timely launch of new products (time to market) and to reaching the target volume of a new product at the planned date (time to volume).

By integrating new product development and supply chain planning, you can ensure that key programs have the needed production and supplier resources available. This integration speeds time to market because it allows the company to implement engineering changes more quickly. Integration with sourcing ensures that suppliers bring the best technology to your products and services. And integration with the returns process ensures that information about defects and poorly understood features is used to improve existing products and develop better new ones.

Design for manufacturing (DFM) and design for supply chain (DFSC) are two practices in which product development and supply chain processes are closely intertwined. DFM ensures that designs are easier to assemble and test, and consume fewer resources. DFM also drives greater flexibility by ensuring that products are modular and by allowing for customization of end-customer orders in the late stages of production.

DFSC goes even further because it ensures that products are also easier to order, pack, ship, install, and maintain. In addition, it supports sustainability by determining how resources such as energy are to be used in production and delivery. DFSC also shapes the degree to which resources can be recycled once the product has reached the end of its useful life. Taken together, DFM and DFSC practices lower costs, improve quality, accelerate order fulfillment, and drive a sustainable supply chain.

IKEA is a leader in integrating product development and supply chain processes to provide consumers with stylish furniture at reasonable prices. Standardized modular designs are built from component parts that fit into flat packages. These compact boxes allow for efficient transport to IKEA stores and are manageable enough that customers can take the packages home themselves. This delivery model reduces costs for both IKEA and its customers.[2]

Marketing and Sales

Supply chain planning requires integration with marketing and sales processes in order to give companies the best view of customer demand, get input on customer and market priorities, and evaluate the need for, and impact of, promotional activities. For production, integration ensures that customer, market, and product priorities drive scheduling.

Designing order fulfillment processes by market segment or key account requires a service menu that is consistent with the commercial aspects of the value proposition. The service menu typically covers product customization, unique packaging, and minimum order quantities, in addition to target delivery lead times. For each order, the marketing and sales process must also provide information on pricing, customer-specific terms and conditions, and the guidelines on customer priorities needed to execute orders.

Finance

Supply chain planning must be integrated with the finance process to ensure the quality of financial information. Shareholders expect companies to provide reliable, high-quality financial information, and they don't like surprises. Forward-looking statements on financial performance must take into account the outputs of supply chain planning for order intake, margins, and cash positions. All supply chain liabilities, both internal and external, must be recognized and reported in line with company and regulatory requirements. Key supply chain risks in procurement, production, and order fulfillment need to be integrated into the financial outlook. This information is critical also for achieving the company's treasury and working-capital strategies.

Good working-capital management also requires strong integration with supply chain execution processes. Defining payment terms—and ensuring that both suppliers and customers comply with them—is critical. In industries in which delivery penalties and liquidated damages apply, companies use this information to determine which customers should receive supply first, and to deal with suppliers that are late with deliveries.

STANDARDIZE AND HARMONIZE PROCESSES
ACROSS THE ENTERPRISE

Equally important are the rules that govern how the selected supply chain processes are applied across your organization. Specifically, you will need to set *standardization and harmonization rules* that determine the degree to which processes are consistent across businesses, product lines, and geographic locations. Standardization means identical processes, whereas harmonization means defining acceptable variants of processes that are suitable in view of customer and market requirements or that are appropriate for the company's level of process automation. These important decisions simplify the supply chain and allow you to leverage investments in common tools, processes, and capabilities.

These rules need to be extremely clear. For example, do they cover processes, information systems, or both? Beware of overdoing it: don't try to impose identical ways of working across multiple businesses or product lines. Each may require its own processes to support strategic goals or market specificities. You may be better served by harmonizing processes— agreeing on standard processes as well as acceptable variances.

A leading provider of bathroom fixtures and furniture was operating in two major market segments. The primary segment was wholesale distributors that supply multiple sales channels, including small retailers. The smaller—but more profitable—segment comprised specialty city-center retailers with showrooms.

While wholesalers held inventory as part of their business model, the specialty retailers had limited storage space—sometimes none at all. Consequently, the bathroom fixture manufacturer needed specific ordering and delivery processes that would ensure each complete bathroom suite was delivered to retailers on time.

Initially, the manufacturer tried to standardize its order-fulfillment process, using the same processes for distributors and retailers alike. This, however, led to many partial deliveries and disaffected specialty retail customers. After sales declined, the manufacturer moved to two differentiated order-fulfillment processes so that it could meet the unique needs of the two market segments. The company, however, retained a standardized production process for use with both segments.

This approach—standardizing and harmonizing processes—has some important benefits. It provides a foundation for training people on proven ways of working, thus increasing the skills of operational teams. It also allows companies to share best practices worldwide, which can accelerate performance improvements across the organization. At the same time, it makes it easier to transfer work between locations in cases of peak demand—helping to optimize revenue while keeping fixed costs down. No less important, standardization and harmonization make it possible to use common information systems, thus lowering costs associated with deploying and operating these systems.

KEY PROCESSES FOR END-TO-END SUPPLY CHAIN MANAGEMENT

A process architecture is only as good as the processes that go into it. So, the first step in designing the architecture is to identify the processes to be included.

Many companies use different terms for the same activities and group their supply chain activities in different ways. To reduce confusion, we use the following terms: *Plan, Source, Make, Deliver, Return,* and *Enable* (Table 2.1).

These six terms aren't arbitrary choices—they're part of the Supply Chain Operations Reference (SCOR®) model, a standard reference model that we helped develop. (See Sidebar, "The SCOR Model," on page 69.) SCOR refers to these major processes as "process types."[3] Each of the major processes consists of activities that fall into one of three categories: Planning, Execution, and Enabling. (See Sidebar, "Three Process Categories.")

Table 2.1 Key Processes for End-to-End Supply Chain Management

	Process	Description
Planning	Plan	Supports balancing demand and supply to develop execution plans in line with overall business priorities
Execution	Source	Acquires externally produced goods or services in order to serve customer orders or future demand
	Make	Transforms resources into saleable goods and services in order to serve customer orders or future demand
	Deliver	Takes orders and delivers the goods and services to customers
	Return	Manages the return of goods for maintenance or repair, or because of environmental or quality issues
Enabling	Enable	Supports planning and execution such as the management of business rules, product and master data, performance measurement, and compliance and risks

THREE PROCESS CATEGORIES

Altogether, there are three types of processes:

- *Planning activities* ensure, using information on supply and demand, that the right resources are in place for the supply chain to function.

- *Execution activities* are the supply chain in action: Source, Make, Deliver, and Return are activities that companies conduct to produce products and services and get them to customers.

- *Enabling activities*, often referred to as Enable, are the actions needed to ensure that supply chain planning and execution processes are effective. Enabling activities include performance management, risk management, and regulatory compliance.

Most managers tend to focus on the execution activities because those activities are concrete. Planning activities are more abstract. They involve forecasts and decisions that are not clear-cut. That degree of uncertainty makes some managers uncomfortable.

The same goes for enabling activities. Many are essential decisions that lack a black-and-white answer. Sometimes even the parameters for those decisions aren't clear, and you have to start by defining your options. Consider business rules, for example. If you have limited manufacturing capacity and too many orders, which customers do you focus on? The most profitable? Those with the most pressing delivery dates? How to set customer priorities is one of many business rules you will need to define. Other enabling activities, such as managing key supply chain data, are more easily understood.

Supply chains can operate—at least for a short time—with weak planning and enabling activities. But that's like driving a car with the "check oil" light on. It won't be long before things start to go really wrong. Companies that excel at planning and enabling activities are able to perform consistently and can more rapidly adapt their processes as their business strategy evolves.

PLAN

Also referred to as "supply chain planning" or "integrated business planning," the Plan major process entails the activities needed to guarantee that your company has the right resources to satisfy demand and can allocate those resources in line with business objectives such as profitability, market share growth, and working-capital targets.

Plan is unique among the major processes in one important respect. While the execution processes—Source, Make, Deliver, and Return—consist of the activities that help the company produce and deliver products to customers, Plan sets the stage for carrying out those activities. For example, Plan processes provide Source processes with information on the necessary materials and their required volumes for the production of goods or services. Likewise, Plan processes provide information on the volume of goods or services that should be produced by Make.

Plan is critical to superior business performance because it allows a company to balance demand and supply. That is, it makes it possible to form the best possible view of demand and to ensure that the right quantity of goods and services will be on hand to meet that demand, while ensuring that these decisions support overall financial goals. The Plan process involves collaborating with many internal functions—including sales, product line management, general management, and finance—as well as with customers and suppliers to consider alternatives and make decisions on the best courses of action. Table 2.2 shows the advantages enjoyed by companies that excel in Plan.

Planning excellence is based on three key principles.

Using Timely and Accurate Information

Because both demand and supply are dynamic, what's accurate today probably won't be accurate tomorrow. On the demand side, accurate planning requires information on customer demand that is based on data such as end-user consumption, the sales pipeline, downstream inventory levels, and competitor intelligence. On the supply side, good planning requires an understanding of the critical resources—labor, manufacturing capacity, and materials—needed to satisfy demand. This includes both internal resources and the resources of key suppliers. Every functional team contributing information to the planning process needs to synchronize its reports to the calendar used for balancing demand and supply. Sales management,

Table 2.2 Metrics of Top Performance in Plan

Plan	Best performer advantage over	
	Average	Median
Forecast accuracy	**27%** more accurate	**20%** more accurate
Plan cycle time (forecast and replan)	**6x** faster	**5x** faster
Supply chain–related finance and planning costs (% of COGS)	**56%** lower spend	**36%** lower spend

for example, needs to review the sales pipeline before providing demand information.

Building Risk Management and Resilience into Your Plans

Planning needs to go beyond the typical quarterly and monthly balancing of demand and supply to include assessments of worst-case scenarios. Companies must mitigate the major risks to their supply of raw materials and components in the event of a natural disaster, financial crisis, or political unrest. One important strategy is to segment your supply base so that you can develop differentiated governance agreements, proactive measures of performance, and risk management approaches.[4]

It's also a good idea for companies to plan for events in which they have more control, such as new product introductions. In this instance, planning needs to determine, among other things, whether current suppliers are able to ramp up production if demand suddenly jumps so that the company will not be caught shorthanded. Planning also needs to work with procurement to confirm that suppliers are on strong financial footing.

Consider Rolls-Royce, a U.K.-based leader in aircraft engines. Through its sales and operations planning (S&OP) process, the company discovered that even though overall demand was growing, a drop in demand for just one product could put several key suppliers in financial difficulty. Rolls-Royce believes that S&OP provides an ideal forum for capturing and managing such risks and that, for this reason, a risk manager is integral to a successful S&OP team.[5]

Aiming for Simplicity

Make planning processes as simple as possible and focus on developing plans that are realistic and executable. This is often hard to do because there are so many factors to consider: demand at multiple levels (country, market segment, product, and brand), the different kinds of resources needed (materials, production, testing, and transportation), and the various locations involved (internal plants and partner locations). At the same time, it's important to prioritize the way resources are used across several parameters, including products with the highest margins and global key accounts. Given all these moving parts, optimizing resources across the supply chain can quickly become infeasible. Instead, simplify the process by focusing on critical, or bottleneck, resources, and set no more than two decision criteria for prioritizing markets and customers in case supplies become scarce.

SOURCE

The second supply chain major process, Source, entails putting the right capacity, materials, and services in place for production. For external suppliers, Source typically involves global and regional sourcing as well as local procurement and material-management teams. It includes strategic activities, such as selecting suppliers and managing relationships with those suppliers, along with tactical activities such as purchasing, scheduling, receiving, inspection, and authorizing supplier payment.

Source process excellence contributes to superior business performance by ensuring that resources are available when needed—at the right quality and cost and at the target level of inventory. Table 2.3 provides a picture of some of the metrics associated with top performance in Source.

Excellence in Source is built on three key principles.

Focusing on the Total Cost of Ownership (TCO)

Many companies focus on getting the lowest purchase price for sourced materials, but this is a shortsighted approach that often backfires. A low-cost

Table 2.3 Metrics of Top Performance in Source

Source	Best performer advantage over	
	Average	Median
Production materials availability (time to increase by 20%)	**9x** faster	**9x** faster
Raw materials inventory (days of supply)	**84%** less inventory	**72%** less inventory
Materials acquisition costs (% of COGS)	**64%** lower spend	**54%** lower spend

vehicle, for instance, isn't a bargain if it breaks down frequently, needs to be replaced soon, or can't be replaced easily. When determining the value of a purchase or contract, be sure to consider all associated costs. The first major goal should be to ensure supply availability, which may require dual sourcing of the individual items or services. Even though this increases upfront costs, it reduces the risk of lost production time or missed orders due to insufficient supplies.

To reduce TCO, set cost improvement objectives not just for the product or service but also for the entire supply chain. For instance, ready-to-use goods may cost slightly more, but they eliminate the need for inspection or preparation, leading to TCO reductions during production. Another consideration is flexibility: a company that places firm orders with suppliers months ahead of time in order to lower costs and then experiences inventory mismatches and write-offs may be better off placing orders later and paying more.

Aligning Sourcing Strategy and Span of Control

Given both supply chain risks and corporate social-responsibility standards, companies must be able to manage deep into their supply chains to ensure that they have a sufficient span of control. Visibility into immediate suppliers' operations is not enough. Companies also need to understand what is happening at each supplier's supplier and beyond—tiers 2, 3, and so on—especially considering that many specialized companies are small and not completely financially stable. Small problems that start on these tiers often generate larger consequences as they cascade through the supply chain.

Managing more deeply starts with selecting the right suppliers and drawing up the right agreements with them, but it ultimately requires visibility and timely corrective actions. Visibility can be secured through such means as risk assessments and audits, ongoing supplier monitoring, and supplier-driven disclosure. It may also be necessary to help a supplier develop capabilities in areas such as environmental responsibility.[6]

Maintaining an Enterprisewide Focus

Choosing suppliers that can service the entire organization worldwide, and making large-volume purchases from these suppliers, can provide economies of scale. At the same time, using the same commodity teams, specifications, and evaluation criteria to manage the global supply base provides economies of scope. An enterprisewide focus also creates opportunities for a more tax-efficient supply chain. Locating decision-making authority for purchasing in a tax-efficient jurisdiction, for example, can reduce costs.

MAKE

The third supply chain process is Make, or production, which involves transforming resources into saleable goods and services. For organizations whose production activities are conducted by partners, high proficiency in collaboration is essential. (See Chapter 4.)

Production process excellence contributes to superior business performance by ensuring that resources are transformed into saleable goods and services with the right level of quality, at the budgeted cost, according to the required schedule, and meeting any regulatory requirements that may exist. Table 2.4 shows the advantages enjoyed by companies that excel in Make.

There are three principles for process excellence in Make.

Aiming for Flexibility, Not Just Low Costs

Flexible production makes it possible to generate higher revenue without raising the level of fixed assets. There is no single benchmark for

Table 2.4 Metrics of Top Performance in Make

Make	Best performer advantage over	
	Average	Median
Internal manufacturing capacity (days to increase by 20%)	**20x** faster	**10x** faster
Work-in-process inventory (days of supply)	**12x** less inventory	**7x** less inventory

manufacturing flexibility, however, because capital-intensive industries such as cement production generally have a higher level of fixed assets than more labor-intensive industries such as clothing. Yet in both types of industries, the choice of operating model has an impact on flexibility. For example, a cement company can produce bagged cement to stock; alternatively, it can wait until a customer order is received before packaging the cement, thus assembling to order.

Companies with flexibility are also able to make last-minute adjustments to the production schedule without endangering commitments already made to other customers. Therefore, high-quality information (about, for example, order status, production capacity, and material availability) is essential.

One company renowned for manufacturing flexibility is Toyota. Developed back in the 1970s, the Toyota Production System (TPS) streamlined the production process while increasing flexibility, thus helping the automaker set the industry standard for on-time delivery. The flexible manpower line, a key aspect of the TPS, ensures that a production line can meet changing requirements without lowering productivity.

Synchronizing All Manufacturing Activities
Suppliers can respond better to a change in demand if they are kept up to date, so it's important to provide information on production schedules, material consumption, and inventory levels. Companies also should work with suppliers to define rules that should be followed for replenishment, including flexibility levels, cycle times, and stock levels. Formalized processes and accountabilities for production rules, information, and performance data need to be established internally and with supply partners.

Setting and Monitoring Quality Standards
Consistent quality is fundamental, so it's key for everyone involved in manufacturing activities to have access to data concerning quality. Companies should capture such data at each step of the production process and

analyze the information using a structured approach such as Six Sigma. All products should be traceable at the lot and unit level so that quality problems can be quickly identified and corrected. Information concerning quality should be provided to product management and R&D on a regular basis so that new products can be designed for manufacturability.

DELIVER

The fourth supply chain major process, Deliver, starts when you receive a customer order and includes all the activities needed to complete that order, from providing a price quote to collecting payment (Figure 2.3). Deliver is closely linked to the other major processes and requires that the customer order be clear and executable for Source and Make activities.

Delivery process excellence contributes to superior business performance by ensuring that your customers receive your goods or services on time and at required standards of quality and cost. Top performers in the delivery process achieve the superior performance of the metrics shown in Table 2.5.

Figure 2.3 Delivery Subprocesses

Order creation	Order management	Warehousing	Transportation	Invoicing and cash collection
1	2	3	4	5

Table 2.5 Metrics of Top Performance in Deliver

Deliver	Best performer advantage over	
	Average	Median
Perfect order fulfilment (as a % of total orders)	**27%** higher quality	**19%** higher quality
Days sales outstanding	**47%** fewer days	**49%** fewer days
Order management costs (% of revenue)	**64%** lower spend	**58%** lower spend

We recommend the following three principles for Deliver process excellence.

Cutting Costs and Time with "Straight-through Processing"

Straight-through processing makes order information available to all involved departments simultaneously. As a result, they can more easily work together and communicate with the customer, increasing efficiencies and reducing cycle times. Straight-through processing requires making customer order information visible to all relevant functions: order management, credit approval, manufacturing (making to order), engineering (engineering to order), warehousing, transportation, and invoicing. With this approach, execution activities can be synchronized across departments, and Deliver activities can be conducted more smoothly and quickly.

Setting Up End-to-End Tracking and Traceability

Because customers expect complete visibility into the status of their orders and shipments, this capability is rapidly becoming a basic customer requirement. Internally, key-account managers should have access to full order information for each of their accounts—from order signal to cash collection. In some industries, managing supply chain risks such as counterfeiting, theft, and spoilage requires the ability to seal packaging and track shipments from the point of production to the point of delivery.

Building Sustainability into the Delivery Process

Delivering products while consuming less energy and reducing carbon emissions has become important, requiring new thinking in many areas. In many cases, changes in packaging make it possible to ship more products in a given container. It's also worth looking at the location of distribution centers relative to customers. For a company that receives shipments from many sources to fulfill a customer order, it may be wise to consolidate all line items in a local warehouse before delivering the order. Consolidation allows the company to deliver the complete order in one shipment, reducing the number of transportation hours needed. Another useful approach is to use transportation scheduling to create the most efficient loads for a given carrier. And route-planning tools can improve the efficiency of vehicles on the road by ensuring the most efficient itineraries for each vehicle.[7]

RETURN

The final execution major process, Return, involves collecting and processing previously sold products according to customer agreements, government regulations, and business policies. Return covers all activities from return authorization to financial settlement. The primary drivers behind returns differ by industry, but they typically include the return of defective or unsatisfactory products, incorrect orders, excess channel-inventory returns, refurbishment or reuse, and government-mandated recycling and take-back programs. Each of these categories has its own set of required activities.

Essentially, Return is a reverse supply chain process. It involves, among other things, capturing item-level data from the point of return, tracking a product until disposition, and managing warranties for the complete product life cycle. It also requires capturing a range of analytics, including the reasons for returns, originating location, costs, and credits.

The Return physical network has its own challenges. For example, returns typically feature small volumes of many different items with irregular frequency. Companies must find a way to collect, sort, and distribute this array of items as efficiently and economically as possible. Central collection points are one way to aggregate volume in a cost-effective manner.

For Return process excellence, follow these three key principles.

Including Returns in Product Life-Cycle Thinking

A product that has been designed with returns in mind can create value even during the end-of-life phase. Integrate the particular Return constraints of your industry into the earliest phases of the product life cycle.

For example, Xerox, a global leader in document technology and services, was among the first companies in its industry to design its machines with remanufacturing, reusing, and recycling in mind. The company's innovative solid-ink technology eliminates the need for cartridges, resulting in a 90 percent reduction in office waste compared with similar color laser products. Xerox also has developed eco-friendly strategies for dealing with traditional plastic cartridges. The Xerox Green World Alliance recycling program uses a patented process to recover and reuse raw materials from used Xerox cartridges. As a result, millions of cartridges and toner containers are reused or recycled annually.[8]

Basing Return Policies on Total Cost of Returns

For returns of defective, wrong, or unsatisfactory products, set up an explicit return policy for each item sold. Customers want these kinds of returns to be processed quickly and easily. For other types of returns, such as refurbishment or reuse, specific policies are also necessary. Will you take back only your products or also those of a competitor? Is there a minimum quantity that needs to be returned per transaction? While these policies need to be based on their transaction cost, it is important to always keep customer service in mind.

Consider using an external returns specialist. This decision should be based on the nature of the return, the total cost of the return—including assessment, collection, sorting, and disposal—and your company's existing return capability.

Providing Return Information Quickly to Guide Both Disposal and Preventive Actions

Consistent information flow on the reasons for returns is a valuable source of insight. With the right set of facts regarding individual returns, procurement can deal with suppliers appropriately, while production, engineering, and logistics can learn to take corrective action in their respective areas. Moreover, return managers can use data on costs, credits, and revenue to manage reverse supply chain operations.

TESTS FOR A GOOD SUPPLY CHAIN ARCHITECTURE

Once you've developed your company's major processes and organized them into a coherent whole, you will need to evaluate them to make sure that they will create the value needed in a sustainable way. A robust supply chain process architecture satisfies three tests:

- *End-to-end scope.* The architecture encompasses all interactions between internal functions as well as interactions with suppliers and customers.
- *Strategic fit.* Processes feature practices that truly support your supply chain strategy.
- *Reliability.* Processes are integrated, documented, and supported by high-quality data.
- *Adaptability.* Processes are adjusted to reflect organizational learning and changes in strategy.

END-TO-END SCOPE

Your architecture should encompass the entire supply chain—from the supplier's supplier to the customer's customer (Figure 2.4). In addition, it should delineate the activities in which you'll collaborate with your customers and suppliers.

Figure 2.4 End-to-End Supply Chain Process Architecture

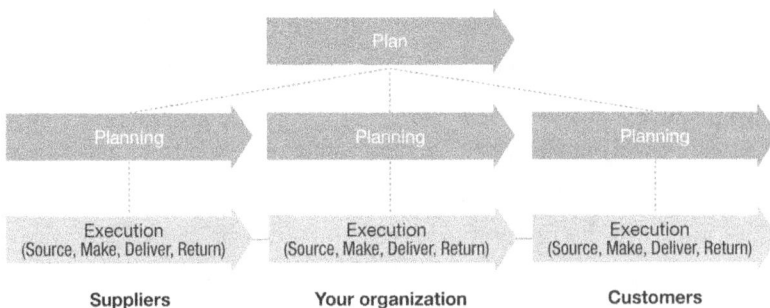

Consider a global manufacturer of computer peripherals that lagged behind its competitors in delivery performance. Despite having more than 80 days of finished-goods inventory, the company delivered only 75 percent of customer orders on time, compared with the industry leader's 90 percent on-time-delivery rate. To address these challenges, the company launched a number of supply chain improvement projects and invested in a costly, worldwide Enterprise Resource Planning (ERP) system to do a better job of managing orders, manufacturing, procurement, and accounting.

During this initiative, however, a closer look at operating practices revealed that the company had focused on achieving objectives in individual functions at the expense of company-level outcomes. For example, manufacturing had redesigned its production facilities and set up just-in-time supplier deliveries, reducing total production time to industry best-in-class levels. Similarly, the logistics team had achieved industry-leading transportation costs by mandating full loads for trucks that moved products from plants to distribution centers. But because the company's supply chain lacked an end-to-end scope, these practices within individual functions did little to improve overall delivery performance.

To turn the situation around, the company refocused its improvement efforts, placing emphasis on improving end-to-end performance. Shorter order-fulfillment lead times became a top priority. To accelerate the planning cycle, the company implemented a weekly planning process that involved sales, manufacturing, purchasing, and logistics. And to reduce production and transportation times, the company consolidated customization activities into one regional center and shipped directly to customers.

Although these internal actions improved overall performance, the company realized it also needed to work with suppliers if it was to meet its delivery-performance targets (Figure 2.5). Many of those vendors required long lead times and did not allow changes to existing orders; this, in an industry in which new product introductions are a constant, resulted in a buildup of obsolete inventory. To solve this problem, the company more closely integrated its business processes with those of key-component suppliers. It implemented

Figure 2.5 Collaborative Planning in the Extended Enterprise

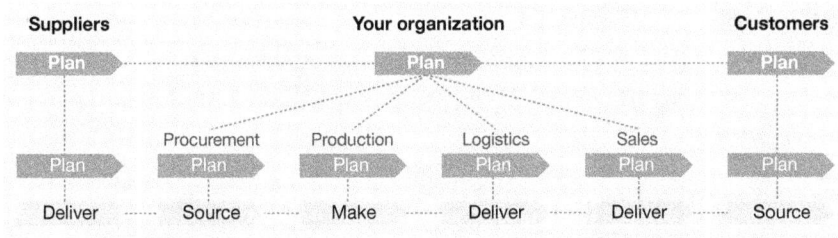

Suppliers	Your organization	Customers
Plan	Plan	Plan
	Procurement Production Logistics Sales	
Plan	Plan Plan Plan Plan	Plan
Deliver	Source Make Deliver Deliver	Source

vendor-managed inventory, which made suppliers responsible for ensuring that there were adequate component inventories at final-assembly factories. This new collaborative-planning process cut supplier lead time by 50 percent for some key components and greatly increased supply chain flexibility and on-time delivery to customers.

STRATEGIC FIT

Before implementing new practices, you will need to assess the value of each and ensure that it supports the basis of competition (Table 2.6). Will adopting the new practice improve working capital, customer service, return on assets, or supply chain costs? Will the practice differentiate the company, or is it a minimum requirement just to be in the game? In some cases, practices that were once considered cutting-edge have become the industry standard.

Amazon, for example, introduced a number of practices, such as self-serve order visibility for consumers, which helped establish the company as a leader in Internet retailing. Known for offering the "Earth's Biggest Selection," the company sells millions of different products, but it stocks only its top sellers. Amazon sells the vast majority of its offerings through partner companies, or it purchases them from distributors when necessary.

Providing a shipment date is easy when the product is in stock: the customer is told that the product "usually ships within 24 hours." But Amazon cannot give customers an exact delivery date for the many products that

Table 2.6 Aligning Supply Chain Processes with the Basis of Competition

Primary basis of competition	Differentiating supply chain practices	Critical supply chain processes
Innovation	• Design for supply chain	• Source, Make, Deliver
	• Collaborative innovation and planning with suppliers	• Plan, Source
	• Dedicated new product introduction (NPI) supply chain	• Source, Make
Customer experience	• Customer visibility on order status	• Deliver
	• Postponement	• Source, Make, Deliver
	• Customer collaborative planning	• Plan
Quality	• Traceability at product and lot levels	• Source, Make, Return
	• Full life-cycle tracking of sold products	• Make, Delivery, Return
Cost	• Integrated factory planning and scheduling	• Plan, Source, Make, Deliver
	• Raw-material and manufacturing-process standardization	• Source, Make
	• Design for manufacturing	• Source, Make

are provided by other companies because it does not have direct control over the delivery schedule. For these items, therefore, Amazon provides delivery commitments on the basis of recent actual lead times, saying, "usually ships in X days."

Despite its inability to follow the best practice of providing precise delivery dates when the order is placed, Amazon nonetheless maintains extremely high customer-satisfaction ratings. It's easy to see why. Customers can check their order status at any time after placing an order, and Amazon proactively notifies them when their product has shipped. The company also provides links to the carrier's website, allowing the customer to track the status of an order and the scheduled delivery date while the order is in transit. The result: customers benefit from an unparalleled array of products, while Amazon optimizes its inventory investment and keeps supply chain costs low.

To avoid the trap of choosing costly, leading-edge practices that provide only marginal support, analyze the contribution that new business practices will make. You can do this by identifying the metrics that will be affected and by understanding their impact on service, cost, and working capital.

RELIABILITY

The supply chain architecture must also be highly reliable, providing documented processes, accurate data, and integrated technology. Otherwise, your supply chain will be prone to errors as a result of the significant effort it takes to coordinate activities across departments and locations.

Documented Processes

Supply chain processes need to be documented not only to support quality management and related audits but also to provide the work instructions that operational teams need for their day-to-day work. While process development and management practices apply to all business processes, they're especially important for the supply chain because of the cross-functional nature of many of its activities. In addition, because many of today's supply chains involve multiple locations around the globe, clear and unambiguous processes are fundamental to get everyone working in a synchronized way.

Process documentation needs to be accessible to operational teams. It needs to be easy to consult as well as easy to understand. Often documentation is highly technical because it's been prepared by experts; it may, therefore, need significant simplification before it's ready to use. We recommend that before you declare the job finished, you should test any newly developed process documentation with operational teams to make sure it is easy to use.

Defining supply chain processes is the easy part. The bigger challenge is upgrading processes on the basis of experience and achieved performance.

Upgrading processes, which needs to be done on a regular basis, requires clear process ownership. It's usually clear who the owners of functional processes such as manufacturing are; however, ownership of processes that cut across multiple functions—for example, planning and order fulfillment—are often difficult to determine.

Accurate Data

Processes are only as good as their lifeblood of supporting data. The thousands of supply chain activities conducted every day depend on a wide range of data: master data (including supplier lead times, material masters, prices, and terms and conditions), transaction data (sales orders, inventory data, and purchase orders), and analytics that compare actual performance with targeted performance. Yet many organizations struggle to keep critical data accurate. One study estimates that even for the average company, almost 20 percent of master data are out-of-date and incomplete.[9] And in many companies, basic transaction information, like order data, is no better.

Here's an example: when implementing a new supply chain planning solution, a company entered standard defaults for supply lead times, with every intention of updating the data before the "go-live" date. No one, however, got around to updating the supplier lead times with accurate data. Because material orders were generated on the basis of inaccurate lead times, there was too much inventory of some materials and too little of others.

Like the supply chain process itself, supply chain data are challenging to manage given that multiple functions are involved in data entry, management, and deletion. So make sure that data quality assurance is a part of your ongoing supply chain process management.

Data structuring and cleaning are top priorities for companies with advanced supply chain practices. These companies use data quality indicators and automate data management processes through applications that support data quality checking and data cleaning. They also ensure proper data governance starting with the assignment of data owners. Many companies have established a separate data-management department and distinct data-management roles (for example, a head of master data management).[10]

Integrated Supporting Technology

The thousands of activities and millions of pieces of data that a supply chain needs to run effectively can't be fully leveraged without supporting technology. The scope of supply chain technology is vast. Internally, execution processes are supported by ERP applications and planning processes, which are typically supported by supply chain planning solutions. This is only part of the picture: other tools and applications are needed to support collaboration with suppliers and customers. Supporting technology is also required for enabling processes, such as those used in master data management and performance analysis and reporting.

The best supply chains have an integrated flow of information that matches the work flow. Unfortunately, too many companies use nonintegrated applications that require manual data reentry, changes in data formats, and multiple quality checks. This results in "applications islands," stand-alone applications that support only one piece of the end-to-end process (Figure 2.6). When links between processes and information systems are missing, there are higher risk of errors, longer cycle times, and added costs.

Integration is an ongoing challenge in most companies. For example, a company wanted to track forecast consumption to ensure that it was balancing demand and supply. The process required gathering data from two separate sources: an existing CRM application that held customer order data and a new planning application that contained information about incoming supply. But because the two systems described products in completely different ways, the company was forced to deploy a tool that translated the elements of a customer's order into planning items.

Figure 2.6 Application Islands Do Not Support Process Integration

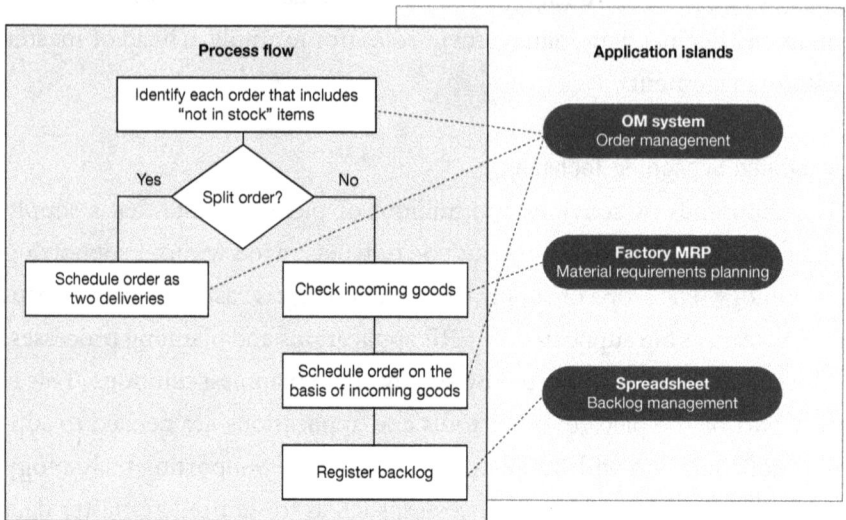

ADAPTABILITY

Once established, your overall supply chain process architecture should be relatively stable, though improvement and upgrading of processes should be done on a continuous basis. Performance evaluation of a given process (Plan, Source, Make, Deliver, Return, or Enable) can trigger a revised analysis of the underlying activities, identifying key changes required to meet the company's objectives. And every day, you can apply lessons learned inside your organization—along with insights gleaned from other companies through benchmarking—to identify new practices that can lead to better performance. Dedicate resources and establish governance to ensure these new practices are integrated into your supply chain process architecture and supporting information systems.

Major revisions of the process architecture are necessary only if changes are made to the supply chain strategy or if end-to-end supply chain goals, such as on-time delivery to customers, order-fulfillment cycle times, and working-capital objectives, cannot be attained. We'll explore major changes of this nature in Chapter 7.

THE SCOR MODEL

Because supply chain architectures can be so complex—involving hundreds of activities in each process and requiring integration not only among processes but also between the supply chain and other business functions—many companies find it difficult to evaluate their performance objectively. To address this issue, we helped develop the Supply Chain Operations Reference model, or SCOR. SCOR provides a process framework and standardized terminology that allow organizations to examine their supply chain architecture across consistent parameters and to ensure that it achieves their specific business objectives.[1]

SCOR consists of four major components: *performance*, a set of standard metrics and strategic goals that companies can use to assess their supply chain execution; *processes*, the specific processes and interactions between processes; *practices*, the activities and sub-processes that lead to better process performance; and *people*, the skills employees need to perform the processes successfully.

SCOR is managed by the Supply Chain Council (SCC), a global nonprofit that establishes cross-industry standards for supply chain management. SCC's membership includes hundreds of corporations, universities, government agencies, and other organizations with large global supply chains. These organizations apply SCOR to assess and improve their supply chain performance, using benchmarks and other improvement tools that SCC provides. Since its initial release in 1996, SCOR has evolved and will likely continue to evolve as the science of supply chain management advances.

FOUR SCOR LEVELS

SCOR breaks the supply chain into four levels, though it directly addresses only the first three: process types, or major processes; process categories; and process elements. For these levels, the model standard-izes terminology. By contrast, processes at the fourth level—operable processes—are highly detailed, work-flow-level tasks that are custom-ized to an organization's specific strategy and requirements. For this reason, they are not included in the model. The benefits that typically come from using SCOR are listed in the figure below.

Benefits of Using Each Level of SCOR

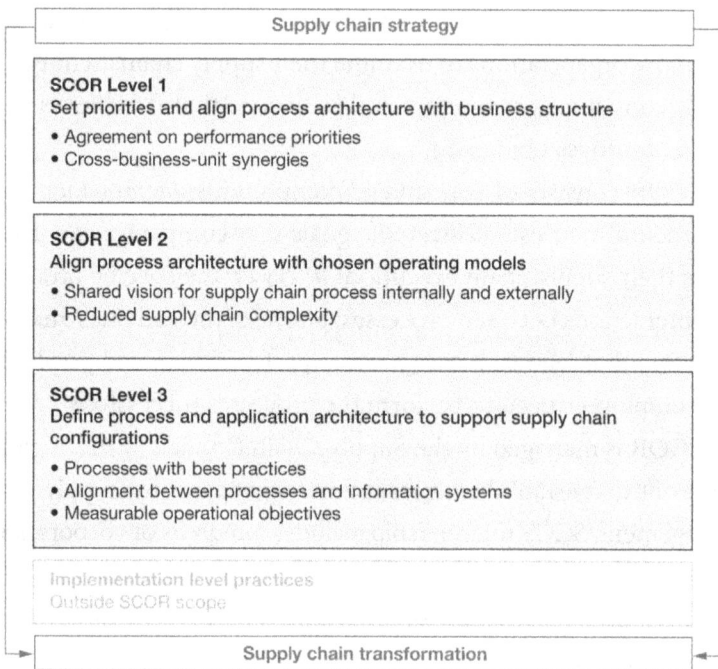

Supply chain strategy

SCOR Level 1
Set priorities and align process architecture with business structure
• Agreement on performance priorities
• Cross-business-unit synergies

SCOR Level 2
Align process architecture with chosen operating models
• Shared vision for supply chain process internally and externally
• Reduced supply chain complexity

SCOR Level 3
Define process and application architecture to support supply chain configurations
• Processes with best practices
• Alignment between processes and information systems
• Measurable operational objectives

Implementation level practices
Outside SCOR scope

Supply chain transformation

SCOR Level 1—Process Types, or Major Processes

Level 1 focuses on the six major supply chain processes—Plan, Source, Make, Deliver, Return, and Enable—and is used to define the overall scope of the supply chain. At this level, the company refines its strategic objectives: the business priorities that the supply chain must support.

Business processes and organization domains are also aligned at this stage. Here, it's critical to make sure that specific processes are associated with the high-level business structure (including business units, product lines, and regions) and supply chain partners. This is key for driving process standardization across the supply chain. Choices at Level 1 often drive IT costs, because different processes across business units typically involve multiple software applications as well as implementation and maintenance costs.

A leader in the consumer electronics industry was losing market share to competitors that had a stronger focus on specific market segments. Long organized as a single centralized business structure, the company needed to transform to multiple business units to compete more effectively. Given the critical importance of materials costs—up to 85 percent of product cost in that industry—as well as product quality and time to market, management decided to maintain centralized functions and assets across all six processes: Plan, Source, Make, Deliver, Return, and Enable. However, each business unit was to have its own inventory policies so that it could meet the specific service requirements of its particular markets.

SCOR Level 2—Process Categories

At Level 2—also called the configuration level—you'll choose the specific processes under each major process that will be needed to realize your supply chain strategy; you'll also choose the relevant operating models. The key Level 2 SCOR process categories are the make-to-stock, make-to-order, and engineer-to-order processes.

You can use these processes to describe the existing supply chain configurations. Typically, companies create a geographical map that shows where customers, suppliers, warehouses, factories, and order desks are located, and they use the process categories to describe the major physical and informational flows. In essence, this is a description of the processes in use today. SCOR refers to this as the "as is" state.

The next step is to develop and test improvement options for "to be," the ideal future state. But be aware that the SCOR Level 2 analysis may show that some processes cannot be optimized because of existing limitations, such as excessive transition costs. In other words, you may not be able to execute all of your to-be requirements in the near term, and so will need to develop a road map to reach your target configuration. (See Chapter 7.)

A commercial aircraft contractor was struggling to consistently meet the requirements of one of its major customers, an aircraft manufacturer. Relationships among internal sales, logistics, and manufacturing operations were complex; in addition, the contractor had to coordinate material, information, and financial flows with its own subcontractors located on three continents. As a result, deliveries to the aircraft manufacturer were increasingly late. And when the manufacturer asked to reschedule orders, the contractor had to contact its suppliers before confirming a delivery date—a process that took several weeks. These problems caused the contractor to lose credibility with the aircraft manufacturer.

In response, the project team used SCOR to determine where the problems lay. SCOR helped the team map order management, procurement, physical distribution, supply chain planning, and financial flows at the company as well as with subcontractors. The team thus was able to associate each activity with a SCOR Level 2 process category. Standardizing process category definitions this way meant that each company in the supply chain, both internal and external, was using the same process terminology for the first time.

The SCOR analysis allowed the team to identify several opportunities for simplifying the supply chain. For example, major subassemblies had previously moved through multiple internal warehouses before they were available for final assembly. This caused significant delays yet added no additional value to the product. The team real-

ized that a change in process and information systems would eliminate these unnecessary steps and shorten the delivery cycle by several
weeks.

Although the entire process took several months, it delivered dra-
matic results. Supplier on-time deliveries improved by more than 20
percent, and the amount of time needed to confirm an order dropped
sharply. Today, the company can confirm customer orders in two
to three days rather than two to three weeks. These improvements
helped the company restore its credibility with a major customer.

SCOR Level 3—Process Elements

In Level 3, the company further develops its supply chain architecture
by adding to its SCOR Level 2 design the required inputs and outputs,
metrics, practices, information systems support, and people skills.
Level 3 analysis can reveal a number of opportunities to streamline
your supply chain. It can help you reduce the complexity of processes and information systems; it can also help create better linkages
between processes. Moreover, the analysis is useful for eliminating
duplicate activities in multiple locations and for reducing process
cycle times.

In addition, Level 3 analysis provides the opportunity to determine which best practices, applications, metrics, and organizational
models would best serve the to-be supply chain. This typically involves
identifying issues associated with existing processes and information systems such as gaps, missing data, and insufficient integration
between systems.

Case in point: A large retailer needed to reduce inventory levels
without sacrificing service. The company had spent months mapping
its key processes and analyzing potential improvement opportunities.
However, the project team was not able to agree on the ideal to-be
supply chain.

To break the deadlock, the team mapped its current processes using SCOR Level 3. An analysis of the Plan Source (sP2) process elements revealed that the company had optimized its supply chain to move high volumes of consumer favorites that were purchased every day in predictable volumes (see the figure below). However, as an examination of a subelement (sP2.1) revealed, the company was not using real-time data from stores to develop planning requirements for suppliers. Although each store placed orders with the warehouses on the basis of its estimate of current demand, the warehouses were pulling inventory from suppliers on the basis of historical demand patterns for all products.

Using Plan Source (sP2) for Better Performance

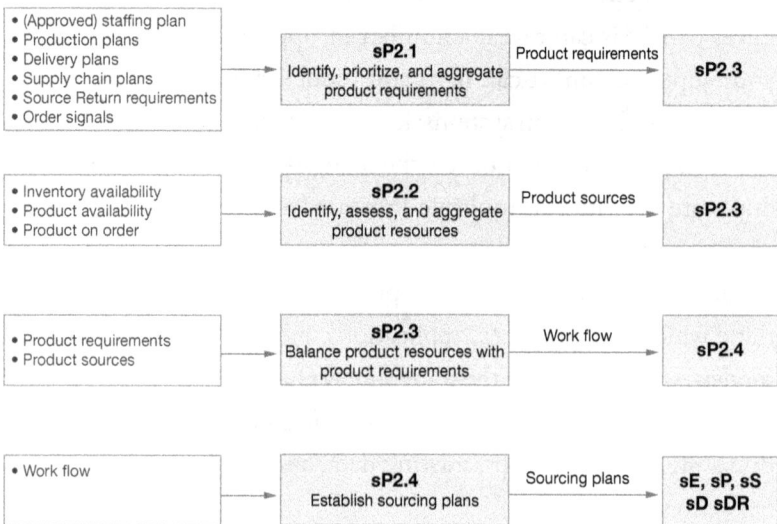

Inputs	Process	Output	Next
• (Approved) staffing plan • Production plans • Delivery plans • Supply chain plans • Source Return requirements • Order signals	**sP2.1** Identify, prioritize, and aggregate product requirements	Product requirements	**sP2.3**
• Inventory availability • Product availability • Product on order	**sP2.2** Identify, assess, and aggregate product resources	Product sources	**sP2.3**
• Product requirements • Product sources	**sP2.3** Balance product resources with product requirements	Work flow	**sP2.4**
• Work flow	**sP2.4** Establish sourcing plans	Sourcing plans	**sE, sP, sS sD sDR**

© Supply Chain Council, 2012

That was fine as long as current demand was consistent with historical levels. In reality, however, demand patterns for many products were highly variable, particularly for new products, store-level promotions, and the periodic introduction of seasonal merchandise. These events distorted demand patterns, creating a baseline demand that was appropriate only for a specific time period.

To solve this problem, the team realized it would be necessary to implement major changes to the planning process. This included introducing collaborative planning with suppliers during promotions and new product introductions.

As these examples show, SCOR provides a structured approach for developing the supply chain process architecture, thus paving the way for better overall performance. The model's top-down approach allows companies to see the big picture before going into greater levels of detail. And its hierarchical structure, which breaks down processes into subprocesses and activities, makes it possible to see how changes will affect existing supply chain operations. This insight helps companies better understand potential risks, needed resources, and implementation timelines. Equally important, it provides a solid basis for both improvement and ongoing management of the supply chain.

---

1.   Supply Chain Operations Reference Model, Revision 11.0, Supply Chain Council, October 2012.

KEY TAKEAWAYS

- To function effectively, supply chains require a process architecture that encompasses the six major processes: Plan, Source, Make, Deliver, Return, and Enable.

- The six processes are interdependent, so you must integrate and coordinate them. In addition, your supply chain process architecture must mesh well with other enterprise processes, including marketing and sales; product, service, and technology development; customer service and support; and finance.

- Companies typically focus their energy on the major execution-related processes—Source, Make, Deliver, and Return—as these are more tangible and easier to work with. However, planning is crucial, as are the enabling activities that support each process. Planning and enabling activities may be more abstract, but ultimately, they are the key drivers of supply chain performance.

- The complex organizational structures of most companies require setting standardization and harmonization rules for supply chain processes. These rules determine the degree to which processes and systems are the same across production sites, product lines, and business units.

- A robust supply chain architecture satisfies four tests—it provides end-to-end coverage, meaning it encompasses all interactions from your suppliers' suppliers through to your customers' customers; it has "strategic fit" in terms of specific processes and practices; it is reliable, meaning all six major processes are documented, integrated, and supported by high-quality data and integrated information systems; and, it is adaptable—with adjustments to processes based on strategic changes and organizational learning.

ESSILOR:
BUILDING AN EFFICIENT SUPPLY CHAIN TO SERVE THE COMPANY'S MISSION

"Being able to serve, in a fast and economical manner, the 4.2 billion people who need lenses to live a better life, from our 19 plants, means an efficient supply chain at the heart of our strategy. This is my dream."

—HUBERT SAGNIÈRES, CEO, ESSILOR

Every year or two, you go to an optician, who gives you a vision test and takes various eye measurements. Fast-forward a few hours or a couple of days: Voilà! Your glasses are waiting for you. Each lens is designed to perfectly suit the specific vision requirements of your left and right eyes while also taking into account how the two work together. In short, they are extremely personalized.

Thanks to ophthalmic-lens manufacturer Essilor, this is a familiar occurrence for millions of people in thousands of locations around the world. With more than 160 years of experience in the lens business, France-based Essilor Group—the name comes from the 1972 merger of Essel and Silor—is the world's largest producer of corrective eyeglass lenses. In 2011, Essilor sold 385 million lenses in more than 100 countries, and revenue should be close to €5 billion in FY 2012.

Essilor is committed to providing people everywhere with high-quality vision. This goes beyond ensuring that people have glasses with the right prescription. Given the link that has been established between bad vision and a variety of problems, including poor health, subpar scholastic performance, compromised safety, reduced productivity at work, and even criminal behavior, Essilor is committed to helping the greatest number of people possible to see properly, in order to improve their quality of life.

"Essilor's mission is to bring good vision to people around the world to increase their quality of life," says Paul du Saillant, chief operating officer. "Our growth strategy is based on four pillars: innovation in products and services, development of the top and middle range of products, international growth via partnership and acquisition, and stimulation of demand to increase market size and fulfill our mission. Our supply chain has been one of our key strengths in executing this strategy. It is a real competitive advantage."

INNOVATION AND CUSTOMER SERVICE: A WINNING COMBINATION

Essilor is well known in the industry for its innovative products. In 2012, for the second year running, the company was listed as one of the world's 30 most innovative companies by the U.S. magazine *Forbes*. Having invented the progressive lens under the brand Varilux back in 1959, the company continues to make new product development a top priority today. Every year, Essilor launches more than 200 new products: in 2011, 45 percent of sales came from products less than three years old. Among its latest innovations is the UV Crizal lens. The most complete anti-UV lens created to date, Crizal helps protect the eyes from rays that cause cataracts and blindness.

For Essilor, however, innovation also plays an important role in the way lenses are made. Over the past few years, the company has developed digital surfacing technologies that make it possible to polish lenses so that they are not only much more accurate but also thinner, lighter, and more flattering for the wearer. To make the best use of these new high-definition technologies, Essilor made changes in its manufacturing processes. The company also developed new optical equipment that allows opticians to capture the information—for example, the degree of eye rotation—that's needed for lenses that are so precise.

The Varilux S series, introduced in 2012, is the most recent result of these innovations. Based on the latest advances in optics and a deep understanding of human physiology, it is the first progressive lens to offer wide-angle vision correction without compromising stability in motion. By eliminating this trade-off, the Varilux S series marks a breakthrough in optics development.

To fuel its innovation engine, Essilor relies on its Centers of Innovation and Technology (CIT), acquisitions, and strategic partnerships with a number of companies with advanced technologies—for example, Nikon, known worldwide for its high-quality lenses. Essilor also acquired a number of companies, including Johnson & Johnson Vision Care's ophthalmic-lens business, The Spectacle Lens Group, whose proprietary technology can be used to make progressive lenses more personalized.

The focus on innovation explains why, in 2011, Essilor produced approximately 650,000 different SKUs, which is an astounding number of products by any count. This number represents all the different high-end and midrange lenses—including all the various frames, coatings, tints, and brands—that Essilor produces to meet the needs of its different customer segments.

While all of this translates into ultrapersonalized products, it also adds a great deal of complexity to the end-to-end supply chain—both the "good" complexity that is critical to competitive advantage and the "bad" complexity that can add unwanted costs and delays. This is especially challenging in light of the company's other key priority: high-level customer service in the form of short lead times. Essilor has consistently been able to achieve both goals because of its innovative approach to the supply chain.

TWO TYPES OF LENSES, TWO OPERATING MODELS

Essilor sells lenses to many different types of retail customers, ranging from international retail optical chains to small independent opticians. The value proposition of the retail location is to offer high-quality glasses that can be turned around quickly. One Essilor client, for example, was founded on the promise that a customer can walk into one of its stores needing a new pair of glasses and walk out wearing them an hour later.

Providing personalized products with short lead times is a tall order, because Essilor's supply chain needs to produce and deliver two major types of lenses, finished and semifinished. Finished lenses correct a single vision problem like myopia (nearsightedness), whereas semifinished lenses address presbyopia (farsightedness), a dual vision condition that people develop in middle age.

Essilor has met this challenge by developing two distinct operating models. Finished lenses are made to stock, while semifinished lenses are a combination of made to stock and made to order.

FINISHED LENSES

The end-customer visits a glasses store (either retail chain or independent), where an optician asks whether he wants the glasses to have any of a variety of features, including glare resistance, scratch resistance, and UV protection. The optician sends the prescription purchase order to Essilor. This is a retail business that is very local by nature, with hundreds of thousands of sales points sending in orders every day.

Upstream, the lenses are mass-produced in factories dedicated to making finished lenses. During this process, two molds are created for each lens—a convex mold for the front (outer) side of the lens and a concave mold for the back (inner) side.

After the lenses are molded, a number of coatings and tints are added to meet the needs of opticians and retail customers. The lenses are then shipped to regional distribution centers (DCs), where they are held as inventory. (Lenses can, however, be shipped directly to large accounts.) Upon receiving a purchase order from an optician, the local DC sends the store the lenses that fit the specific requirements of that order. Usually, the optician then edges and mounts the lenses in a frame of the end-customer's choosing, though this activity can be subcontracted to an Essilor finishing center.

Finished Single-Vision Supply Chain

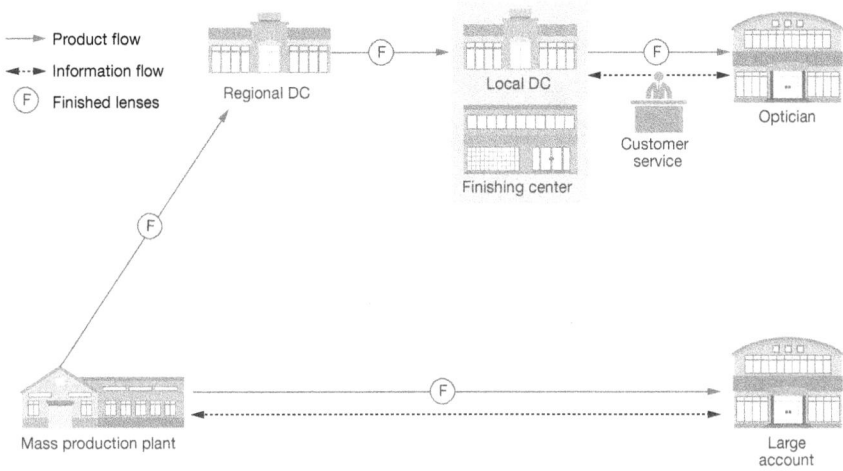

Source: Essilor

SEMIFINISHED LENSES
Essilor finalizes its semifinished lenses in one of two ways, either in local prescription labs (Rx local labs) or in mass-production labs (Rx export labs).

Semifinished Lenses, Local
In this operating model, the end-customer visits an independent optician. After taking eye measurements, the optician (or large account) sends the prescription, along with a list of the specific coatings requested by the end-customer, to the local Essilor prescription laboratory (Rx local lab). This lab

belongs to Essilor or to one of its partners; alternatively, it may be a laboratory that is not part of the Essilor network. These premium progressive lenses are distinguished from finished lenses in four ways: there is a wider variety, they are appropriate for a larger number of eye prescriptions, they are of a higher quality, and they can be ordered with a greater number of coating options.

Upstream, semifinished lenses (clear and polarized) are mass-produced in a dedicated plant that prepares only the front surface of the lenses. These lenses are shipped to a regional DC, where they are held and subsequently sent to fill the stock of labs.

After receiving a prescription from the optician, the lab polishes the back surface of the lenses and adds the coatings and tints requested by the optician. Surface finishing in the labs thus makes it possible for Essilor to produce many different combinations of lenses while at the same time keeping the number of lenses in inventory low.

The Rx local lab sends the lenses back to the optician, who edges and mounts them in a frame for the end-customer; alternatively, the labs can do the edging and mounting. The whole order-fulfillment process—from the customer's first visit to having glasses available for the customer—takes only two days.

Semifinished and Export Supply Chain

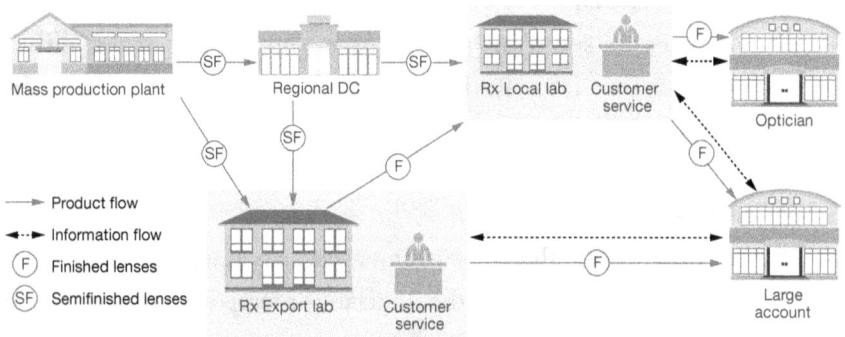

Source: Essilor

Semifinished Lenses for Export

A few years ago, Essilor added six lower-cost prescription labs to the supply chain "Rx export labs," which are mass-production labs located in low-cost countries. Instead of being finalized in regular Rx labs, a portion of semifinished lenses are sent from the mass-production plants and regional DCs to Rx export labs. These labs then ship the lenses to local labs and large accounts in markets worldwide for last-mile consolidation. The Rx export lab in Mexico, for instance, supplies lenses to retail chains in the United States. Only a few megastores have their own labs for finalizing lenses.

"The capability of the carriers used to transport product between countries in different continents has evolved, as has IT," notes Vice President of Supply Chain and Rx Strategy Eric Javellaud. "So we were able to build export labs in low-cost countries while retaining proximity to developed markets. This makes it possible to fulfill customer orders in just five days: two days in the lab to surface and treat the lens, one day for transportation from the lab to the store, and two days in the store to do the edging and mounting."

DEVELOPING THE GLOBAL END-TO-END SUPPLY CHAIN

Up until the 1970s, Essilor produced its lenses in France and sold them mostly in Europe. Over the next 20 years, the company expanded internationally, setting up regional manufacturing and distribution facilities to be close to its customers. Essilor's first factories outside Europe were in the continental United States and the Philippines, followed by plants in Mexico, Puerto Rico, and Brazil.

In the late 1990s, Essilor decided to go truly global, acquiring and partnering with companies to expand its operational footprint. Unlike some companies, the lens maker developed its supply chain as an integral part of its growth strategy. The goal was to grow in developed markets while establishing a presence in emerging ones. To this end, Essilor built new factories in Thailand and China; the company also acquired a number of lens makers in China.

At the same time, Essilor acquired or partnered with a number of Rx lab companies in the United States and India. This bolstered the company's capacity to produce quality progressive lenses in regions with high demand.

Notably, the companies that joined the Essilor network were not forced to change all their processes immediately. They did, however, have to adopt Essilor's worldwide codification of products and use the same electronic data interchange standards for placing orders. In return, they were given access to Essilor's advanced production technology. Even more important, they became part of Essilor's global supply chain and could enjoy the attendant steady customer demand and global economies of scale.

To support the global supply chain, Essilor put global sourcing and planning processes in place. The first step was to consolidate the various IT systems used by operations worldwide into one integrated end-to-end system. "We set up an ERP system that connected all the relevant operational functions—order management, procurement, purchasing, and so on," recalls Gérard Tourenq, vice president of worldwide logistics. "This has enabled the company to set up the same processes in every region worldwide."

The global IT system also enables Essilor to manage a tremendous amount of information coming from the end-customer—the dozens of different types of progressive lenses as well as the wide range of coatings and tints. Essilor's IT system is robust enough to convey such information to both Rx labs and Rx export labs alike.

At the same time, Essilor set up a global supply chain organization. Each of the company's four regions—America, Latin America, Europe, and AMERA (Asia, the Middle East, Russia, and Africa)—has a supply chain department. A global team works on processes and practices with a focus on planning, plant scheduling, and inventory management, while in each zone—that is, each subset of countries in a particular region— managers are accountable for providing demand information and for driving inventory replenishment.

As a result of these global initiatives, Essilor became the first in its industry to develop a truly global supply chain. By 2011, the company had 19 manufacturing plants—4 in Europe, 9 in southern Asia, 1 in Japan, 4 in North and Central America, and 1 in Brazil—and 390 Rx labs.

BALANCING INVENTORY WITH SERVICE

By any standard, Essilor manages an enormous number of SKUs, which grows steadily as new products are added to the portfolio. In this situation, excess and obsolete inventory presents a major challenge, and makes it essential to find the right balance between costs and service.

For Essilor, the solution is to generally keep little if any inventory at its plants. As they are produced, lenses are shipped to regional DCs or to Rx labs. The network varies by region: the United States is very centralized, but lead-time requirements in Europe, with its various transportation challenges, necessitate a DC in practically every country.

Moreover, the global planning process covers forecasts and inventory sizing for each subsidiary. In addition to biannual reviews, there's a monthly sales and operations planning process. The purpose is to develop an achievable plan that is based on forecast demand, sales targets, and the operational capabilities of Essilor, external partners, and suppliers. Each month, forecast updates are used to size inventory and manage plant loads.

In the United States, Essilor implemented a replenishment process that's based on real-time sales. When an order for a pair of progressive lenses arrives at one of the 127 U.S. labs, it is filled with semifinished lenses sitting on the lab shelf. Within 24 hours, those lenses are replaced automatically by the nearest DC. The following Monday, the DC places a replenishment order online, which generates make-to-order production at a plant in Mexico or Asia. Regardless of where the production takes place, replenishment processes are a collaborative effort of the entire supply chain: the laboratories, the Essilor subsidiaries, the geographic regions, and the global supply chain organization.

Essilor has refrained from fully automating some of its planning processes—a decision that underscores the company's interest in balancing cost savings with service. "By keeping some steps dependent on human decision, we have the flexibility to change the product mix when needed," explains Tourenq. "If you optimize everything, what's optimized could end up being a constraint."

MASTERING COMPLEXITY

Producing some 650,000 SKUs and managing deliveries to some 200,000 ship-to points requires extremely good management of complexity. In addition to differentiating flows for finished and semifinished lenses, Essilor has greatly streamlined the delivery process. The company has worked steadily to consolidate the number of U.S. distribution centers, which had multiplied as a result of several acquisitions. Essilor has also pushed back the final packaging process so that it occurs after receipt of a customer's purchase order, thus eliminating the need for repackaging in the event of a last-minute order change. In addition, the lens maker has begun shipping directly to customers where possible.

Essilor has also consistently turned to technology to manage complexity. This includes the use of digital surfacing, which makes it possible to create different prescription surfaces at a late stage of production. At the same time, the company has invested in advanced technologies that make it possible to track individual customer orders as they progress through the supply chain.

Taken together, these practices have had a major impact, both operationally and financially. Not only is Essilor recognized for service in the industry, its inventory as a percentage of sales declined from an index of 100 in 1999 to one of 81 in 2011.

BUILDING IN ADAPTABILITY AND RELIABILITY

Being global is great, but it is not enough: a natural disaster can suddenly throw a supply chain off course. Such events can be especially problematic for a company that views its customer service as a source of competitive advantage.

Essilor deploys a number of strategies to mitigate the risk of disruption. First, it has built a closely linked network around its Rx labs and distribution centers. This allows the company to adjust production, capacity, distribution, and pricing with little advanced notice.[1]

Essilor has also made a point of placing redundant plants and additional inventory in vulnerable parts of the supply chain. Its large network helped the lens maker weather the flooding in Thailand in late 2011.

In addition, Essilor has taken steps to standardize its process architecture worldwide. The company is standardizing manufacturing processes to facilitate moving production from one plant to another. It is also standardizing distribution processes in order to shift inventory easily between DCs, while securing the distribution network with a business continuity plan. At Essilor, adaptability also means being able to develop new supply chain setups to meet customer needs. In response to requests by retail chain customers, the lens maker has started developing value-added services, taking over some of its customers' supply chain responsibilities. For some large retailers, Essilor has built a supply chain to provide lenses and to manage the vast number of frames they sell.

Essilor's emphasis on flexibility makes sense in an industry where technological change is a constant. Every new development, whether it's the next generation of progressive lenses (there have been four so far) or the next manufacturing process, makes it crucial for the supply chain to be able to adapt readily and easily.

THE NEXT 2.5 BILLION

Worldwide, 4.2 billion people are in need of visual correction. Yet nearly 60 percent go without glasses, either because they cannot afford them or because there's no optical store nearby. Most of those 2.5 billion people live in emerging markets, 50 percent are under the poverty line, 60 percent are in rural areas, and 30 percent are children. By 2030, if nothing is done globally, there could be as many as 3.5 billion people in need going without correction.

Making visual health accessible to the greatest number of people is for Essilor both an ambition and a responsibility. The company aims to help reverse, by 2020, the rise in the number of people lacking access to visual correction.

To this end, Essilor is innovating with new products and business models and using partnerships and new competencies to develop offerings that address customer needs. And a number of local initiatives are helping to distribute lenses to the people who need them: mobile optical shops in rural India, screening projects in China, and charity initiatives led by the Essilor Vision Foundation.

Making a lasting contribution to society is one of the key objectives of Essilor as a company—and an energizing purpose for its teams.

CHAPTER THREE

DISCIPLINE 3: DESIGN A HIGH-PERFORMING SUPPLY CHAIN ORGANIZATION

Companies across industries have had to rethink the design of their supply chain organizations. The best designs address three major questions: Who in the organization should be responsible for which activities? How should the organization be structured? What skills are critical for top supply chain performance?

In today's world, where globalization, volatile demand, and frequent disruption pose constant challenges to global supply chains, the role of the supply chain organization is more critical than ever. That's because the supply chain organization is responsible for driving the supply chain strategy.

But creating a strong supply chain organization isn't easy. For one thing, it's difficult to find people with the right skills and knowledge. It's also difficult to know which organizational structure will work best and who should be responsible for what.

To add to the challenge, today's most effective supply chains differ greatly from those of the past. Twenty or thirty years ago, many companies regarded their supply chain organization as a group of separate functions responsible for tactical execution—buying raw materials, for example, or manufacturing and delivering products. They included such departments as procurement, production, and shipping and receiving; those departments took direction from what were considered to be more strategic functions, such as product development, sales, or marketing. It was rare to find a senior executive who had come up through the operations organization; indeed, most operations managers found they had limited pathways to senior-management roles.

Things have changed a great deal. Recognizing the supply chain's strategic importance, companies are increasingly designing their supply chain organization to encompass the six major processes of Plan, Source, Make, Deliver, Return (in some instances), and Enable. They are also implementing the policies and procedures, information systems, and reporting relationships needed to support those end-to-end major processes. Moreover, they're ensuring that their supply chain organization has strong relationships with other internal functions and departments and with external partners so that the supply chain organization can play a role in everything from product design to service and support.

Designing a supply chain organization with these capabilities doesn't necessarily require your company to overhaul existing operations or invent new departments. What's key, rather, is making sure the organization includes the people responsible for executing and continually improving each process. In some cases, this may require large-scale restructuring that will group together the people who support a stream of work that crosses traditional organizational boundaries. In other cases, it may involve relatively small modifications designed to bolster true cross-functional management. That might mean consolidating two departments to eliminate a process handoff, or it might be as simple as reallocating responsibilities within a particular group.

With these points in mind, this chapter offers guidelines for designing a supply chain organization: the activities essential for the design and the distinguishing characteristics of a well-designed organization.

THREE ACTIVITIES ESSENTIAL FOR DESIGNING YOUR COMPANY'S SUPPLY CHAIN ORGANIZATION

First, a basic definition is in order. We define the supply chain organization as the group that consists of every company employee who handles the Plan, Make, Source, Deliver, Return, and Enable processes. These people all report to the organization leader, who may be called the chief supply chain officer, the vice president of supply chain, or something similar.

To design an effective supply chain organization, a company must excel at three major sets of activities that are interrelated and mutually reinforcing (Figure 3.1):

- Defining the roles and responsibilities
- Selecting the right organization structure
- Putting the right skills and talent in place

Although the activities are presented here in a sequence, there is no prescribed order for pursuing them. Your company can start with any one of the three, provided that you treat the organization design process as an iterative one.

Figure 3.1 Interrelated Activities for Designing a Supply Chain Organization

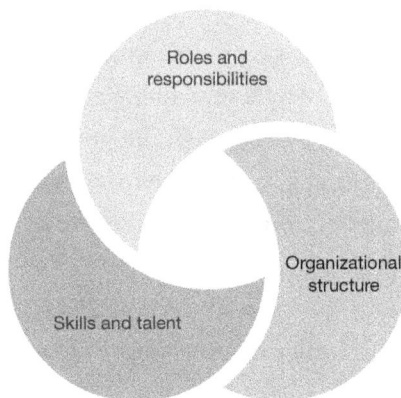

DEFINING THE ROLES AND RESPONSIBILITIES

Consider all the tasks and activities that need to occur in order for the supply chain to function well. (See Chapter 2.) Can you state clearly who is doing what within your existing supply chain organization? If not, your supply chain organization is probably not living up to its full potential. Every essential role needs to be clearly defined, as does the responsibility for executing it.

As an example, consider the process for ensuring that purchased materials meet your company's quality specifications. Many companies describe their incoming inspection process this way: "First, materials are received at the loading dock. Next, the quality of incoming materials is validated through a standard sampling plan." This process description, though oversimplified, is not unlike the process documentation or standard operating procedures used in many companies: it states what needs to happen. But it leaves out critical information about who is responsible for executing each of these tasks. Here's a better way to document this process: "The receiving team records the receipt of incoming materials, then inspects the materials to validate their quality."

The difference is subtle but important. Every activity needed to support your supply chain strategy must be owned by an individual or a team. It's surprising how often companies do not observe this practice.

Consider a company that was producing configure-to-order products in a crowded market dominated by several major players. Customers expected delivery within a few days, even though the process of selecting, validating, assembling, and testing a specific product configuration could easily stall. Those delays could be considerable: some 15 percent of orders were at least three weeks late.

Many of the delays were due to technical problems—like an infeasible configuration or an order that included obsolete options—that only a member of the sales-engineering team could resolve. When customers called to complain, they found that their account managers knew neither the reason for the delay nor when the order would be delivered. Account managers were equally frustrated, because they weren't alerted when an order was stalled or a new ship date was set. These issues put the company at risk of losing sales to competitors.

The management team mapped out the order management process step by step and took a close look at who was responsible for making sure each step happened. A RACI chart (Figure 3.2; also, see Sidebar "What Is RACI?") immediately revealed the problem: no one was made responsible for communicating to the customer when to expect delivery or, in cases where there was a delay, what the new delivery date was.

Figure 3.2 Example of Order Management RACI Analysis

	Account manager	Order administration	Sales engineering	Assembly and test
Select and validate configuration	A		R	
Determine price	A		R	
Communicate price to customer	A	R		
Receive and enter customer order	I	A		
Calculate ship date based on standard lead time		C		A
Communicate initial delivery date to customer	I	I		
Resolve technical issues	C	I	A	
Update ship date	I	I	C	A
Communicate updated delivery date to customer		I		C

A: Accountable   C: Consulted   I: Informed   R: Responsible
◀ No responsible or accountable function designated

WHAT IS RACI?[1]

RACI is an acronym derived from the four potential roles that an individual or function could play relative to a specific activity:

- **R=Responsible.** An R designates the person(s) or function(s) responsible for completing a particular activity or step in a process. Responsibility can be shared.
- **A=Accountable.** An A designates the person or function ultimately accountable for ensuring that the activity is completed. There can be only one A for a decision or activity.
- **C=Consulted.** A C designates the person(s) or function(s) that must be consulted before a decision or activity is finalized.
- **I=Informed.** An I designates the person(s) or function(s) informed of the results once a step is completed.

A RACI chart can help a company clarify roles and responsibilities in cross-functional processes. You structure the chart by identifying the individuals or functions that participate in a process (presented as columns), the key activities taking place (presented as rows), and the primary outcomes for process elements that contain a judgment or decision. Activities apply to a role or need, not to the specific person currently responsible for the task. Once you've created the chart, you enter the appropriate RACI code in each applicable cell.

After you've populated the chart, you need to resolve any ambiguities and problems. The presence of many Rs in a column indicates that a function may be overloaded or have insufficient focus. And a lack of Rs and As signifies that the role is a candidate for elimination. If every box in a row is filled in, ask whether that many functions really need to be involved in the activity in question. If there are no As, ask why no one's accountable. Some group or person must have accountability for the activity.

---

1.   J. Mike Jacka and Paulette Keller, *Business Process Mapping: Improving Customer Satisfaction*, 2nd ed., Hoboken: John Wiley and Sons, 2009, 257.

Following the analysis, the company modified the order management process to clarify the sequence of activities and the responsibility for executing the activities. The assembly and test group would determine the completion date; order management would notify the account manager of the planned ship date and update it whenever there was a delay. Similarly, the account manager would notify the customer of the delivery date and update it as necessary.

SELECTING THE RIGHT ORGANIZATIONAL STRUCTURE

Defining supply chain roles and responsibilities helps you understand all the activities that need to happen for your company's supply chain to run smoothly. But these activities need to be organized such that an entity—a group, function, or individual—is responsible for making sure that each activity happens, and an entity is accountable for each outcome.

Take, for example, the activity of validating and booking a customer order. This seems simple enough, but if it's carried out incorrectly, it can have a major impact on revenue reporting or, worse, can result in noncompliance with legal requirements. When you examine the order management process at your company, is there a clear view of who sets the requirements for considering an order booked? Who carries out this activity? Who makes sure it's completed? Who needs to be informed that an order has been entered and booked? Who needs to be consulted if a problem arises? How you answer these questions—especially regarding the R and A roles—has direct implications for your supply chain organization's structure. It affects how information and materials flow through your organization, who interacts with whom to handle the activity, who reports to whom, what span of control individuals have, and how job descriptions are defined.

There isn't one answer for what a supply chain organization should look like. The right structure is one that most effectively enables execution of your company's business strategy and that allows your supply chain to deliver the required operational performance. You can think of this as arranging responsibilities and accountabilities in a way that ensures that all the processes and activities that make up each major process are under the purview of one senior executive.

Three types of supply chain organization structures can help your company meet these imperatives: centralized, decentralized, and hybrid (Table 3.1). Though the structures differ in important ways, each can support your business strategy and improve your supply chain's performance—providing you use the right criteria.

Table 3.1 Choosing the Optimal Supply Chain Organizational Structure

Organizational structure	Advantages
Centralized	• Leverages economies of scale • Consolidates global demand and supply, allowing optimized decisions about what products to make, sell, and distribute—and where • Allows dissemination of policies, procedures, and process consistency across the whole company
Decentralized	• Accommodates cultural differences between business units and/or geographies • Optimizes supply chain processes for a product, unit, or region • Enables business units to operate with autonomy
Hybrid	• Encourages development teams to share components and/or suppliers • Uses corporate standards for certain business elements, but gives flexibility to business units in how these standards are executed

Centralized

In a supply chain organization with a centralized structure, core processes are managed at the corporate level and are deployed across multiple business units, regions, or product groups. Companies use a centralized model because it can provide economies of scale, reduce redundancy, and allow global common policies and procedures. Centralized sourcing, for example, allows a company to consolidate material spend, and thus improve its purchasing power with key suppliers. And centralized supply chain planning provides global visibility into supply and demand, making it easier to optimize revenue and margins across multiple products and geographies.

IBM is a company with a centralized supply chain organization. In the past, the company had 30 distinct supply chains, one for each of its business units, and each unit had its own supply chain organization. Then IBM took the significant step of creating its Integrated Supply Chain (ISC) organization, a stand-alone business unit charged with making and delivering IBM products and services to customers. Consolidating all core supply chain functions, the ISC was designed to provide front-end customer support, manufacturing, procurement, and logistics services across 59 countries.[2]

Decentralized

A decentralized supply chain organization puts responsibility for the Plan, Source, Make, Deliver, Return, and Enable processes in the hands of business units, regions, or product groups. Each division has the authority to manage its supply chain independently of the others and thus is free to negotiate its own contracts, select its own suppliers, and control its own inventory.

Decentralized supply chain organizations are common in large, complex companies that sell many different kinds of products. It's often the case that the company has grown through mergers and acquisitions and decides to retain the various supply chain organizations it inherited along the way. Take Johnson & Johnson, which consists of more than 250 operating companies located in 57 countries around the world. The operating companies are organized into three distinct segments: Consumer Health Care, Medical Devices & Diagnostics, and Pharmaceuticals.[2]

With oversight provided by a central organization called the Group Operating Committee, each of the three segments functions as its own operating company. Senior management at each operating company is responsible for that business's strategic plans, as well as for its day-to-day operations, and each company manages its own end-to-end supply chain. Although certain corporate standards, such as J&J's approach to corporate social responsibility (CSR), influence the design and management of each operating company's supply chain, individual management teams determine how to meet the CSR standards.

Hybrid

A hybrid supply chain organization (Figure 3.3) centralizes some supply chain processes while allowing divisions or regions to manage others. Most commonly, a company selecting this structure centralizes sourcing responsibility but lets divisions manage their own planning, manufacturing, and delivery, yet all kinds of permutations exist. Hybrid companies may, for example, centralize responsibility for negotiating partnerships with providers of outsourced services, while leaving day-to-day management of these relationships to division heads.

Consumer goods giant Unilever provides an apt example of a company with a hybrid structure. With dual headquarters in the Netherlands and the United Kingdom, Unilever sells more than 400 product brands—think Lipton, Dove, and Surf—across four major product categories: Foods, Refreshment, Home Care, and Personal Care. Revenue in 2011 was €46.5 billion.

Only recently did Unilever adopt a hybrid organizational structure, however. Until the late 1990s, all of the company's supply chain activities

Figure 3.3 Example Hybrid Supply Chain Organization

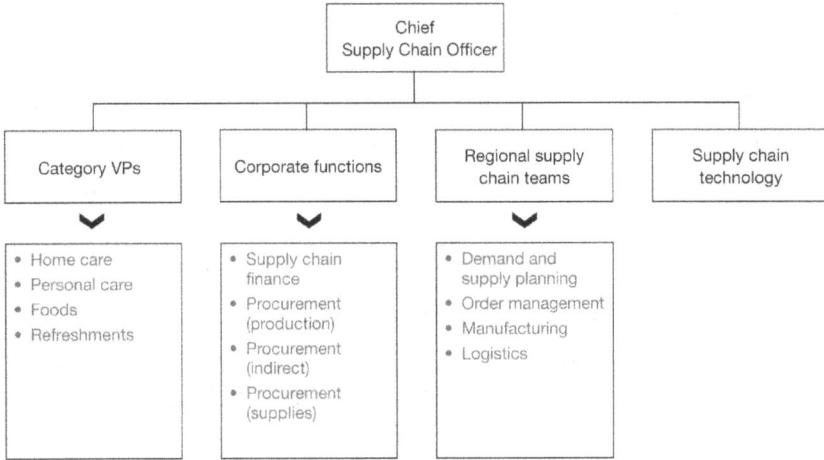

```
                        ┌─────────────────────┐
                        │        Chief         │
                        │ Supply Chain Officer │
                        └─────────────────────┘
        ┌───────────────────┬──────────┴──────────┬───────────────────┐
┌───────────────┐  ┌──────────────────┐  ┌──────────────────┐  ┌──────────────┐
│ Category VPs  │  │Corporate functions│  │ Regional supply  │  │ Supply chain │
│               │  │                  │  │   chain teams    │  │  technology  │
└───────────────┘  └──────────────────┘  └──────────────────┘  └──────────────┘
       ▼                   ▼                    ▼
┌───────────────┐  ┌──────────────────┐  ┌──────────────────┐
│ • Home care   │  │ • Supply chain   │  │ • Demand and     │
│ • Personal care│  │   finance        │  │   supply planning│
│ • Foods       │  │ • Procurement    │  │ • Order management│
│ • Refreshments│  │   (production)   │  │ • Manufacturing  │
│               │  │ • Procurement    │  │ • Logistics      │
│               │  │   (indirect)     │  │                  │
│               │  │ • Procurement    │  │                  │
│               │  │   (supplies)     │  │                  │
└───────────────┘  └──────────────────┘  └──────────────────┘
```

were managed at the local level. Although this arrangement provided local autonomy for regional organizations, it hindered operational efficiency across the enterprise.

As it grew globally, Unilever restructured the way its businesses were organized, creating two major divisions that encompassed all of its products worldwide. Shifting P&L responsibility away from the local organizations provided new insight on which materials were common across its product categories. Major supply categories, such as dairy products, tea, fragrances, and oils, emerged.

To leverage its global scale while remaining agile locally, Unilever adopted a hybrid supply chain organizational design.[3] Teams in each of Unilever's eight geographic regions, or "clusters," are responsible for what the company calls "front-line functions." They manage the day-to-day business, including demand-and-supply balancing, customer order management, manufacturing, and logistics.

At the same time, Unilever's corporate supply chain organization manages 95 percent of procurement. Consolidating demand in this way makes it easier to hedge against price volatility. It also gives Unilever clout to demand that products, such as palm oil, be farmed sustainably.[4] The corporate supply chain team also manages other functions that cut across the company, such as customer service and quality, to ensure that they are seamlessly integrated with cluster operations. This leaves the category vice presidents free to focus on product innovation and brand building. The cluster supply chain teams, corporate supply chain functions, and category vice presidents are all managed by the chief supply chain officer, Pier Luigi Sigismondi.

These changes have made the supply chain a real strategic asset. It has played an important role in Unilever's effort to double the size of its business while simultaneously bolstering product quality and cost savings. For this reason, in 2012, Gartner ranked Unilever one of the world's ten best supply chains. As CSCO Sigismondi notes, "Our supply chain represents the backbone of Unilever's success and is making the difference to our business, thanks to our unique blend of global scale and local agility."[5]

Centralized, Decentralized, Hybrid: How to Choose?

Above all else, the choice of supply chain organizational structure should be based on how best to support the company's business strategy. A company's business strategy should be stable, but it will certainly evolve over time—and the supply chain organization should evolve with it.

Consider a business that's planning to enter a new geographic market. In this new market, the enterprise may face local sourcing or employment regulations or find that the cost to transport products from existing production locations is prohibitive. If the business currently uses a centralized structure, it may want to consider a shift to a hybrid strategy that facilitates the tailoring of processes and infrastructure to local requirements.

A supply chain organization's structure should also reflect the company's culture. An enterprise that wants to foster an entrepreneurial spirit may not find it advantageous to use a centralized structure that dictates how supply chain work gets done.

There's also the issue of complexity. Even if a company has sound reasons for establishing a decentralized supply chain organization, multiple procurement or planning organizations may create so much complexity that the resulting costs eliminate the advantages.

Finally, consider whether local autonomy will be advantageous or disadvantageous. Some management teams find that it makes sense to start with a centralized organization that can help align processes and behaviors. The company may then shift to providing more autonomy to business units or geographies.

A recent PwC study found that many high-performing companies prefer to use a hybrid model (Figure 3.4). They centralize many of their core strategic processes, such as new production introduction, procurement of strategic materials and services, and supply chain centers of excellence, and they manage up to 75 percent of their customer order, service, operational procurement, and delivery functions at a regional level.[6] These companies get the benefits of economies of scale for procurement as well as the flexibility and responsiveness that are possible with regional manufacturing and distribution.

Figure 3.4 Global vs. Regional Management

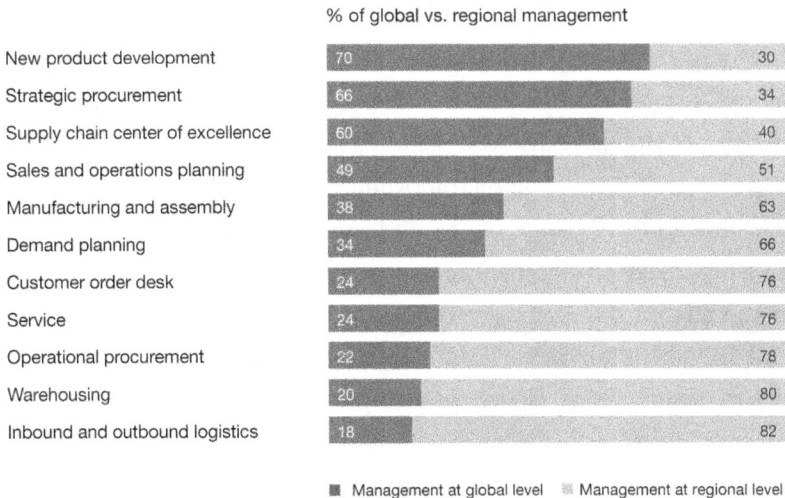

% of global vs. regional management

	Management at global level	Management at regional level
New product development	70	30
Strategic procurement	66	34
Supply chain center of excellence	60	40
Sales and operations planning	49	51
Manufacturing and assembly	38	63
Demand planning	34	66
Customer order desk	24	76
Service	24	76
Operational procurement	22	78
Warehousing	20	80
Inbound and outbound logistics	18	82

■ Management at global level   ▧ Management at regional level

Note: Some numbers in the chart total more than 100 because of rounding.

Source: *Next-Generation Supply Chains: Efficient, Fast, and Tailored,* Global Supply Chain Survey 2013, PwC, 2012.

Whichever structure you choose, be sure that you can provide the right information technology to support it. A centralized structure without fully integrated information systems between business units or geographies won't be able to deliver on the promised advantages of aggregation and economies of scale. Likewise, a decentralized structure that can't translate disparate data into consistent information about the state of each business won't be able to provide a true picture of how the company is performing as a whole.

PUTTING THE RIGHT SKILLS IN PLACE

In addition to defining the key roles and structure of your company's supply chain organization, you need to ensure that people with the right skills, talents, and interests fill each role. This is much harder now than it was ten years ago. Today's high-risk business environment demands that supply chain professionals have skills of a whole new order.

Supply chain leaders need to be fluent in the language and mechanics of supply chain management, such as material requirements planning, inventory management, and production control. But these are just the basics. People also need strong analytical abilities to extract business insights from the vast amounts of data now available to supply chain professionals. They need deep process knowledge, a desire to serve customers, and an understanding of their company's corporate social-responsibility policies. In addition, they must be adept at handling tools aimed at improving overall performance, such as advanced planning and scheduling or logistics optimization systems. Particularly important, because of the cross-functional and cross-company nature of the end-to-end supply chain, supply chain professionals need broad operational experience and strong communication and relationship-management skills.

Sound like a tall order? It is. Nearly 60 percent of executives report that acquisition and development of supply chain talent is critical to their company's success. That's one reason why executive recruiters are so busy these days. It's also why so many companies are revving up their internal training programs and boosting compensation packages for successful supply chain managers.

Breadth of Experience

For the most part, supply chain management skills are highly transferrable across industries. Carlos Garcia, senior client partner for executive recruiting firm Korn/Ferry's supply chain practice, notes that some of the most successful executives have a broad range of experience. "The best supply chain people have sat in every seat," he says. "They not only understand the core supply chain processes but have experience with other functions such as sales, marketing, finance, and engineering."[7]

Increasingly frequently, new supply chain executives come from a different industry altogether. In fact, some of the most sought after are people with experience in multiple industries and geographies; many started their careers in functions unrelated to supply chain. Certainly, many highly successful supply chain executives have remained in the same industry throughout their careers. But breadth is becoming an increasingly important qualification.

Communication and Relationship-Management Skills

Supply chain roles used to require mostly technical skills—choosing and managing suppliers, running efficient production facilities, understanding the mechanics of materials planning. Those skills are still critical, Garcia notes, but they're really just the price of admission. While today's supply chain managers need to be grounded in the basics of each core process, they also need to be skilled in communication, persuasion, and the nuances of managing relationships in a matrix, or "dotted line," organization. These skills have become increasingly important as more companies operate in numerous locations around the world.

As an example, in a matrix organization, one person may be responsible for developing relationships with companies that provide contract-manufacturing services in numerous geographies, while local managers handle day-to-day operations. The local managers may report directly to the general manager of their region and at the same time answer to the executive responsible for global contract manufacturing. Supply chain managers need to be adept at retaining control over activities that aren't in their direct reporting hierarchy.

Strong relationship-management skills can also help supply chain professionals deftly handle the conflicts that can arise in companies over seemingly competing objectives. For instance, people who manage procurement are evaluated on criteria such as how much they pay for materials, the quality of what they purchase, and whether materials are delivered on time. Meanwhile, those in charge of CSR must ensure that all purchases meet standards for labor, ethics, and sustainability. It's very likely that raw materials certified as fair trade, conflict free, or carbon neutral will be more expensive—a situation that can put the CSR and procurement organizations at odds with one another. A skilled supply chain executive will know how to balance the two groups' objectives in ways that serve the company's overall strategy.

BUILDING A TALENT PIPELINE

In any organization, balancing the competencies needed with the competencies on hand is critical. As supply chains become longer and more complex, the skills needed to manage them change as well. A lack of available talent is a huge concern for senior executives. A recent annual PwC survey of more than 1,250 corporate leaders found that 43 percent of CEOs are finding it more difficult than in previous years to hire people in their industry, and that these constraints are having a quantifiable impact on corporate growth. In the same study, one in four CEOs reported that they were unable to pursue a market opportunity or have had to cancel or delay a strategic initiative because of a talent crunch (Figure 3.5).[8]

What happens when the demand for supply chain skills outstrips the supply? Where do you look for talent? Competitors, other divisions in your own company, people who have the potential to grow into a new job, executive recruiters, informal networking, and people from industries other than yours—all of these constitute worthwhile sources of talent. But first you need a strategy for leveraging them. What trade-offs do you need to make? Is a job candidate who seems perfect for a particular role asking for more money than you're willing to pay? How do you balance the trade-offs?

Figure 3.5 Impact of Insufficient Talent

% of companies reporting impact of talent constraints

Our talent-related expenses rose more than expected

43

We weren't able to innovate effectively

31

We were unable to pursue a market opportunity

29

We cancelled or delayed a key strategic initiative

24

We couldn't achieve growth forecasts in overseas markets

24

We couldn't achieve growth forecasts in the country where we are based

24

Our production and/or service delivery quality standards fell

21

Source: *Delivering Results: Growth and Value in a Volatile World,* 15th Annual Global CEO Survey 2012, PwC, 2012.

There are different ways to answer these questions. Your decisions will often require a trade-off analysis that considers numerous factors, such as experience level, training requirements, and impact on customer service.

The experience of one company, a provider of logistics services, offers a case in point. The company anticipated 15 percent growth in its workforce over the next year and had a choice between bringing in new college graduates or more-seasoned professionals who commanded higher salaries. A comparison of payroll expenses for the two scenarios showed clearly that hiring junior staff provided substantial cost savings.

Digging deeper, the company examined various components of the overall costs related to hiring experienced versus inexperienced employees. It looked at the initial cost of compensation and benefits; recruiting; education, training, and development; relocation; and opportunity cost (Figure 3.6). "Opportunity cost" was defined as the cost to the company of work considered unsatisfactory by customers, work not done at all, and employee dissatisfaction due to excessive overtime—all issues that are more likely to crop up with less-experienced employees. The analysis showed that

Figure 3.6 The Relative Cost of Inexperience

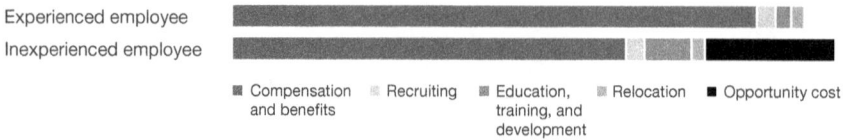

Experienced employee
Inexperienced employee

■ Compensation   ▨ Recruiting   ■ Education,   ▨ Relocation   ■ Opportunity cost
and benefits   training, and
                                    development

"lower cost" employees would actually cost more over the long term. As this company discovered, the total-cost-of-ownership principle that applies to material assets applies to human assets as well.

Rather than bringing in new staff, many companies choose to develop existing employees' supply chain skills. Some offer tailored leadership-development courses that help turn promising managers into senior executives. Others offer supply chain academies or boot camps that provide employees with a solid overview of supply chain processes in a short amount of time. "We can find a tremendous amount of capability at the entry level. Many people, in fact, come in with advanced degrees that are a testament to their industry and technical know-how," a senior supply chain executive in the electronics industry says. "But when they have strong education credentials and minimal practical experience, the challenge is in how they problem-solve. That, to me, is very teachable."

Companies shouldn't underestimate the importance of improving their talent. It's as strategically important as having a best-in-class manufacturing operation or demand-planning process.

OTHER DEFINING CHARACTERISTICS OF EXCEPTIONAL SUPPLY CHAIN ORGANIZATIONS

An effective supply chain organization is thoughtfully and skillfully designed. It has the appropriate structure, clearly defined roles and responsibilities, and people with the right skills. But the best supply chain organizations have several additional distinctive characteristics.

A SEAT AT THE TABLE

The most effective supply chain organizations put one senior executive in charge of all the core processes and provide him or her with a set of cross-functional performance objectives as well as the resources needed to meet them. Whether the title is vice president of operations, chief supply chain officer (CSCO), or some other designation, companies are increasingly including the head of their supply chain function in the C-suite. Indeed, one study found that 25 percent of Fortune 125 companies had a single executive in charge of an integrated global supply chain.[9]

However, formal titles displayed on an organization chart are far less important than how actual relationships and responsibilities work within a company. If the most senior supply chain executive has only limited involvement with key functions such as product design, sales and marketing, or finance, the supply chain organization will lack sufficient influence and will be unable to operate as an integrated team.

Even companies that use a decentralized organization model should have a supply chain executive at the most senior level in the company. After all, companies that have independent product groups or regions still have global vice presidents of sales, marketing, and other mission-critical functions.

When the leader of the supply chain organization is a member of the executive management team and has input into major strategic decisions, it's much more likely that the company will be able to deploy a differentiating supply chain strategy. Unilever is a case in point: the CSCO is appointed at the board level, raising the profile of the supply chain organization.

But companies need to go beyond conferring a senior-level title. Many companies remain locked in a traditional paradigm in which sales, marketing, and development are considered the architects of the company's strategic direction, and procurement, production, and distribution are thought of as tactical executers. Despite problems with high inventories, late shipments, or missed revenue opportunities, many companies fail to see supply chain management as a critical area of expertise or appreciate its potential strategic value. Unless the supply chain leader has a clear mandate, major opportunities may go to waste.

STRONG CORE CAPABILITIES

Leaders of the best supply chain organizations know which activities are—or have the potential to become—strategic differentiators for their company. They and the rest of the C-suite keep these critical activities in-house or outsource them to only the most trusted of partners. And they contract out other activities that may be better performed by third-party providers that offer an ever-expanding menu of services.

Less-thoughtful leaders can fall victim to a potential peril of outsourcing—what we refer to as "thinning the core." This occurs when a company over-relies on supply chain partners to manage many of its day-to-day supply chain activities. Some companies have suffered disastrous consequences when staff that was left within the organization had little personal experience with core operations processes, such as materials planning or demand management. Mike McNamara, CEO at Flextronics, a Singapore-based electronics manufacturing services provider, notes that many companies working with Flextronics had allowed their core to become too thin. "It's important for us to have people within our customers' companies with whom we can 'talk supply chain,'" he says. "We see a lot of companies who are no longer capable of performing some very critical activities."[10]

This is an issue for a company that, like Flextronics, is developing the parameters that will govern its relationships with customers—and when it's attempting to execute supply chain processes on a day-to-day basis. "If there is no one within the customer's organization who can develop a long-term demand plan," McNamara says, "it's very hard for us to get set up in the way that will serve them most efficiently."

Although these risks still exist, the concept of outsourcing has become mainstream; most companies don't view using a manufacturing- or logistics-services provider as moving something "out" of their own company. These service providers are simply additional strategic supply chain partners. However, don't underestimate the difficulty of transferring these capabilities to a

Figure 3.7 The Dangers of Over-Relying on Outsourcing

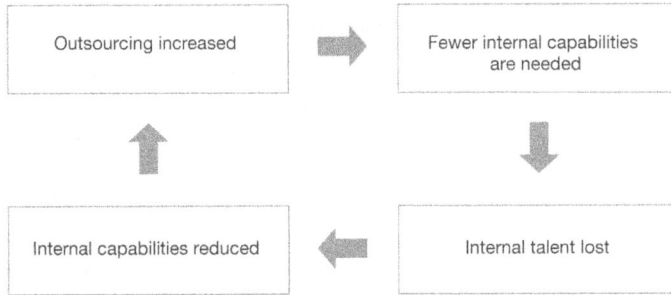

new partner and managing the resulting complexity. Over-reliance on out-sourcing can also set in motion a cycle in which fewer internal capabilities are needed, internal talent is lost, internal capabilities are reduced—and the company outsources even more (Figure 3.7).

If you decide to outsource any of your company's core supply chain processes, you'll need to develop and maintain a core competency centered on managing outsourcing partners and processes effectively. If you're out-sourcing production, for example, you'll need to have a deep knowledge of the manufacturing process within your industry and for your specific products. You will also need the ability to perform due diligence for manu-facturing and engineering talent, manage contracts, and monitor produc-tion output. Familiarity with demand planning will also be essential, as will the ability to measure the contract manufacturer's ongoing activity. No less important, you'll have to understand the local customs where the partner is based. You'll also need to be able to manage several strategic partnerships as well as cross-functional teams simultaneously. It will be especially challenging to ensure that people who don't report to you still perform the way you expect them to.

To avoid thinning your company's core, start with a list of key supply chain processes and the core competencies needed to execute those pro-cesses. But don't just consider present needs: your company's longer-term business strategy is just as, if not more, important. Summarize the skills that will be needed to create or defend competitive advantage, to help grow the business, and to ensure customer satisfaction. Next, identify any gaps between the skills needed and those already in place. Finally, get consensus on whether to develop these skills in-house through training and targeted hiring or to use supply chain partners to fill the gaps.

Leading companies use this approach when deciding what to outsource and what to keep in-house. They keep strategic processes such as S&OP, strategic sourcing, and product development in-house, while outsourcing approximately 50 percent of their warehousing and logistics activities and 35 percent of their manufacturing and assembly (Figure 3.8).[11]

ADAPTABILITY

The best supply chain organizations evolve in response to changes not only in the external business environment but also in a company's strategies. Expanding into new regions, adding a product line, updating CSR guidelines,

Figure 3.8 Outsourcing Preferences

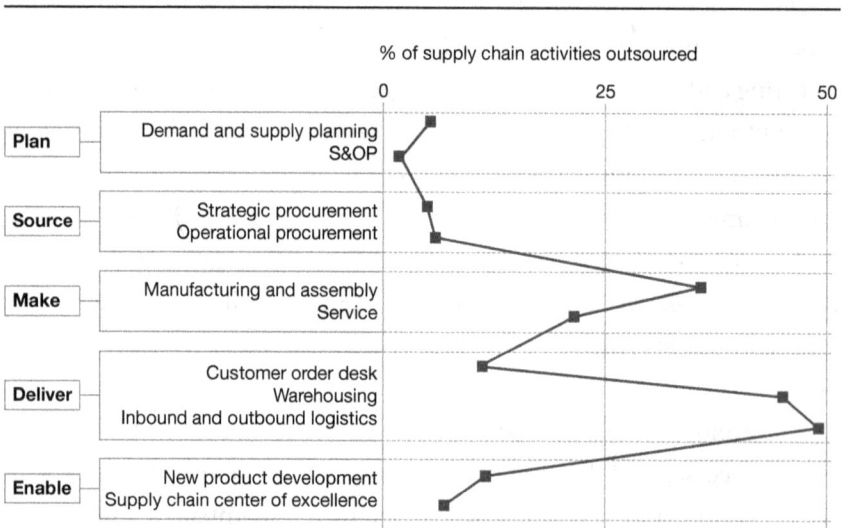

Source: *Next-Generation Supply Chains: Efficient, Fast, and Tailored,* Global Supply Chain Survey 2013, PwC, 2012.

acquiring a company, modifying the target customer base—any of these changes will likely require major adjustments within your company's supply chain organization. These changes may affect roles and responsibilities, organizational structure, or required skills. In fact, strategy changes often render existing skills obsolete and create the need for new ones.

Likewise, a shift in strategy or a desire to improve operations in general can call for alterations in your supply chain organization's design. If your company consolidates its supply base, adds a distribution location, or transitions to an outsourcing model, you may need to add or modify certain supply chain processes or structures. You may also need to bring in new capabilities related to local operating environments.

A California-based manufacturer of sophisticated telecommunications equipment discovered this firsthand. In the early 2000s, the company faced strong shareholder dissatisfaction. The management team was in a bind. The company's Silicon Valley plant was outdated, inefficient, and expensive, but outsourcing manufacturing to an overseas partner would mean entrusting a complex product-customization process to an entity outside the company's span of control. After considerable due diligence and analysis, senior management decided to transfer production to a manufacturing partner in Taiwan.

For the manufacturing transfer to succeed, the company needed to maintain strong relationships with suppliers of critical components while shifting responsibility for day-to-day purchasing of these components to the new manufacturing partner. It was also critical to ensure that end-customer requirements could be collected, integrated, and acted on as quickly as possible—a challenging objective given the distance and cultural differences between the two companies.

With these considerations in mind, senior management implemented several major changes. Specifically, they introduced processes that would help ensure availability of critical components before orders were actually taken and thus reduce order fulfillment delays. They also created a new department charged with the entire order-execution process to eliminate information gaps that had caused confusion about who was responsible for delivery performance. In addition, they tightened links between customer order management, planning, and procurement by physically moving the groups closer together and by requiring that order commitments be confirmed in person.

That's not all. With the new outsourcing arrangement, the company had lost the ability to modify production schedules as customer requirements were changed or refined, which was a common occurrence. As a result, it had to provide the manufacturing partner with a forecast of production requirements well in advance of when products were actually needed. That demanded a rethink of the planning and procurement skills that were needed. "Our new model meant that the buying and materials planning tasks were going to blend," notes the vice president of global operations. "You can't just take a tactical buyer who has been placing purchase orders by following system-generated recommendations and suddenly turn him into a planner who can make decisions without completely concrete data. We had to do a lot of retraining and, in some cases, some strategic hiring to develop the organization we wanted."

The organizational restructuring followed the schedule of the manufacturing transition and allowed the company to meet an aggressive deadline without adversely affecting customer service levels. At the same time, the sharpened focus on planning helped cut inventory liabilities dramatically. The reconfigured supply chain organization played a key role in the company's ability to support its new supply chain strategy—and to realize its benefits.

Look closely at most supply chain organizations and you'll see that they are a mix of design and evolution. That's because designing a supply chain organization isn't about following a recipe, it's about recognizing how the organization can add value to the business and then identifying ways to get there. A seasoned CSCO notes, "You see what happens—what works and what doesn't—and then you do more of the things that are working."

But it's not just trial and error. Your company's business strategy should drive how you structure your organization, the competencies you need to have, and your requirements for skills and experience. Get that right, and you can make changes to your business strategy while ensuring that your organization is fit for purpose, resilient, and flexible.

KEY TAKEAWAYS

- Globalization strategies, market uncertainties, talent wars, and the mainstreaming of corporate social responsibility are compelling companies to rethink how they design their supply chain organization.

- Companies that take an integrated approach to their supply chain organization see the organization as a source of competitive advantage. They structure it to cover Plan, Source, Make, Deliver, Return, and Enable processes. And they put one person in charge of the entire function.

- Possible structures for a supply chain organization include centralized, decentralized, and hybrid. Each type of structure offers diverse advantages, and the most appropriate choice will meet several key criteria.

- In exceptional supply chain organizations, roles and responsibilities are clearly defined, which encourages accountability.

- Today, supply chain excellence requires skills of a whole new order. To put the right skills in place, executives must source talent inside and outside the company as needed.

- In addition to selecting the right structure, clarifying roles, and acquiring the right skills, the best supply chain organizations have a "seat at the table." They take care not to "thin" their core competencies by over-outsourcing or outsourcing the wrong supply chain activities. And they continually revisit their designs to accommodate internal and external change.

HAIER:
PURSUING THE CUSTOMER-INSPIRED
SUPPLY CHAIN

On August 28, 2008, Zhang Ruimin, the CEO of the Haier Group, announced that as of the next day the company's central distribution center would be shut down. From then on, Haier products would no longer be sent to a central warehouse, where they would sit waiting until retail customers placed their purchase orders. With the new "zero inventory" strategy, Haier would have to ensure that the supply chain ran so smoothly that products moved without a hitch from the factory directly to retail stores.

This decision was revolutionary: the supply chain organization now had to deal with goods coming off the product line and no place to house them. Yet just three weeks later, the company had put in place a process that ensured a seamless flow of product from the factory all the way to the customer. Limiting factory storage space—the factory can accommodate only one day's worth of production—continues to provide a means to reinforce the discipline.

This episode is just one example of the innovativeness of Haier's approach to its supply chain strategy and the value that approach has provided. With the belief that there is always room for improvement, the company takes its supply chain very seriously, constantly examining and adapting it as needed.

The journey has been unusually short. In just 27 years, Haier has gone from being a small refrigerator factory in Qingdao, China, to the world's largest brand of white goods—refrigerators, washing machines, air conditioners, and water heaters—as well as a major producer of TVs, small appliances, and smartphones. In 2011, Haier topped the list of major appliance brands worldwide for the third consecutive year, according to Euromonitor[1] International's rankings. Revenue in fiscal-year 2011 totaled CNY 150.9 billion ($23.3 billion), translating into a 7.8 percent global market share.

"Haier's supply chain is a competitive core competence for the company," says Liang Haishan, executive vice president of the Haier Group and president of the Haier White Goods Group worldwide. "Every step of the way, the supply chain has proved a critical asset, helping Haier keep its eyes on the customer."

BECOMING THE NUMBER-ONE WHITE-GOODS BRAND IN CHINA

Known in its early days as Qingdao Refrigerator Company, Haier got its real start in 1984, when Zhang Ruimin was appointed managing director. At the time, the company was grappling with major quality and infrastructure problems. In one year, three different managing directors had come and gone, and Zhang expected he'd have the same experience.

A PRIORITY ON QUALITY

Zhang's first step was to address the quality issues. After determining that 76 fridges fresh off the production line had defects, Zhang took up a sledgehammer and set an example by smashing the defective fridges to bits. The number that day was 76, he told them, but it could be 760 tomorrow and 7,600 the day after.

Zhang understood that to succeed against competitors, which in those days numbered more than 100, it was critical to produce refrigerators that were unparalleled in quality. An avid student of Western management practices, Zhang looked abroad for guidance. In 1985, he forged a partnership with Liebherr Group, a premium German refrigerator manufacturer, to transfer technologies and equipment.

In the years that followed, Chinese demand for refrigerators skyrocketed, owing to population growth and rises in personal-income levels. Under Zhang's leadership, the Qingdao Refrigerator Company focused on enhancing quality and building brand strength rather than on expanding output. The strategy worked. When overproduction by competitors led to an enormous surplus of refrigerators and deep discounts, Zhang refused to lower prices in the conviction that quality would prevail. Competitors were forced to shut down their operations, while the Qingdao Refrigerator Company thrived.[2]

The company—which changed its name to Haier in 1992—began expanding its operational footprint in China. Over the course of the decade, Haier acquired several home-appliance companies that had been performing poorly and added their manufacturing facilities to its asset network.

During this period, Haier also began developing what would become its greatest source of differentiation: innovativeness based on close interaction with the customer. It set up a computerized after-sales service center— the first Chinese white-goods company to do so. This was critical, because it allowed the company to monitor product performance and provide maintenance and repair services to many thousands of customers.

THE RETAIL NETWORK

Not surprisingly, Haier's retail-customer base grew as well. In the early years, growth occurred primarily in China's urban areas. More recently, demand has grown in rural areas as a result of the 2009 state agrarian policy, which provided subsidies for refrigerator purchases as a way to stimulate growth during the Great Recession.

To facilitate distribution to rural consumers, the company accelerated the development of its retail network. Haier stores began cropping up all over China. Today, Haier has 6,000 county stores, 24,000 town stores, 150,000 vendor contractors, and 19,000-plus service centers.

Haier has aligned its retail network with China's tier system, which categorizes cities based on economy scale and population size. In tier 1 cities (Beijing, Shanghai, and Guangzhou) and tier 2 cities (provincial capitals), consumers can purchase Haier refrigerators at multibrand retail channels. These include Wal-Mart and China's leading appliance and electronics retail stores, Gome and Suning. Consumers in tier 3 cities like Qingdao get their fridges at those stores as well as smaller stores that carry only Haier products. In tier 4 towns and villages, consumers also go to Haier-branded stores, though in some rural villages, the shop often consists of no more than a kiosk marked by an umbrella.

Wherever consumers are located, the retail store plays a critical role in Haier's value proposition. All stores serve as a place where consumers can learn about and purchase the model that best fits their needs. The Haier-branded stores also serve as maintenance and repair centers. People can contact a toll-free hotline and bring their appliances to the nearby Haier store for repair.

THE PEOPLE ON THE FRONT LINE

Whether the retail store sells many brands or just Haier, Haier employees are there to support retail customers as they select their refrigerators. Approximately 30,000 of the company's 80,000 employees are in sales, which is roughly the same number Haier has in manufacturing. Large by any standard, the sales force allows the company to enjoy an exceptionally high level of interaction with end-customers. Explains Yang Qiaoshan, Haier's general manager of market operations for China, "This approach means the customer has a better buying experience, while the company gets the information it needs to develop products that are better suited to customer requirements."

Not only are the sales staff very knowledgeable about Haier products, they are key to ordering and inventory management. Using a proprietary system called eStore, they provide a continual feed of data from stores throughout China to inform the sales and operations (S&OP) planning process. This ensures that the people involved in the supply chain organization always know how many fridges of each model have been sold each week, and this knowledge helps them estimate how many will be ordered in the coming weeks.

The information provided from each store is critical. More frequent—and therefore more accurate—demand signaling drives production planning and has helped Haier cut inventory by almost half and reduce inventory of raw materials as well as finished goods by almost three-fourths.

PRODUCT INNOVATION COMBINED WITH
SUPPLY CHAIN INNOVATION

Urban and rural end-customers vary greatly in their lifestyles. Haier's operating models are designed to satisfy the gamut.

The factories are set up to facilitate mass production of dozens of refrigerator models, which translate into hundreds of unique products across Haier's strategic model, with its low-end, value, and high-end brands. More than 80 percent of refrigerators are made to order. The remaining are "made to commit," which are more-customized products that are configured on the basis of the retailer's commitment to sell them.

The refrigerators are all produced in Haier industrial parks, where factories and suppliers sit side by side. In the Qingdao Industrial Park, Haier Refrigerator Division 1, a plant focused on two- and three-door fridges, produces nearly 2 million units a year.

Haier is able to profitably produce as many types of refrigerators as it does for several reasons. First, the company has integrated supply chain considerations into design. Each refrigerator is designed in modules: five main systems (outer frame, door, electrical controls, cooling system, and packaging) and 23 subsystems. Haier uses modularization to speed up the design process and to facilitate the manufacturing process. "Platforming and modularization are the means for integrating modular design, modular supply, intelligent manufacturing, and virtual-network marketing," notes Zou Xiwen, a senior executive responsible for modularization of products at Haier. "They are key to end-to-end management of customer requirements."

Collaboration with suppliers plays a major role in modularization. Take, for example, the refrigerator cooling system. To assemble a compressor unit in the past, Haier would procure the compressor, evaporator, and condenser from several different suppliers. Recently, Haier reduced the number of suppliers to just two, and asked them to provide entire modules. Using a new collaborative-design process, Haier worked with these suppliers to develop a cooling system that reduced refrigerator power consumption by 30 percent and time to market by 33 percent.

Haier's profitability is also due to Haier Logistics, a subsidiary that takes care of logistics, both inbound and outbound. On average, 1,000 full trucks leave Haier factories every day with finished products. This capability makes it possible for retail customers to promise end-customers speedy delivery. It also allows Haier to stand by its guarantee of 24-hour delivery in many locations; in some Haier stores, in fact, it's possible to buy a fridge in the morning and have it delivered that afternoon.

Haier also focuses avidly on working capital. "Cash is like air" is a mantra the company lives by—the idea being that you can live without water and food for a few days, but you cannot live without air. Accordingly, in addition to very tight inventory management, the company doesn't ship an order until the retail customer has paid in full.

But above all else, it's the focus on the end-customer that drives Haier's growth and profitability, from R&D all the way to after-sales service and support. Ideally, no product is developed without taking account of what customers want, and no product is manufactured without a real customer order. Notes Executive Vice President Liang, "With better-designed products, we create greater value for the customer—and for Haier as well."

BECOMING A GLOBAL LEADER

Haier's global-expansion efforts are fueled by the same customer focus that made the company so successful in China. Whether it's fridges with a video-messaging device integrated into the door for European families or mini-fridges built to fit under desks for U.S. college students, Haier has consistently developed products with features that speak to its customers' needs.

DIFFICULT FIRST, EASY LATER

In 1990, Haier launched a three-step strategy that defied conventional business wisdom. Instead of starting with developing markets, Haier first targeted what it considered "difficult" markets—that is, Western markets with developed economies. And instead of offering low-priced products as many Chinese companies did, Haier looked for unfilled niches and created products that filled those niches without compromising on price. Haier believed this strategy was critical for building brand equity.

Haier's Global Footprint in 2011

Americas		China	
R&D centers	2	R&D centers	2
Production centers	4	Production centers	17
Point of sale	10,860	Point of sale	105,547

Europe		Asia Pacific	
R&D centers	4		
Production centers	3		
Point of sale	12,622		

Africa and Middle East		Asia Pacific	
R&D centers	0	R&D centers	2
Production centers	7	Production centers	14
Point of sale	3,750	Point of sale	10,453

Source: Haier

Accordingly, Haier's first substantive venture outside China was the United States—which, with its high cost of manufacturing and many competitors, certainly qualified as "difficult." Haier products—compact fridges—were already being imported to the United States by a New York–based import company. To break into the U.S. market in a big way, Haier inked deals with the biggest of the big-box stores: Home Depot, Best Buy, and Wal-Mart. At the same time, Haier established an industrial park—its first outside China—in South Carolina. It also established a warehouse in New Jersey for storing goods imported from China.

STAY IN

Recognizing that niche products were only a way to gain entry to difficult markets, Haier decided to start producing mainstream products. The company viewed this as critical for becoming a major brand in those markets. To realize this goal, the company deployed a "three in one" approach—localized design, production, and marketing—to understand local customer requirements and to satisfy their needs.

TAKE THE LEAD

Haier then focused on becoming a brand cherished by local consumers. The strategy was to sell innovative products that differentiated Haier as a trendsetter. To take one example: for people in Africa, where power outages were a common occurrence, Haier developed a no-frost freezer able to keep food frozen for 100 hours. The freezer's success confirmed the company's number-one position in the Nigerian market.

Haier supplemented its three-step expansion strategy with the occasional acquisition. The most important of these was the 2011 purchase of the white-goods and consumer-appliance business of Sanyo. This move gave Haier a firm foothold in the Japanese market.

Today, Haier's operational footprint spans six large regional markets in addition to China: the Americas, Europe, the Middle East, Southeast Asia, East Asia, and South Asia.

GLOBAL AND DOMESTIC SUPPLY CHAINS: COMMON LINKS

Although Haier's domestic and international growth trajectories differ markedly, the supporting supply chains have some important things in common.

First is the global supply chain organization. Haier consistently staffs its overseas operations with local managers who have experience in leading white-goods companies. These managers then hire local teams and develop local sales and distribution channels.

Second are the common processes that Haier has developed to drive collaboration across functions and across geographies. Haier has a single point of global leadership for defining harmonized supply chain processes, including demand planning, procurement, manufacturing, logistics distribution, and order delivery. "Given the breadth of our organization, we need common ways of working such as standardized language, processes, and KPI definitions to collaborate effectively," notes Haier's vice president of supply chain, Lim Chin Chye, who oversees the company's global supply chain. "Haier adopted the SCOR® model to achieve this."

Another critical element is the S&OP process. Executives from headquarters in China and the regional sales offices worldwide align sales and manufacturing plans on a weekly basis. This is no small challenge, given that more than 200 refrigerator SKUs are produced for China and an additional 400 are manufactured for the rest of the world.

No less important, Haier emphasizes the same performance metrics across the company's domestic and global supply chains: velocity, predictability, and flexibility. When it comes to measuring velocity, Haier deploys a number of metrics: order fulfillment time as well as the different components of order fulfillment (order to manufacture, order to ship, and so on). Using a proprietary system, the company can see predictability and velocity performance by key account as well as by factory, so it can take action as needed.

At Haier, supply chain performance management goes well beyond tracking and reporting performance. Under Haier's "individual goal alignment" model, targets are directly assigned to individuals and teams. These targets include forecast accuracy, which is assigned to sales teams; order-to-delivery cycle time, which is assigned to supply chain planning teams; order-to-ship cycle time, which is assigned to factory management teams; and order daily clear, which is the number of orders placed in a day and a target for production line teams. Unlike in many other organizations, there are consequences for not meeting targets. If a district sales manager orders too many fridges and therefore exceeds target inventory levels, his compensation is reduced; if he sells more than were ordered, compensation is increased.

NO EVERLASTING SUCCESS

Haier has come a long way in the past 27 years, but the journey is far from over. Opportunities for growth in China remain considerable. With only 24 million people earning more than 3,500 RMB a month, which is the threshold for paying income tax, the standard of living is bound to rise. This will likely open up a whole new market for Casarte, Haier's high-end brand.

Setting its sights on a more global operation, the company is firmly committed to its "three thirds" strategy: one-third of products will be manufactured and sold in China, one-third will be manufactured in China and sold abroad, and one-third will be sold and manufactured abroad. Haier is not there yet, but it is well on its way.

In the Haier museum in the company's headquarters in Qingdao, you can read in large letters the slogan "No everlasting success." The constant search for improvement and refusal to accept the status quo is part of the Haier DNA.

While it's difficult to predict the path the journey will take, one thing seems certain. Haier will continue to challenge the way it is operating in order to stay at the top of its industry—and the customer-inspired supply chain will continue to be critical to success.

CHAPTER FOUR

DISCIPLINE 4:
BUILD THE RIGHT COLLABORATIVE MODEL

Smart collaboration with your company's supply chain partners can generate a wealth of strategic and financial benefits for you and your partners. But to reap those benefits, it's essential to understand the full range of potential collaborative models and to implement the ones that best suit your company's needs—while avoiding the risks inherent in partnerships.

As companies today focus on strengthening their core capabilities, they are forging increasing numbers of partnerships in multiple regions to drive faster, less-costly innovation and manufacturing of products and to expand their customer base globally. In a world of shorter economic cycles, more frequent natural disasters, and much political instability, these partnerships have become more critical to success than ever. Indeed, in a recent survey of 374 senior supply chain, sourcing, and operations executives, nearly 60 percent of respondents said that collaboration was strategic to their business.[1]

But partnerships have become more challenging as well. As their reliance on strategies and resources that are not under their direct control grows, companies must do more than collaborate—they must collaborate effectively. That means understanding the many forms of collaboration and what each can and cannot accomplish.

UNDERSTANDING COLLABORATION

What exactly is collaboration? We define it as the means by which companies in a supply chain work together toward mutual objectives through the sharing of ideas, assets, information, knowledge, risks, and rewards. "Collaboration" can refer to a wide range of joint activities, from information sharing among business units to complex, long-term product development and marketing projects.

Regardless of the form it takes, an effective collaborative relationship can deliver major strategic and financial benefits to all the parties involved (Table 4.1). It can accelerate a company's push into markets with steep barriers to entry, for example, by providing access to expertise and technology too costly or difficult to develop internally. Equally important, collaboration can deliver cost savings or increased revenue—or both.

THE COLLABORATION SPECTRUM

Collaboration partners in supply chain management can be customers, suppliers of materials, or suppliers of services that support supply chain operations, such as manufacturing or logistics. The extent of the collaboration may vary by type of partner and strategic importance to your company.

Table 4.1 Benefits of Collaboration

Benefits to customers	• Better forecast accuracy and customer service • Lower order-management costs • Better allocation of promotional budgets
Benefits to suppliers	• Reduced inventory • Lower warehousing costs • Better availability of materials
Benefits to service providers	• Faster time to market • Increased innovation • Lower landed cost • More-reliable delivery • Flexible capacity development • Lower capital expenditures and reduced depreciation

However, most collaborative relationships are established and maintained in similar ways. Companies can draw upon various types of collaborative relationships (Table 4.2).

The spectrum of ways companies can collaborate is wide. This holds true regarding both the relative depth of collaboration and the relative number of relationships (Figure 4.1). For most companies, the number of transactional relationships is much higher than the number of synchronized relationships.

Note the absence of distinct boundaries shown between the different degrees of collaboration. That's because collaboration is a continuum, not a set of clearly delineated management practices. Nor is the spectrum a path to a mature collaboration capability; it's a characterization of the relative number of relationships in which it is feasible to engage.

Table 4.2 Four Ways to Collaborate

Degree	Description	Features
Transactional	Partners agree to a set price for a specific offering over a set period of time or for specified purchase volume and/or dollar amount	• Focuses on minimizing effort associated with day-to-day transactions, often when decisions to do business with particular suppliers are based on price • Requires little effort, investment, and information sharing
Cooperative	Partners share information about commitments, forecasts, inventory availability, purchase orders, or order and delivery status	• Requires higher level of information sharing • Data are sent manually or electronically from one partner to the other ("pushed") or accessed by the receiving partner ("pulled") • Data type and format are standardized
Coordinated	Partners rely on each other's capabilities and commit long-term to the relationship	• Relies on two-way information flow between partners and tightly coordinated planning and execution processes • Requires high level of negotiation and compromise • Requires proprietary systems for information exchange
Synchronized	Relationship moves beyond supply chain operations to include other critical business processes	• Partners may invest in joint R&D projects, supplier development, and intellectual property development, thus generating mutual strategic value • Partners share physical and intellectual assets and personnel • Partners jointly develop information

Figure 4.1 The Collaboration Spectrum

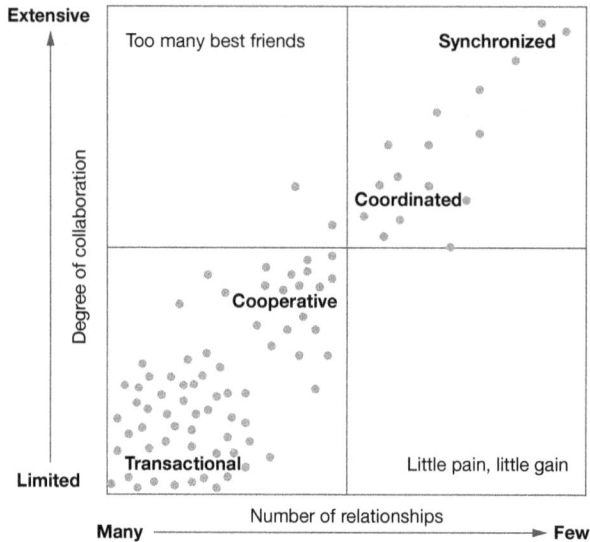

Every relationship with a customer or supplier probably involves a certain degree of collaboration. But before your company sets out to systematically establish relationships with its supply chain partners, we suggest taking the time to understand the degrees of collaboration along the spectrum, identify your company's specific needs, and consider which type of collaboration, with which suppliers, would best help you address your needs most effectively. For most companies, having a small number of deeply collaborative relationships is preferable to attempting to collaborate deeply with numerous partners. Later in this chapter, we'll discuss how to determine the degree of collaboration that is best with each supply chain partner.

Transactional Collaboration

Transactional collaboration is the most basic and by far the most widely used collaboration model within any company. A transactional relationship occurs any time a customer and a supplier agree to a set price for a specific product, either over a set period of time or until sales of the product reach a specified volume and/or dollar amount. The buyer gets a fixed price over the life of the agreement in exchange for purchasing a minimum quantity of the product, and the seller has less of a challenge with materials and production planning.

This form of collaboration aims for the efficient and effective execution of transactions between partners. This isn't to say that transactional relationships don't offer strategic value. But partners in such relationships aren't chosen with a view to reducing overall supply chain management costs or increasing revenue. Instead, they are meant to improve the ease with which transactions are conducted—for example, by eliminating the need for constant renegotiation. With less strategically important supply chain partners, companies tend to focus on minimizing the effort associated with day-to-day transactions rather than on developing long-term relationships.

Furthermore, transactional relationships rarely require sophisticated information systems and, as a result, many companies don't provide and respond to information electronically. For this reason, many transactions are performed manually.

Cooperative Collaboration

Cooperative relationships use a higher degree of information sharing than transactional relationships. Cooperative supply chain partners may provide automatic commitments and confirmations. Or they may share information on forecasts, usage, inventory availability, purchase orders, and order and delivery status. Usually, one partner posts information that the other partner reviews and acts on. In this one-way communication, data are sent manually or electronically ("pushed") from one partner to the other, or published in a manner that's accessible by the recipient ("pulled"). The type and format of the data provided are usually standardized.

Capture and provision of point-of-sale (POS) data is a common example of cooperative collaboration. POS data are automatically gathered as a consumer's purchases are put through a checkout process. The retailer collects POS data on the quantity and price of every product purchased.

These data are often enriched with related information such as promotions or special purchases that are spurring higher volume. The supplier can use these data in the planning process, having a better understanding of recent customer buying behavior and sales patterns as well as the circumstances that are influencing demand.

Coordinated Collaboration

In a coordinated relationship, supply chain partners work even more closely together and rely more heavily on each other's capabilities. Therefore, this degree of collaboration requires a two-way flow of information between partners as well as tightly synchronized planning and execution processes. Because the infrastructure and processes needed to support this type of information sharing are more complex than in the cooperative model, many companies reserve coordinated collaboration for more strategically critical supply chain partners.

Vendor-managed inventory (VMI) is a good example of coordinated collaboration. As the term implies, the supplier is responsible for ensuring that the customer has sufficient materials on hand. Some VMI programs are manual—the supplier physically walks through the customer's site to monitor inventory levels, or kanban cards (signals of needed inventory) are sent from the buying organization to the supplying organization. But most programs in place today are automated. In some cases, the supplier determines inventory needs remotely, by means of forecasts and past usage. In other cases, the supplier uses current consumption rates, POS data, or inventory levels. In either approach, effective data transmission is the key to successful VMI.

A coordinated relationship is rarely undertaken lightly. Unlike transactional and cooperative relationships, it requires extensive negotiation and a long-term commitment from both partners. Given the high level of data sharing, secure systems are needed for exchanging information. Putting the required processes and tools in place takes time and money; the expectation is that both parties will benefit from the efficiencies created as the relationship proceeds.

Synchronized Collaboration

The greatest depth of collaboration on the spectrum, synchronized collaboration, occurs at the upper right quadrant of the framework. In this model, the collaborative relationship includes critical business processes in addition to the supply chain. Partners may invest in joint R&D projects, supplier development, or intellectual property (IP) development. The sharing of physical and intellectual assets may even extend to personnel. Synchronized collaborations can also take the form of strategic alliances, in which one company licenses a technology to another, or in which two companies work together to build one product into another.

A familiar example is a PC that comes with application software already installed. Synchronized collaboration can also take the form of joint development of products or services, shared information, or new and better ways of working together.

Joint development can yield great value. When it comes to development of new offerings, a company that includes key material suppliers or manufacturing partners on its development team is far more likely to create product designs that are compatible with best-in-class supply chain performance. (See Sidebar "Joint Development Through Synchronized Collaboration.") Companies in synchronized collaborations often share a product-data-management system, whereas companies in other types of collaborative partnerships usually just exchange product data.

In any synchronized collaboration, information is jointly developed rather than just transmitted or exchanged. Moreover, synchronized collaboration tends to focus on a strategic vision of the future rather than on near-term planning and tactical execution. Long-term financial investment in partners is a hallmark of this type of collaboration. A preference to work extensively with a partner to resolve disputes or concerns about contractual expectations—rather than simply severing ties—is another defining characteristic.

JOINT DEVELOPMENT THROUGH SYNCHRONIZED COLLABORATION[1]

Through joint development, supply chain partners can achieve significant process improvements by connecting their operations in new ways. These improvements enable them to work together more effectively and to share resulting efficiencies.

Joint Development Through Synchronized Collaboration

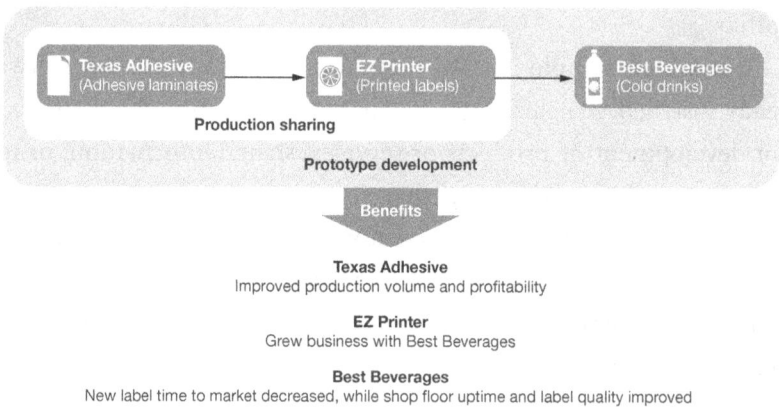

| Texas Adhesive (Adhesive laminates) | → | EZ Printer (Printed labels) | → | Best Beverages (Cold drinks) |

Production sharing

Prototype development

Benefits

Texas Adhesive
Improved production volume and profitability

EZ Printer
Grew business with Best Beverages

Best Beverages
New label time to market decreased, while shop floor uptime and label quality improved

An apt illustration is provided by joint development efforts among a label company that, for the purposes of this discussion, we will call "Texas Adhesive," and Texas Adhesive's supply chain partners, "EZ Printer" and "Best Beverages." Texas Adhesive makes adhesive labels for beverage bottles. Its customer, EZ Printer, prints the labels and sells them to Best Beverages, which affixes them to its cold-drink bottles.

Texas Adhesive secured an agreement from Best Beverages to switch from paper labels to laminate, which were superior both functionally and aesthetically. But EZ Printer quickly realized it was caught in the middle. The printer would lose money if it paid the higher price that Texas Adhesive was charging for laminate and sold the laminate labels at the price Best Beverages was willing to pay.

To drive down costs, Texas Adhesive and EZ Printer codeveloped a unified production schedule that optimized manufacturing runs at both facilities. They also set up a system whereby operators at EZ Printer provided constant feedback to Texas Adhesive about issues they encountered with the laminate labels, such as wrinkles in the material and other defects. Texas Adhesive used this feedback to make improvements, resulting in productivity improvements and cost savings for both parties.

Extending the effort, Texas Adhesive and EZ Printer worked with Best Beverages to codevelop a prototyping tool that allowed all three companies to design and test labels together. The joint approach helped the Texas Adhesive label designers and the Best Beverages marketing team to see which designs worked best in the label-manufacturing and label-application processes. And all parties involved could explore ways to create labels that met the three companies' priorities.

Each of these supply chain partners benefited from the joint-development initiative. For Texas Adhesive, production volume and profitability improved. EZ Printer's business with Best Beverages grew. And Best Beverages saw its time to market for new labels decrease, while shop floor uptime and label quality improved.

---

1.   Based on Francis Gouillart and Mark Deck, "The Craft of Co-Creation: Taking B2B Collaboration to a Whole New Level," *PRTM Insight*, 2011.

FINDING THE RIGHT PLACE ON THE SPECTRUM

Each relationship with a supply chain partner has its own place on the collaboration spectrum. As you design your collaboration strategy, you need to identify which partners are best suited for each type of relationship. The collaboration spectrum offers a set of options. There's no right or wrong place to be along the diagonal band, but there are areas outside the band that you'll likely want to avoid when choosing a collaboration model.

First, there's the area that we like to call "Little Pain, Little Gain." In this quadrant, companies collaborate on a limited basis with a relatively small percentage of their supply chain partners. The investment and risk involved in this model are low—and so is the return. While financial benefits can certainly accrue from limited collaboration, the Little Pain, Little Gain model may not be a commercially effective basis for a complete collaboration strategy, because the benefits you'll get are not worth the required investment.

The second area to avoid is the one we call "Too Many Best Friends." In this quadrant, the objective is very deep collaborative relationships with numerous supply chain partners. Interestingly, developers of collaboration tools often describe this as the optimal model, pointing out that advanced technologies enable collaboration that is both broad (many supply chain partners) and deep (extensive collaboration with each). Although this level of integration is possible, it's usually not practical—mainly because aligning a large group of partners with your business objectives and getting them to change their operations in accordance with your company's interests is extremely difficult.

Most collaborative relationships today are transactional or cooperative. They tend to focus on a narrow set of supply chain activities—typically procurement and manufacturing. And even though they are certainly considered collaborations, they are not expected to deliver lower inventory levels, better customer service, more efficient use of human resources, or faster, more reliable delivery. That's because the investment required of each partner is low, and the resulting value won't necessarily advance either company's strategy, enable entry into new markets, or provide access to new technologies or skill sets.

Transactional and cooperative collaboration usually do exactly what they are designed to do: deliver modest to moderate improvements in the execution of day-to-day transactions. That doesn't mean that transactional and cooperative relationships don't have value. And they should not be considered merely a stepping stone to relationships that are more

complex and strategic. Advanced collaboration needs a greater investment, continuing maintenance, and ongoing vigilance against circumstances that could harm the relationship. It's not right for every customer/
supplier relationship.

As companies move away from the traditional model of vertical integration, the need for deeper collaboration with select supply chain partners
intensifies. Deciding to divest an internal competency doesn't eliminate the
need for that competency—it simply moves the source of the competency
beyond your company's direct control. The ability to successfully manage
these external relationships can in itself become a critical competency.
(See Chapter 3.)

It's a major challenge to balance what's theoretically possible, what's
needed to support the business strategy, and what's practical in terms of
managing day-to-day operations. The fact that the collaboration spectrum is different for every company means that what's optimal in terms
of number and type of collaborative relationships varies widely. Although
many companies are a long way from their optimal range, the number
of cooperative and coordinated relationships is growing. But the ability
to reach an optimal state of collaboration is limited by the availability of
partners prepared to work with you.

Furthermore, the deeper and more extensive a collaborative relationship becomes, the more critical it is that all parties firmly integrate their
core supply chain processes. Companies integrate such processes by establishing rules governing which specific processes will be integrated and by
determining the required degree of integration.

Toyota pioneered the collaborative supply chain more than 50 years
ago. The longevity of the Toyota model suggests that strategic collaboration not only works but also can be sustained over a long period of
time. The relationship between Toyota and Autoliv, the world's largest
manufacturer of automotive safety systems, provides an apt example.
When production challenges in Autoliv's Utah plant made it difficult to
deliver products on time, the automaker sent a manufacturing expert

to Autoliv's plant to teach the fundamentals of the Toyota Production System. Within three years, Autoliv's manufacturing processes were completely transformed—to the benefit of both companies.[2]

THE PATH TO SUCCESSFUL COLLABORATION

Your company's success in building collaborative relationships depends on whether you and your partners are able to execute according to your mutual agreements. While every partnership is different, the following guidelines for success apply to all:

- Master internal collaboration before trying to work with external partners.
- Segment partners, then define the appropriate degree of collaboration for each.
- Trust your partners but protect your interests.
- Share benefits, gains, and losses.
- Use technology to support your collaborative relationships.

MASTER INTERNAL COLLABORATION FIRST

Internal collaboration can generate important benefits, such as economies of scale and scope, greater efficiency, knowledge sharing, and less duplication of effort. It also helps test your company's readiness to achieve common goals by aligning processes, systems, and organizational structures—all in a low-risk environment. Finally, internal success provides proof that the benefits of collaboration are real. For all these reasons, it can set the stage for external collaboration with supply chain partners.

But internal collaboration is challenging. That's because in companies that are organized by business units or functions, people tend to focus on maximizing performance in their own "silo" instead of in the company overall. And they may have difficulty seeing how their actions and decisions affect people in other units or functions. Thus, they may not immediately see how new ways of interacting can generate advantages for the company as a whole. Business units may also have incompatible information systems. Without a common data platform, shared functionality, and standardized metrics, these disparate systems can block effective collaboration.

To overcome these challenges, senior managers must be able to articulate—in concrete, specific terms—the kinds of benefits that internal collaboration can generate for the business. They also need to dispel the perception of internal collaboration as a zero-sum game, where improved performance in one department necessarily comes at the expense of another. Finally, they must ensure that their company's existing infrastructure doesn't discourage collaboration because of a real or perceived negative impact on a function or business unit.

At Logitech, the need for internal collaboration is clear. Logitech makes products for use in PC navigation, gaming, Internet communications, digital music, and home entertainment. The company has a worldwide supply chain, selling in retail outlets around the world, on web-based retail sites, and through relationships with original equipment manufacturers (OEMs).

For its products sold in retail stores, Logitech relies on eye-catching packaging to project an image of quality and innovation. For many products, this means form-fitted, clear packaging that highlights the product's look and feel from any angle. But the package also needs to be well suited to retailers' displays, which may require products to stand on a shelf or hang from a rack.

These marketing and sales considerations, however, may conflict with what works best for supply chain operations. For example, packaging designs can limit the number of product units that can fit on a pallet for shipping.

But at Logitech, decisions about the look and feel of packaging are the domain of marketing, not the supply chain organization. Moreover, once a product-package combination has been designed and marketed, modifying the design is difficult. That's because retailers see a packaging change as a whole new product and therefore may want to exchange anything they already have on hand for the "updated" version of the product.

To address these issues, Logitech asked its marketing and supply chain organizations to collaborate in the package design process. Managers encouraged them to make compromises, with a goal of developing a package that would meet both groups' objectives. The designs resulting from this collaboration have enabled Logitech to get products to customers much more efficiently, while communicating the innovation and quality of the products within.[3]

SEGMENT YOUR PARTNERS, THEN DEFINE THE
DEGREE OF COLLABORATION FOR EACH

A world in which your company is tightly linked to all of its supply chain partners—customers and suppliers alike—may sound appealing. But it's nearly impossible to achieve, and it's not likely to be cost-effective. Intensive collaboration is complicated and challenging, and it requires a major investment in resources, processes, and systems. Moreover, not all customers are equally profitable, and not all suppliers are equally valuable. And many potential partners may not be capable or even willing to support the level of collaboration you want.

For these reasons, it makes sense to segment your partners before embarking on a collaboration program. This is not unlike the approach that marketing professionals take to segment their target customers: they do it so that they can allocate resources to customers who will deliver the biggest return on investment (ROI).

How should you approach segmenting your partners? No doubt, you have a list of customers, suppliers, or commodities you consider key or strategic. But what factors cause you to label them as such? Is it the size of the company? The price of materials or services? An enterprise's dependence on you—or you on it? A company's value to you in terms of revenue generation?

It's inherently risky to base a partnering decision on one or two such simple criteria. We recommend evaluating potential partners along multiple dimensions. Mapping a potential partner along these dimensions can help determine what type of relationship will best support your strategy. The dimensions to consider include the following:

- *Strategic importance.* How essential to your company are the potential partner's size, business volume, technology, expertise, materials/components, and market position? The more critical the partner is to your business, the more deeply you should plan to collaborate.

- *Anticipated relationship longevity.* How long do you expect this partnership to last—months or years? A short-term partnership probably doesn't warrant the intense effort and financial commitment of coordinated or synchronized collaboration.

- *Number of potential partners.* Are there other companies that can provide the same quality, volume, or technical expertise? Would it be easy to transition to another partner? If several other companies can provide what you need, keeping the relationship at a transactional or cooperative level isn't likely to be an issue.

- *Criticality to products.* Is this a supplier whose products or services are essential for the form, fit, or function of yours? Is it feasible to substitute another company's products? Is the partner interested in and able to engage in joint development? If the partner's product is critical for yours, deeper collaboration is necessary.

- *Risk potential.* Does working with this company pose significant business interruption risks? Is it located in a vulnerable geographical area or geopolitical climate? You can help mitigate risk by establishing joint agreements for redundant capacity or guaranteed allocation in the event of a supply chain disruption; that, however, is possible only with a coordinated or synchronized relationship.

- *Contribution to branding.* Do people buy your product because they value a specific supplier of one of its components or associate your brand with theirs? If the answer is yes, you should plan on a synchronized relationship.

- *Other criteria.* Some criteria, such as cultural fit, aren't as easily quantified. If your company and the partner have very different cultures and values, there's a good chance that a cultural clash could stymie your collaborative efforts. If you still consider this supplier strategically important and want to invest in extensive collaboration with the company, you'll need to address these differences. You might, for example, set common social- and environmental-responsibility parameters or establish consistent guidelines for employee empowerment and decision making.

Not all dimensions are equally important. In today's business climate, evaluating business interruption risk is crucial when determining the right level of collaboration. The Japan tsunami and Thailand floods of 2011 revealed the vulnerability of thousands of companies' supply chains. Many of these companies had assumed that suppliers could be easily replaced; it turned out that they could not be.[4] Do your research before turning to a collaboration assessment framework.

Also, consider how important your company is to your partner's business; don't assume that because you consider the partner critical, it will be willing to invest heavily in your company. Be ready to compromise on what you expect from the partner. Electronics manufacturing services (EMS) providers or contract manufacturers in the electronics industry are a case in point. These companies can handle relatively deep collaborations with hundreds of OEM customers because they have the right enabling technology. But they rarely go as far as establishing synchronized planning and execution processes with all of their customers; they reserve that only for the largest or most strategic. For these special customers, the EMS provider is willing to offer special treatment, such as changing its production plans and expediting parts.

The best approach for segmenting partners is to create an assessment framework *before* approaching them. Start by listing the criteria—in clear, unambiguous terms—that a partner must meet to be considered for each of four degrees of collaboration. Decide how many partners of each type you want to have, based on the needs of your business or your previous experience with collaboration. Figure 4.2 shows an example of how a company might establish an assessment framework. Then, rank the prospective partners by how well they meet the different criteria. You may want to create a list of must-have criteria and eliminate any partners that fail to meet them.

Figure 4.2 Partner Assessment Framework

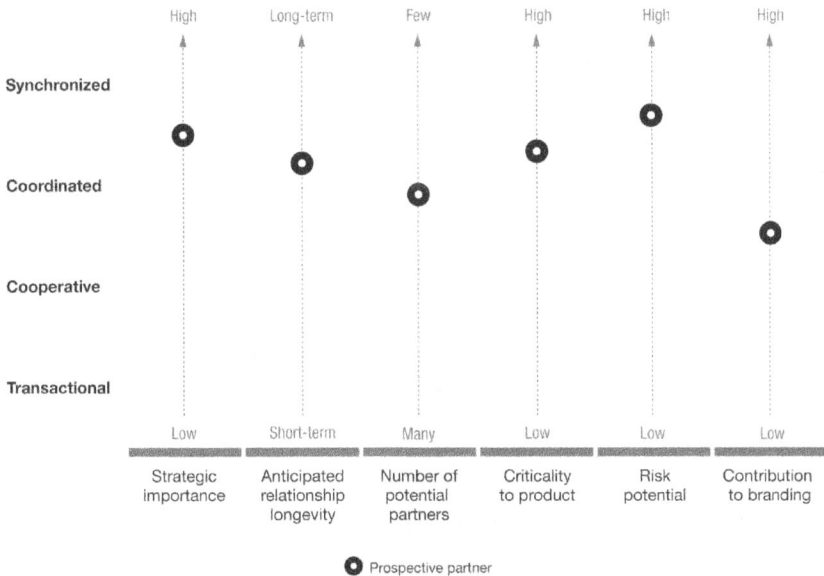

McDonald's is a company that segments its suppliers strategically. For commoditized items, such as napkins and straws, the fast-food giant opts for a limited degree of collaboration and a large number of suppliers at the local level. By contrast, McDonald's limits the number of suppliers that provide critical ingredients like beef, fish, and chicken, and materials like packaging that can be sourced globally. McDonald's works closely with these strategic suppliers to create processes essential for meeting its goals.

Take one example: Because food safety is a top priority for McDonald's, the company invests heavily in close relationships with "grinders" (hamburger-patty producers) to ensure that the product meets McDonald's exacting standards. As Jose Luis Bretones, former director of global supply chain strategy for McDonald's, explains, "It's part of our relationship with them [the grinders] to make sure that the McDonald's brand is protected all the time. That means they have to guarantee there's a barrier between the areas that are producing patties for us and the areas that are producing patties for other companies so that there is no transfer of ingredients and/or cross contamination."[5]

Deeper collaboration creates the greatest value in instances where there is a high concentration of three things: interaction (for example, in-person meetings, phone conversations, or project teams), expertise (an exchange of tacit knowledge or expertise, such as an executive, knowledge worker, or specialist might have), and information (as found in databases, working documents, and archives).

To drive deep collaborative relationships, companies like Cisco, the U.S.-based networking-equipment giant, have defined "collaboration impact zones" along the supply chain. These areas are where exchanges of information and expertise with partners are most frequent and most intense. Managed well, collaboration impact zones can greatly bolster an organization's business and management practices.[6] Establishing collaboration impact zones allows a company to focus on the areas of collaboration that are most critical to ROI.

TRUST YOUR PARTNERS BUT PROTECT YOUR INTERESTS

Effective collaboration is based on building relationships and on sharing both information and the benefits gained as the relationship progresses. That means you shouldn't ask your partners for something without giving them something in return. That "something" can be price concessions, value-added services, or, in most cases, information. If you're willing to set up an infra-structure to automatically send purchase requirements to your suppliers, you should expect to be asked for demand projections so that they can be prepared. Sharing information requires trust; if you aren't willing to provide those projections, you may not have the necessary confidence in your partner.

There's a good reason that many companies are skeptical about making highly strategic information available to collaboration partners: trust is violated all the time. Confidential pricing data make their way into the hands of competitors. Engineering specs are copied. Sales forecasts are communicated to a competitor. A customer is told that it's getting the best price from a supplier—only to discover later that rival companies are getting an even better price from that same supplier. Indeed, concern that a company doesn't share the same goals with its trading partners is significant: nearly 43 percent of participants in a recent study agreed that this was true for their company (Figure 4.3).[7]

Figure 4.3 Concern About Consistency of Partnership Goals

Response to the statement "we worry that we and our partner don't share the same goals."

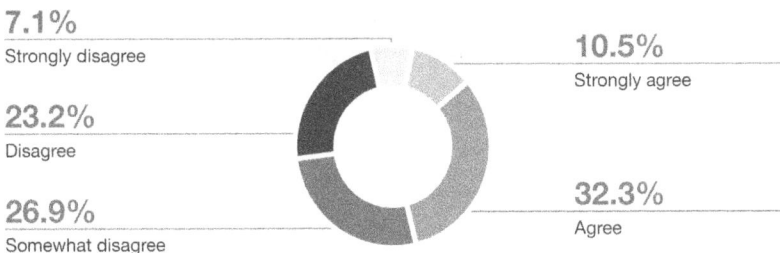

7.1%
Strongly disagree

10.5%
Strongly agree

23.2%
Disagree

26.9%
Somewhat disagree

32.3%
Agree

Source: SCM World, March 2012

Some argue that violation of trust is part of the natural order of business. Willy Shih, a professor at Harvard Business School, notes that in the 1870s, U.S. textile companies sent employees to work in British factories; the employees took notes on textile equipment and brought the information back to their employers. And during the Cold War era, Russians and East Germans stole U.S. computer and chip designs. This, Shih argues, is a normal development pattern.[8]

Whether or not you agree with Shih's philosophy, most companies don't think that just because they are pioneering deep collaborations, they should accept the theft of IP as a normal part of doing business. That's why they do whatever they can to protect their own interests. Yet sometimes all the planning in the world isn't enough.

While no collaboration can be made failsafe, you can take steps to protect your company.

Robust Contracts

At some point, even the most carefully constructed contracts may fail. While there's no guaranteed way to prevent this from happening, the good news is that the concept of protecting a company from a confidentiality breach is more advanced than it used to be. Your collaborative partnerships should typically include a contract or confidentiality agreement that provides a level of legal protection that transcends the "fuzzier" concept of trust. But while a structured contract can minimize risk, don't assume that it will provide a source of legal recourse should the relationship fail. Often, going to court over a contract violation is just too costly to be worthwhile. Instead, use the contract as a tool for clarifying how the relationship will be governed and as a way to define roles and responsibilities.

Cybersecurity

Data transmission is another concern. Although many technologies can encode data, the risk of technology failure is real. As a result, more companies are deploying comprehensive security services that require partners to follow prescribed security practices. Partners may be required to use certain types of passwords and limit server and workstation access to only those employees who have undergone extensive background checks, have signed nondisclosure agreements, and are accessing your information and proprietary designs from stations with approved Internet Protocol and MAC addresses.

To help companies manage information security risk, the International Organization for Standardization has created a comprehensive set of controls that dictate best practices in areas ranging from security policy to business-continuity management. Some companies require their collaboration partners to observe these standards. Because these standards are frameworks for information-security best practices rather than methodologies, companies generally use them to outline the specifics of what they require of their partners. These specifics may include such measures as disaster recovery plans or the consistent use of antivirus protection within all network-connected devices.

But eliminating all information security risk is virtually impossible— and unaffordable. That's because the supply chain is dynamic, with existing partnerships evolving and with new customers and suppliers being added on a regular basis. To determine the right level of security needed, first identify the situations that would cause the greatest business disruption. These might include the unavailability of critical systems, loss of data integrity, or disruptions in ongoing communications with your partners. Then assess and put in place the steps or tools needed to minimize the odds of these events occurring.

SHARE GAINS AND LOSSES

Our definition of collaboration includes sharing benefits achieved in the course of the partnership through "gainsharing." It also means sharing losses incurred.

Gainsharing to Reduce Costs

Formal gainsharing is a well-known way to distribute the financial benefits of a business relationship between supply chain partners. Each partner agrees to work toward lower overall costs and to share the savings. The specifics are usually detailed in a legal contract. The relationship between Navistar International and Menlo Worldwide Logistics offers an excellent illustration.[9]

Navistar, a manufacturer of commercial trucks, buses, and diesel engines, wanted to expand its network of 1,000-plus dealers worldwide. Its supply chain, which operated across three business units—truck, engine, and parts—depended on numerous carriers and third-party logistics providers. Independent logistics organizations within each business unit made it difficult to consolidate requirements across the company, get a clear view of global inventory, or identify failure points throughout the extended supply chain.

In 2008, Navistar entered into an agreement with one of its logistics service providers, Menlo Worldwide Logistics. The Shared Collaboration Model, as the partnership was called, aimed to reduce Navistar's logistics spending by 25 percent in five years while simultaneously improving Menlo's logistics network. If Menlo succeeded in reducing Navistar's logistics spending by 25 percent in five years, Navistar would put those savings toward Menlo's infrastructure improvements.

Select Menlo team members worked at Navistar and vice versa. The exchange proved so successful that eventually it was difficult to distinguish between Navistar and Menlo employees. Early successes included rationalizing Navistar's transportation spending and adopting a new core-carrier program, reengineering the vehicle delivery process, and implementing a Lean materials-flow pilot project at a Navistar manufacturing facility. At the end of the partnership's second year, Navistar had already achieved 11 percent cost savings—significant progress toward the five-year 25 percent goal (Figure 4.4).[10]

Figure 4.4 Gainsharing to Reduce Costs

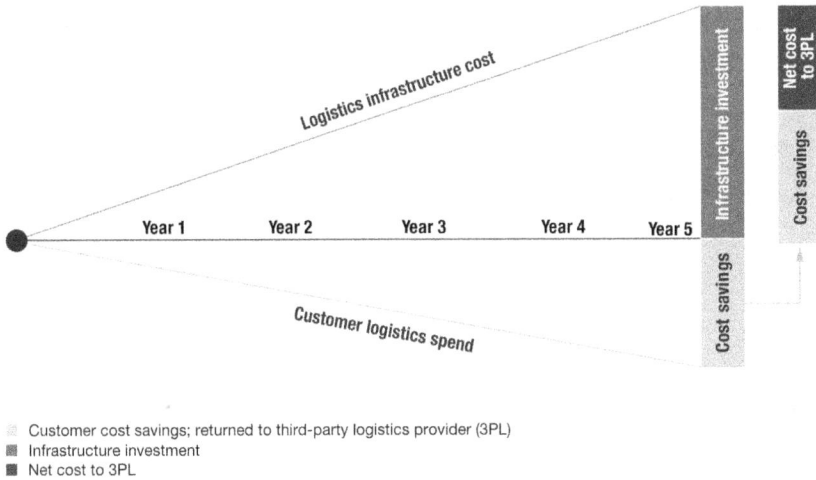

   Customer cost savings; returned to third-party logistics provider (3PL)
   Infrastructure investment
   Net cost to 3PL

Gainsharing to Boost Innovation

Gainsharing doesn't always entail a formal financial agreement. Companies may choose to collaborate on new products and services that allow mutual benefits without strict accounting for spending and savings.

Consider U.K.-based Shutl, an up-and-coming web-based service focused on improving delivery times for online retailers. Although online shoppers can find and purchase anything in seconds, they often have to wait days for delivery. That lag time deters many consumers from online conversion—that is, from making online purchases. It is, in fact, the single greatest challenge for online retailers.

By collaborating with retailers and local courier companies, Shutl has found a way to make delivery exceptionally speedy and cost-effective. Consumers can choose delivery within 90 minutes of purchase or in any hour-long window of their choice, any day they choose; they can then track their orders and watch them "shutling" in real time on a GPS-enabled map. Shutl's technology matches individual deliveries to a courier on the basis of availability, location, performance history, and price. Couriers can bid for delivery jobs by adjusting their pricing to capture business while using whatever capacity they have available. At the same time, the cost of failed deliveries is reduced because the shopper selects when the delivery is to occur.

The value of the collaboration is clear. Shutl has seen demand for its services rise, the retailers have seen large increases in order conversion and the size of the average order, and couriers have profitably put unused capacity to use. The other winner: customers—whose ratings for Shutl are overwhelmingly positive.[11]

Gainsharing with Competitors

Supply chain partners are not the only ones to use gainsharing. Competitors, too, use this practice to their mutual advantage—a strategy often termed "horizontal collaboration." In these relationships, two or more companies agree to share logistics or manufacturing capacity to cut the costs of less-than-truckload shipments, empty backhauls, or underutilized equipment.

Three tire companies provide an apt example. Each faced similar challenges in the U.K. market, where their retail customers demanded delivery within 24 hours of placing an order. As a result, "drop sizes"—the number of tires delivered at one time—were getting smaller as deliveries became more frequent. That meant higher logistics costs and more exhaust, which wasn't doing much for the companies' carbon footprint.

To solve the problem, the tire companies forged a partnership that would take advantage of the fact that they shared the same delivery process as well as many of the same customers and delivery points. The three tire companies agreed on a number of prerequisites, including the need to retain individual brand identities. They also established methods for sharing costs and for providing transparency regarding key performance indicators. Before embarking on the partnership, they established a formal communication process and signed mutual confidentiality agreements. The result: a tremendous reduction in truck miles, costs, and carbon emissions for all three companies.

USE TECHNOLOGY TO SUPPORT YOUR COLLABORATIVE RELATIONSHIPS

Although the advanced capabilities that vendors of supply chain collaboration systems can offer are not essential for successful collaboration, technology can confer important benefits. Most critically, it allows better communication with supply chain partners. Technology thus can help break down barriers between companies, improve the flow of information, and convert data into useful information.

Early Uses of Technology

During the dot-com boom of the late 1990s and early 2000s, many companies were slow to leverage technology in collaborative partnerships. Some companies lacked the required understanding of complex information systems. Others expected to reap the promised benefits without doing the preliminary legwork—the analysis, process redesign, and alignment with the new applications that were needed to gain the full functionality. Moreover, no single e-business standard for transactions and messaging had yet emerged. Collaboration tools had to translate multiple data formats, which limited their appeal.

As a result, many business-to-business portals were simply databases for pushing information. Company A would publish data to a site, then notify Company B that the information was available, or assume that Company B would check the site on a regular basis. Company B would view the information, download it to its own system, and decide whether to take action. These portals were, while limited in functionality, of great benefit to some industries. The pharmaceutical industry, for example, found that the standards needed to use them were a step forward in meeting stringent government-compliance requirements.

Electronic Data Interchange

Until recently, electronic data interchange (EDI) was the primary method of communication used to transfer POS and other data, often with information flowing through a proprietary EDI network. For companies without an EDI capability, private supplier portals, hubs, or extranets remained the alternatives. Most of these tools enabled document and content management; embedded workflows automated the routing of documents, forms, and certain data and tasks. Systems stored data locally and required specific communication protocols to push the data to suppliers. These transactions were also subject to platform and operating system limitations, and the costs to create these systems were borne by the manufacturers that ran them. Only a few companies continue to use them today.[12]

Many of today's collaboration tools now include functionality for supply chain event management, such as a missed supplier delivery or an unexpected customer order. By providing early warnings, and thereby speedy analysis of mitigation options, they strengthen customer–supplier relationships. Industry-standard tools, such as RosettaNet Partner Interface Processess (PIPs) and collaborative planning, forecasting, and replenishment (CPFR), have also gained prominence. Both RosettaNet PIPs and CPFR use standard business-process definitions and consistent formats for the data that flows between them.

Cloud Computing

The advent of cloud-computing services has greatly reduced the investment required for electronic collaboration. Companies no longer have to buy and own servers, applications, platforms, and other computing assets. Instead, they pay service providers for these assets on an as-needed basis and access them through the Internet. (See Sidebar "Cloud Computing's Pros and Cons.") Cloud computing can help companies lower their capital expenditures and quickly scale their computing power up or down to reflect the rhythms of their business.

CLOUD COMPUTING'S PROS AND CONS

Cloud-based computing systems enable companies to leverage supply chain software solutions with minimal investment in computing power and software licenses. The cloud also provides the backdrop for a highly collaborative supply chain network, with high visibility and centralized storage and data handoffs. Simplified, standardized workflows mean that companies can quickly ramp up with little capital expense or organizational distraction. If a service is no longer needed, a company can simply stop using it—and stop paying for it.

For these reasons, cloud computing has the potential to enable collaboration between hundreds of companies on a global scale—an entirely new information-sharing model that can support highly complex trading-partner networks. Just as a social-networking site provides instant status updates to all "circle" members, a cloud-based supply chain network can update all nodes with the current status of common objects such as purchase orders, shipment notifications, or inventory levels by location.

Yet cloud computing also raises concerns about sharing information with supply chain partners. Since very few companies own or operate their entire end-to-end supply chain, decisions about using cloud technology involve multiple partners, creating complexities and sensitivities between the participating organizations. Companies have an absolute need to protect their IP and their customers, because lost or misused data can do irreparable harm. For this reason, companies operating in the cloud must develop trustworthy relationships with partners and a communication infrastructure that can transfer information in a highly secure manner.

As technology continues to advance and companies' ability to leverage it keeps improving, information flow and decision making will also be enhanced. However, even the most sophisticated technology can't compensate for suboptimal processes or the absence of a seasoned supply chain professional's expertise. A good collaborative system can gather data and make recommendations based on a predefined set of business rules, but it can neither gauge the applicability of those rules to the current situation nor calculate the effect of an inappropriate demand on a supply chain partner.

That's because technology is an enabler, not the driver, of success. To make certain that your technology investment pays off, ensure that your organization is set up to leverage it. That may mean changing your organization's structure, processes, incentive plans, and performance measurement. Also be sure to involve your suppliers and customers in the selection and development of processes and systems. Or, at the very least, solicit feedback from them and allow them to influence or enhance the design.

BE READY TO COMPROMISE

When you invite another company to be a collaboration partner, you're asking it to make fundamental changes in how it operates. The further you go along the collaboration spectrum, the more you're asking of your partner. Large, powerful companies may be in a position to force changes in their supply chain partners. Other companies must be prepared to sell prospective partners on the idea of collaboration.

Often, OEMs or EMS providers develop the "master plan" for a collaborative relationship. Suppliers are expected to provide value-added services as the cost of continuing to do business. But if you expect your suppliers to provide more services and take on additional risk at no additional cost to you, your chances of getting these companies on board are small. And even if you do succeed in getting them to sign up, you may find they're unable to meet the requirements you've set for them.

To avoid these situations, work closely with your partners to develop a value proposition they can understand and buy into. Create an agreement that fairly values the added services you want them to provide—and pay them a premium that's appropriate.

Also, remember that successful collaborators make a major effort to compromise with and support their partners. A business may, for instance, share the costs of improving working conditions at factories with its contract manufacturer. Or it may provide a mutually beneficial technology solution to a supply chain partner at little or no cost, and then help the partner get up to speed on using the solution. Hyundai, for example, supported suppliers hard-hit by the Great Recession by increasing funding of their R&D activities and by providing low-interest loans.

Finally, be sure to set up a way to monitor the results of your collaborative relationships. Work with your partners to establish a set of metrics that are consistent with the value proposition and that can be updated and reviewed on a regular basis.

Your watchword in crafting a collaboration model should be *adaptability*: the collaboration model is a work in progress—one that you must continually tweak, and occasionally even overhaul, to keep your company's competitive edge as sharp as possible. As your company's business and supply chain strategies evolve to meet changing priorities and business conditions, you may need to alter the types of collaborative relationships you have with suppliers. In some cases you may need to end them altogether. You may also want to modify the degree of collaboration you have with certain supply chain partners.

TESTS OF SUCCESSFUL COLLABORATION

You're more likely to forge effective collaborative relationships with supply chain partners if you excel on several fronts:

- *Vision.* You have a single, unambiguous picture in mind for your collaboration strategy. This picture should include certain elements, such as a clear purpose and goals for your collaborations with supply chain partners. Your vision should also reflect a firm understanding of your company's current and future desired core competencies to ensure that your collaboration strategy is wholly consistent with these competencies. But when it comes to developing or acquiring needed competencies, start small: focus on a limited set of capabilities, select partner candidates, and choose tasks rather than trying to do everything at once.

- *Business acumen.* You pay close attention to how the advanced systems that support supply chain collaboration are evolving, and you identify the opportunities and the challenges that technology advances present. You also let your business drivers and economic realities shape the nature of collaborative relationships and the way you manage them. And, in parallel with your initial efforts, you assess the organizational changes that will be needed to support collaboration on a larger scale.

- *Accountability.* You know how to align your company's compensation and reward structure with the goals of your collaboration strategy. You also effectively manage your collaboration partners and have a comprehensive metrics program in place that allows you to monitor their performance—and your own—on a regular basis.

KEY TAKEAWAYS

- There are four degrees of collaboration: transactional, cooperative, coordinated, and synchronized.
- Successful internal collaboration can set the stage for excelling at external collaboration.
- Segmenting supply chain partners helps companies determine the right degree of collaboration with each partner.
- Collaboration partners must share gains—as well as losses.
- Technology is an enabler, not the driver, of success.
- Mutual trust and compromise are essential.

KAISER PERMANENTE: THRIVING UNDER PRESSURE

In most developed countries, health spending is rising faster than incomes. The issue is particularly acute in the United States, which not only spends more per capita on healthcare than any other country but also has seen spending rise as a share of national income for decades—from 10 percent in 1985 to 17 percent in 2010 to a projected 25 percent in 2037.[1] Costs have skyrocketed across the board, including hospital stays, doctor visits, pharmaceuticals, lab tests, new technologies, healthcare administration, and health insurance premiums. Ironically, as treatment options become more advanced, fewer people are able to afford them.

The U.S. Patient Protection and Affordable Care Act, enacted by the U.S. government in 2010, is designed to make health coverage more affordable and available. In an industry where employers and consumers for decades absorbed year-over-year cost increases, the Affordable Care Act catapulted most healthcare providers into a new world, where survival will require a laser-sharp focus on cost and efficiency without compromising patient outcomes.

For Kaiser Permanente (KP), by contrast, the Affordable Care Act ushered in the next phase of work, one that was already very much in progress. Since its establishment in 1945, the KP Medical Care Program has focused on high-quality, affordable care. Taking the next step, the company is making innovations in its supply chain that will make it possible for the organization to thrive—not just survive—in the new era.

BUILDING THE KP NETWORK

Headquartered in Oakland, California, Kaiser Permanente is the largest nonprofit health plan in the United States, serving more than 9 million members. The KP organization consists of three separate legal entities: the nonprofit Kaiser Foundation Hospitals, the for-profit Permanente Medical Groups, and the nonprofit Kaiser Foundation Health Plan and its subsidiaries. All told, the Kaiser Permanente organization has 37 medical centers and more than 600 medical offices located in nine states and the District of Columbia. Revenue in 2011 was $48 billion.

With roots dating back to the 1930s, Kaiser Permanente was formed following World War II, when many people could not afford to go to a doctor. The company has remained committed to providing affordable, high-quality healthcare ever since.

Collaboration among the various KP entities has been key to realizing that commitment. KP has carefully coordinated its clinical services—primary, secondary, and hospital care—to promote and provide higher quality healthcare. Additionally, it has put an infrastructure in place to provide quality-of-care

Kaiser Permanente Organization

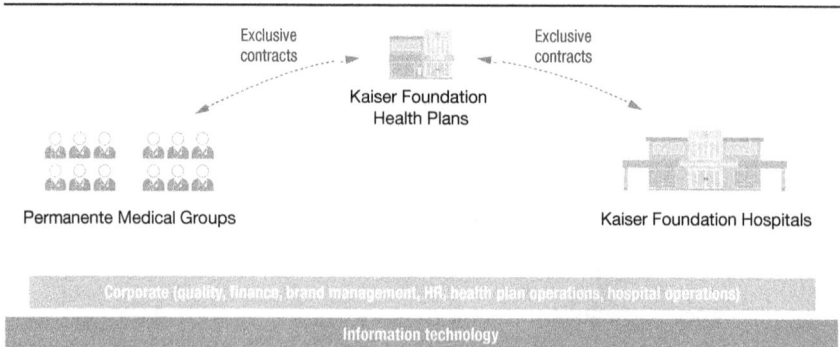

Source: Kaiser Permanente

oversight and to keep everyone focused on a common goal, namely keeping people healthy and out of the hospital.

One of the factors that have made this collaboration work so well is KP's huge investment in cutting-edge information systems, which give KP providers access to patient records all across the program. As a result, virtually every detail about a patient—from doctor visits to postsurgical treatments—is in the system, improving both clinicians' ability to administer high-quality care and patients' experience of the treatment process. Through e-visits and telephone consultations, for example, KP doctors are able to access patient records and consult with patients electronically, resulting in fewer unnecessary visits, better medical outcomes, and higher patient satisfaction.[2]

The focus on collaboration and integrated information systems has made it possible to realize substantial cost savings, which KP shares with its members, offering some of the lowest insurance premiums in the markets it serves. Members typically pay a monthly premium and fixed copayment for visits and procedures and in turn can choose from a wide range of KP clinics, hospitals, and clinicians. People who have traditional fee-for-service plans are more likely to have to contend with skyrocketing premiums, escalating copayments, and out-of-pocket costs that can vary widely depending on the physician seen and the facility visited.

KP's emphasis on health maintenance and low prices encourages members to engage in routine checkups, wellness visits, and lifestyle counseling. In 2011, KP received top marks from the National Committee for Quality Assurance in 20 out of 77 effectiveness-of-care measures—that is, proactive illness-prevention measures such as weight counseling for children, comprehensive diabetes care, and antidepressant medication management.[3]

ADOPTING A NEW APPROACH TO SUPPLY CHAIN MANAGEMENT

As the Affordable Care Act legislation takes hold, the company is looking for new sources of cost savings while continuing to improve the quality of the healthcare services it provides. One key target is the product supply chain; that is, the supply chain for the medical devices and supplies used to deliver those healthcare services.

Medical supplies account for up to 40 percent of a hospital's operating costs, representing the second largest expense after labor.[4] Yet when it comes to managing the supply chain for those supplies, the healthcare sector in general lags other industries.

That was a sobering thought for KP, which spends $2 billion on medical devices and supplies each year. Recognizing that significant change was needed, KP brought in supply chain experts from relevant product-based industries.

Laurel Junk is one such expert, hired in 2009 from biotech pioneer Amgen to be KP's vice president of supply chain. "The burning platform is healthcare reform and the reduced reimbursements that are hitting us in a material way," says Junk. "We're facing the same cost pressures that other industries did. They just got to a critical point much sooner than we did."

INTRODUCING DATA STANDARDS

A key reason why healthcare isn't as efficient as other industries in this area is a lack of consistent and uniform data standards for medical and surgical supplies that would make it possible to identify and describe products in a systematic way. Not only does it mean that each hospital may use a different part number for the identical product (be it gloves, sutures, or instruments) but the product description and the manufacturer can vary as well.

This isn't just a problem for one healthcare network trying to communicate with another; it's a problem within individual systems. And the bigger the system, the bigger the potential problem. Without uniform standards, KP as an organization has found it difficult or even impossible to consolidate all of the numerous requirements for medical supplies, so each KP hospital has had to place its own orders. As one of the largest healthcare systems in the United States, KP has the leverage to secure excellent volume discounts, but only if efficient planning and procurement processes are in place.

But it's not just about efficiency. Common standards allow service providers to more easily share information about medical products or devices used to treat a particular patient. This information can be another useful tool to help providers decide which particular medical products and devices should be used—or, even more important, avoided. That information may be essential in an emergency situation, or when manufacturers issue product recalls.

That's why in 2010, KP helped establish the Healthcare Transformation Group (HTG). A consortium of five healthcare systems, the HTG consists of KP, Geisinger Health System, Intermountain Health Care, Mayo Clinic, and Mercy. The HTG immediately began to push for a standard that would allow healthcare organizations to assign a unique code to every product. GS1® was the standard of choice.[5]

If you've ever gone grocery shopping, you've seen GS1 standards in action in the form of the ubiquitous Universal Product Code (UPC), which is found on virtually all retail products in the United States. The bar codes developed for the healthcare industry look a lot like UPCs. And they perform a similar function, allowing all the players in the supply chain—manufacturers, distributors, and hospital chains—to be on the same page.

Bar Code Standards at Work

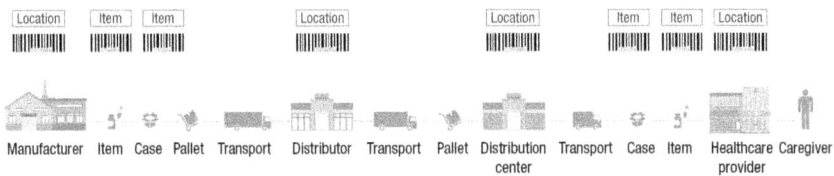

Source: Based on GS1 Standards in Healthcare

Some suppliers have been resistant because of the expense involved, but the HTG has held their feet to the fire. "The five of us said to our top 20 suppliers, 'No bar codes by the end of the year, no business,'" says Junk. "It's a collective voice from the customer side."

ADDRESSING INVENTORY CHALLENGES

Data standards don't just help with the procurement side of the supply chain; they drive internal efficiency and ultimately help to improve the quality of healthcare. Consider the basic activities of putting materials in a specific location when they are received, then taking them out when they are needed for a patient procedure. Failure to record the changes in inventory associated with these activities results in an inaccurate picture of inventory levels. For this reason, hospitals prefer to check inventory in and out by scanning product bar codes. But when multiple bar codes are in use, it's difficult to know which one should be scanned. In some cases, labels are put on top of others, making the right bar code impossible to read.

To avoid these problems, some hospitals rely on manual methods for tracking inventory. But paper-based systems are also problematic. Not only does the process take a lot of time, it's also prone to errors that give an incorrect picture of what's actually on hand. Inventory that drops below a specified minimum is a red flag, causing the procurement organization to order more, often via expensive expediting.

But excess inventory and expedite fees are not the biggest issue. Before any patient procedure, the required supplies must be pulled from inventory. This is usually done via a procedure card. Not unlike a shopping list, a procedure card specifies what medical supplies will be needed for the procedure. But when supplies aren't available in their designated location, the clinician must hunt for them. A 2009 hospital industry survey showed that 70 percent of nurses spend 5 to 20 percent or more of their time each shift searching for supplies.[6] For a 12-hour shift, that's at least 30 minutes and as much as two and a half hours that those clinicians are not tending to patients.

KP is taking a number of steps to solve this problem, which is common among hospitals. For starters, it is shifting responsibility for picking the medical supplies listed on the procedure cards to members of the supply chain staff. This change will free up nursing staff for patient care.

In addition, KP has also defined inventory locations and developed rules for how materials are taken and returned; associating a part with a specific location makes it easier to find. Consistent use of bar codes also helps, reducing manual transactions when products are moved from one location to another or used for a procedure.

Ultimately, an accurate record of the supplies used for specific procedures will help identify the products that are used most often and make it possible to develop demand forecasts and safety stocks more accurately at the individual-item level. More important, because the use of specific supplies will be tied to patient records, the hospital will have a more robust way to accurately track exactly which products were used for each procedure.

TURNING DEMAND PLANNING FROM AN ART TO A SCIENCE

Formal demand planning isn't the norm for most hospitals. That's not surprising, given the number of unplanned procedures, emergency and otherwise, that occur in any given day. KP, however, is pioneering a demand-planning process that takes into account surgeries scheduled in advance. Elective surgeries, for example, may be planned several months ahead of time, with fewer scheduled during the summer and holiday periods. This information, in combination with an accurate view of historical procedure schedules, helps make the picture of future needs more accurate.

KP is also using demand planning to ensure that the right products are available for unforeseen procedures. In the past, the nursing staff usually set inventory targets. Since shortages can be very problematic, the staff is likely to err on the side of ordering too much. "The nurse will say, 'Well, typically, we need 10,'" says Brooke Fan, executive director of supply chain. "Why don't we put in 15, just in case?" Those "guesstimates" could pack a punch. Incremental inventory resulting from an extra 50 percent, multiplied by thousands of parts in hundreds of locations, can run into the millions of dollars, without necessarily eliminating the likelihood of a shortage.

That's why the KP supply chain team has adopted a more analytical approach to predict future needs, looking at how many products of a certain type were used, when they were used, what they were used for, and how long they take to replenish. The team is also looking at the variability in demand and lead time to calculate appropriate safety-stock levels.

With a formal demand plan and accurate inventory levels, each KP hospital can order supplies with the confidence that the right quantity will be on hand and that shortages will be few and far between.

LEADING THE WAY

Data standards, automated transactions, and formal demand planning all play a part in KP's supply chain strategy. Better measurement of how medical supplies are being used—and how effective they are—informs decisions on how much to purchase and when and where supplies are needed. Changes in organizational responsibility allow clinical staff to focus more on patients than on materials management. And the company is tying the usage of specific materials to KP's sophisticated patient-records system, extending KP's reputation as a leader in healthcare information systems.

Advances in medical science and technology have resulted in new procedures, medications, and medical devices focused on increasing the quality of lives and, in many cases, saving them. At KP, these technologies have had a very positive impact on patient outcomes. KP intends to continue making use of the best new technologies while maintaining its position as an affordable and high-quality healthcare option, so that it can keep delivering the best patient outcomes at the lowest possible cost.

This is where the power of the KP organization plays a huge role. With information systems that collect data with each supply chain transaction,

KP can consolidate information across the entire organization, greatly simplifying the procurement process, sharing resources across facilities, and collaborating closely with suppliers and distributors.

To be sure, changes in healthcare law have posed massive challenges for the healthcare industry. Kaiser Permanente, however, is leading the way with the help of a supply chain strategy that faces cost-reduction challenges head on.

CHAPTER FIVE

DISCIPLINE 5:
USE METRICS TO DRIVE PERFORMANCE

You may have formulated a sound supply chain strategy, established disciplined supply chain processes, set up an integrated supply chain organization, and initiated collaborations with supply chain partners. But if you don't know how the supply chain is performing on all of these fronts, you can't identify and address performance problems. In this chapter, we delve into the complex world of supply chain performance metrics—and explore how to use those metrics to assess as well as to manage performance.

Most executives would agree with the adage "If you can't measure it, you can't manage it." Yet most companies lack a supply chain performance measurement program that's robust—that is, one that provides a clear picture of overall performance, pinpoints the root of performance problems, and helps identify improvement opportunities. The reason is simple: establishing such a measurement program is extremely difficult. Just getting agreement from managers throughout the organization on what exactly should be measured can be a major effort, let alone deciding which metrics to use or how to set targets for those metrics.

Many companies have separate scorecards for customer service, procurement, and manufacturing already in place. But relatively few organizations track cross-functional supply chain metrics, such as order-fulfillment lead time or cash-to-cash cycle time, on a regular basis. And in many cases, those companies that track cross-functional metrics do not know how to use these metrics to optimize end-to-end processes within their own company or the larger supply chain.

What's more, many companies' metrics programs tend to focus on financial outcomes, such as profitability, revenue, and return on assets or investment. This isn't surprising, since companies must do financial reporting on a regular basis, and financial metrics are relatively easy to obtain once the books are closed for any given period. In addition, regulations such as the Sarbanes-Oxley Act of 2002 require companies to validate their financial data and document their controls and procedures, placing further emphasis on financial metrics.

While undeniably important, financial metrics in isolation are inadequate measures of performance. They don't provide information on key operational activities that affect financial performance, such as order delivery performance or customer service levels. Moreover, they are, for the most part, lagging indicators: that is, they reveal what a company has or hasn't achieved in the past.

Supply chain metrics, by contrast, can act as forward-looking indicators. They provide the best way to understand whether your supply chain's performance is improving, worsening, or likely to worsen in the future. If performance is getting worse, the metrics can help you correct problems before they turn into crises.

Here's one example: Orders that are delivered late may impact your company's future revenue. That's because customers often consider their most recent service experience with a company when they are deciding whether or not to make another purchase from that company. Delivery delays may also extend your receivables collection period, negatively impacting cash-to-cash cycle time. Thus, quality of service is a valuable leading indicator—even for companies for which customer experience is not the primary competitive differentiator.

That's not all. The right set of supply chain measurements also makes it easier to compare your company's supply chain performance against that of other companies. With these measurements, you can do a better job of communicating performance expectations to people working throughout your supply chain, making it easier to set goals and drive continuous improvement.

What does the word *metric* really mean? A metric is a clearly defined standard of measurement that, in a supply chain context, allows a company to assess quantitatively how well a process is performing. It also allows the company to make comparable assessments with its own past performance as well as with the performance of competitors.

Key performance indicators (KPIs) are high-level metrics that usually form part of a dashboard designed to give senior management an overview of how the business is performing. KPIs are distinctive in that they measure processes that are critically important to gaining competitive advantage: if, for example, a company is competing on cost, it will likely have numerous KPIs related to cost, such as purchase prices for raw materials, labor rates, and logistics costs. In most cases, KPIs do not provide insight into why something has gone wrong; rather, they simply signal that a process is or is not performing as expected. When a KPI is off track, managers need to closely examine the processes and functions that influence it.

One of the challenges of establishing an effective supply chain metrics program is deciding which metrics to track. This chapter focuses on two key concepts: performance measurement and performance management. Using *performance measurement*, you put in place the right metrics for assessing the effectiveness of your supply chain. By contrast, with *performance management*, you track actual performance against targeted performance on all your metrics and use the resulting insights to make needed improvements. In other words, you use performance measures to evaluate how effective your supply chain is in supporting your business strategy. In sum, the act of *measuring* performance provides only visibility; it is *managing* performance that effects performance change.

SUPPLY CHAIN PERFORMANCE MEASUREMENT: SELECTING THE RIGHT METRICS

Supply chain metrics cover all six major supply chain processes: Plan, Source, Make, Deliver, Return, and Enable. How do you select the metrics that will be right for your company? The following guidelines can help:

- Understanding standard metrics
- Linking metrics to your business strategy
- Choosing a balanced and comprehensive set of metrics
- Setting targets for each metric

UNDERSTANDING STANDARD METRICS

You may choose to define metrics that are specific to your industry or your company, but there is also great value in using standard metrics whose definitions are consistent across companies and industries. Standard operational metrics include those intended primarily for internal management, such as total supply chain management cost, return on working capital, and cash-to-cash cycle time (Table 5.1). They also include external metrics that measure performance important to the customer: perfect order fulfillment and order-fulfillment cycle time are good examples. Operational metrics can focus on one function, such as transportation cost, or they can be cross-functional, such as total order-management cost.

The Supply Chain Operations Reference model, or SCOR®, is a framework that provides standard metrics that companies can use to evaluate their operational performance. Each metric in the model has a standard definition and an explanation for how the metric is calculated.

Consistent with its overall structure, SCOR recognizes three levels of predefined metrics. Level 1 metrics are the diagnostics needed to monitor performance at a high level. Note that Level 1 includes both internally and externally focused measures (Table 5.2).[1] Many companies that use SCOR

Table 5.1 Total Supply Chain Management Cost

Category	Costs
Order management	• New product release, phase-in, and maintenance • Customer order creation • Order entry and maintenance • Contract, program, and channel management • Installation planning • Order fulfillment • Distribution • Transportation, outbound freight, and duties • Installation • Customer invoicing and accounting
Materials acquisition	• Materials and commodity management and planning • Supplier quality engineering • Inbound freight and duties • Receiving and materials storage • Incoming inspection • Materials processing and component engineering • Tooling
Inventory carrying	• Opportunity cost • Shrinkage • Insurance and taxes • Total inventory obsolescence: raw materials, work in process, and finished goods • Channel obsolescence • Field-service parts obsolescence
Finance and planning management information systems (MIS)	• Supply chain finance costs • Demand and supply planning costs • Supply chain IT costs (MIS)

Source: PMG

designate their Level 1 metrics as their KPIs. *Level 2* metrics serve as diagnostics for the Level 1 metrics, helping to identify the root cause or causes of Level 1 performance gaps. *Level 3* metrics serve as diagnostics for Level 2 metrics.

LINKING METRICS TO YOUR BUSINESS STRATEGY

Your supply chain metrics must be consistent with your company's key business goals. This is essential for seeing how well your supply chain is supporting the business strategy and for taking the actions needed to improve performance.

Table 5.2 SCOR Level 1 Metrics

	Performance attributes				
	Focused on the customer			Internally focused	
Level 1 metrics	Reliability	Responsiveness	Agility	Cost	Assets
Perfect order fulfillment	✓				
Order-fulfillment cycle time		✓			
Upside supply chain flexibility			✓		
Upside supply chain adaptability			✓		
Downside supply chain adaptability			✓		
Total cost to serve				✓	
Overall value at risk			✓		
Cash-to-cash cycle time					✓
Return on supply chain fixed assets					✓
Return on working capital					✓

Source: *Supply Chain Operation Reference Model*, Revision 11.0, Supply Chain Council, October 2012.

Measuring a few metrics in isolation is a common—and often coun-terproductive—way for companies to use performance-related data. A more effective approach is to start with your company's strategic goals and work backward to identify the supply chain performance metrics that support them. Keep in mind that no predetermined set of metrics is appropriate for all businesses: you'll need to choose supply chain metrics that reflect the performance parameters related to your supply chain objectives.

Consider a PC peripherals producer that competed on cost and rapid fulfillment. The company manufactured in China and Singapore and trans-ported products by sea to regional distribution centers, where they were shipped upon receipt of customer orders. Product standard costs were based on planned material and logistics costs.

The supply chain was designed with the intention of keeping costs low. But the logistics strategy—shipping by sea—added significant lead time. In some cases, transportation to distribution centers took as long as five weeks. Short product life cycles in this context made forecasting difficult. As a result, the company often had to move products by air, incurring expedite fees that nearly tripled transportation costs. In some cases, products had to be unpackaged, reconfigured, and repackaged at regional distribution centers to match customer orders.

These transportation and rework costs were largely invisible to product divisions, since they didn't affect product margin. The costs did, however, raise operating expenses and hurt the overall bottom line, which didn't sit well with executive management or shareholders.

To gain a better understanding of the problem, the company began measuring and reporting metrics specifically related to its basis of competition: low costs and fast fulfillment. This analysis revealed not only that transportation costs were far above the industry average but also that delivery of many orders took longer than the quoted lead times. Further analysis traced these incongruities to inaccurate forecasts and a lack of modularity in product designs. The management team began tracking product-level forecast accuracy, as well as expedite and rework costs associated with specific products. With this understanding of the origins of the excess costs, it was possible to determine how allocating a portion of these costs to specific products would impact margins.

This analysis of the metrics provided the impetus for improving the forecasting process. Moreover, it led the company to design products so that specific configurations would not be assembled until orders were received.

CHOOSING A BALANCED AND COMPREHENSIVE SET OF METRICS

The goal of performance management is not to promote excellence in every dimension but to drive behaviors that best support the business strategy. Yet even when the basis of competition—innovation, customer experience, quality, or cost—is well understood, some companies have a hard time determining where performance excellence is critical and where it's merely "nice to have." A balanced set of supply chain performance metrics is critical to understanding these trade-offs. It includes internally and externally focused, financial and nonfinancial, and functional and cross-functional metrics, as well as metrics that encourage continuous improvement.

Consider for example, the circumstances of a test-and-measurement equipment company whose customers were demanding lower prices. In order to minimize the impact on margins, the management team made the reduction of material costs a priority. The management team pushed the procurement group to negotiate better prices, setting aggressive cost-reduction targets and tying individual compensation to achievement of these targets.

The buyers obtained substantial discounts by purchasing some materials in higher volumes, and they also found suppliers that would charge less for other materials. These efforts resulted in a lower cost per unit for many materials, meeting the targets set by senior management.

After a few months, however, it became clear that the focus on the cost of materials was having a negative effect elsewhere in the supply chain. Buying in volume increased inventory dramatically. And because the shift to less expensive suppliers led the company to use materials of lower quality than those used previously, manufacturing yields dropped, and scrap and overtime rose. As a result, the cost-cutting initiative actually led to an increase in total cost.

The moral of this story is clear: Focusing on functional metrics in one area can drive unwanted behaviors in others and interfere with effective control of the overall supply chain. Functional metrics aren't bad in and of themselves, but they can be detrimental if they are not combined with cross-functional metrics that capture performance across the end-to-end supply chain.

The Balanced Scorecard methodology, developed by Robert Kaplan and David Norton, has done much to communicate the importance of

Table 5.3 The Balanced Scorecard: Four Perspectives

Perspective	Examples of supply chain metrics
Financial	• Cost of goods sold • Labor rates • Transportation cost per mile • Value-added productivity • Asset turns
Customer	• On-time delivery to commitment • Order-fulfillment cycle time • Fill rates • Perfect order fulfillment
Internal process	• Forecast accuracy • Production quality • Production flexibility • Internal cycle times
Workforce learning and growth	• Number of employees holding professional supply chain certification • Number of employees who have completed Six Sigma training

balance and comprehensiveness in performance metrics.[2] This methodology augments financial objectives and metrics with three additional perspectives that are just as important to the execution of a company's strategy: customer, internal process, and workforce learning and growth. Table 5.3 shows examples of supply chain–related metrics that might be associated with each of these four perspectives.

Using Tiered Metrics to Understand Cause and Effect

Part of choosing a balanced portfolio of metrics is understanding cause and effect. SCOR Level 1 metrics provide a view of overall supply chain health, but they don't explain what is actually causing performance to be above or below target. To understand that, you need to break out the different metrics that contribute to high-level performance. SCOR refers to this process as "metrics decomposition."[3]

If, for example, the number of inventory days of supply is well above what you consider acceptable, you'll need to take a look at each type of

Figure 5.1 Using Metric Decomposition to Analyze Performance

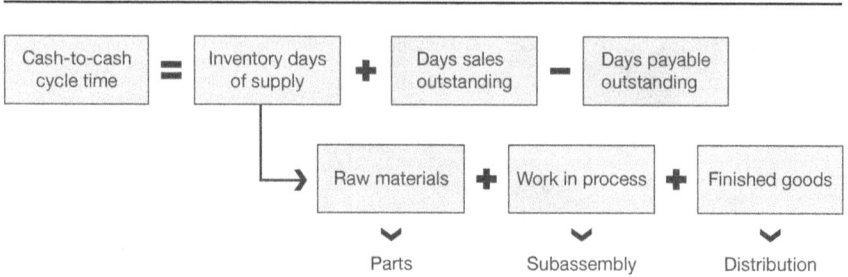

inventory—raw materials, work in process, and finished goods—both internally and among your suppliers and customers (Figure 5.1). Once you have an understanding of where inventory levels are too high, you can look at the underlying processes. Excess inventory is correlated with forecast inaccuracy, long material lead times, poor quality, and demand volatility, so a next logical step is to examine each of these metrics and use your findings to determine which processes require further analysis.

Measuring from Your Customers' Perspective

In order for metrics to support the premise of the supply chain as an end-to-end process, you need to consider the customers' viewpoint. A tire company learned this lesson firsthand after spending more than two years implementing delivery performance metrics across all regions and customer groups.

The company, which sold its tires to retailers, distributors, and repair shops, promised that all tires would be available to customers within one day of ordering. It defined on-time delivery as the percentage of tires received by customers within a day of their placing an order. So an order placed on Monday was considered on time if the tires were delivered on Tuesday.

The company reported great results: calculations showed that most tires were indeed scheduled for delivery the day after they were ordered. Customers, however, were less impressed, complaining that many deliveries arrived late. Their dissatisfaction was in line with an industry-sponsored customer survey that showed the company was performing worse than the competition. This, needless to say, came as a great surprise to the management team.

Closer investigation revealed some major discrepancies concerning what was meant by "on-time delivery." The people manning the order desk didn't "start the clock" until they knew a tire was actually in stock or on its way to the regional distribution center. They could then provide a committed delivery date to the customer. They calculated on-time delivery as the percentage of orders that could actually be scheduled for delivery the next day. But the order desk did not monitor whether deliveries were actually made as planned—only whether they had been scheduled for the following day. The assumption was that if a delivery had been scheduled, it would be on time. Customers, meanwhile, calculated their measurement of on-time delivery as the percentage of orders that were completely filled by the promised date.

As a result of these various discrepancies, interpretation of the exact same performance resulted in a wide range of "on-time delivery" metrics (Figure 5.2).

Figure 5.2 Tire Company Performance: Metrics Inconsistent with Customer Definition

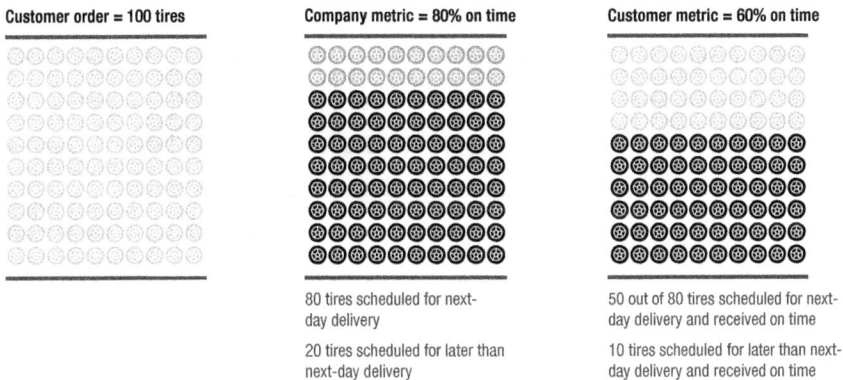

Customer order = 100 tires	Company metric = 80% on time	Customer metric = 60% on time
	80 tires scheduled for next-day delivery	50 out of 80 tires scheduled for next-day delivery and received on time
	20 tires scheduled for later than next-day delivery	10 tires scheduled for later than next-day delivery and received on time

To resolve these discrepancies, the company's management team refined two metrics for order delivery performance. The first was "on-time delivery to commit," which was defined as the percentage of complete orders received on the promised delivery date. The second metric, "order-fulfillment cycle time," tracked the time from when an order was received to the time when the tires were delivered.

When analyzing the discrepancies, the company made an important discovery: customers actually valued an accurate delivery date for their entire order more than they valued turnaround time. This insight led the company to reassess its entire customer-experience strategy and to focus on providing not only speedy delivery but also accurate commitment.

Avoiding Too Many Metrics

When faced with a myriad of metrics, companies often choose more than they actually need. This is especially true when managers put one or two important metrics in place—and gain visibility into operational capabilities and results for the first time. For companies accustomed to using solely financial metrics, data that offer insight into the performance of key supply chain processes are extremely powerful. The natural inclination is to want such data for all processes.

Consequently, companies develop new metrics even when it isn't feasible to monitor them all on a regular basis or to take action on the basis of the results. Many, for example, produce a monthly operations report that includes every metric under the sun. Each department—for example, procurement and manufacturing—is usually responsible for completing the sections covering its scope of responsibility. Before the advent of electronic document distribution, such reports would be collected in a voluminous binder for distribution to a long list of individuals. Today, these reports are posted online.

Compiling the operations report is no small undertaking. "We spend hours chasing down data to include in our section. When we're done, we've crunched hundreds of numbers and produced almost 40 different metrics," notes an order management director at an industrial-equipment company. "But after all that work, I'm not sure anyone ever looks at them."

Small wonder this order-management director doesn't see the value of the information he is required to produce: when too many metrics are monitored, it's difficult to distinguish those that provide real value from those that are simply possible to calculate. Of course, if you have too few metrics, you won't get a comprehensive picture of your supply chain's performance.

Determining which are the right metrics to deploy is an iterative process. Management teams may start out with too many or too few, revising their approach as needed. For instance, they may decide to add certain metrics that cover major supply chain processes and that are most closely tied to the company's business strategy. Or they may realize that some metrics don't link strongly enough to the business strategy and, therefore, can be eliminated. There is no one correct number or correct list of metrics any company should have; rather, it depends on each company's unique circumstances.

SETTING TARGETS FOR EACH METRIC

Once you've selected your supply chain metrics, you need to set a target for each. Do you want to reduce transportation costs per mile by a certain percentage? Decrease order-fulfillment cycle time to a specific number of days? Keep labor rates under a particular dollar figure?

Target setting is somewhat of an art. You want your targets to motivate the right behaviors, but how do you decide what levels of performance to strive for with each metric? The following practices can help.

Conducting Internal Benchmarking

If your company is large, you should measure the performance of comparable functional areas, divisions, business units, and facilities within your enterprise using consistent definitions. For instance, compare the performance levels of a set of manufacturing facilities, warehouses, distribution centers, purchasing organizations, and order management groups. Identify best-in-class business units or divisions and use their metrics as benchmarks for similar functions within the company.

Collecting internal benchmarking data is simpler than obtaining performance data from other companies. Still, you should monitor your internal-benchmarking effort closely. On rare occasions, internal benchmarking can trigger unproductive competition among business units. In extreme cases, business units may try to "game the system" to deliver winning results. If you see this happening, take immediate action to reset behavior.

Conducting External Benchmarking

Compare your company's performance against that of other companies. You may choose to limit the comparison to companies within your own industry, or you may want to include companies in other industries as well. External benchmarking helps you understand what level of quantitative performance is possible and, more important, which practices might deliver this level of performance. Be sure to study companies in other industries that have supply chain characteristics similar to yours—production processes, distribution channels, or other structural similarities that allow for a valid comparison.

To conduct external benchmarking, you'll need to collect a lot of performance data from other companies—as well as your own. Many companies are reluctant to provide such data directly to competitors or even to noncompetitors. To get around this roadblock, consider participating in benchmarking surveys managed by independent third parties, such as benchmarking-service providers or industry associations. These organizations specialize in defining relevant supply chain metrics and in working with participating companies to ensure that the data collected are unambiguous and accurate.

Once you have collected data, analyze any performance gaps between your company and your comparison group. A scorecard that provides a graphic representation of your company's performance compared with that of a select population could help highlight areas of opportunity (Figure 5.3). Investigate the causes behind any performance problems and

Figure 5.3 Level 1 Key Performance Indicators (KPIs)

		Population performance, by quintile				
KPI metrics		Major opportunity	Median		Best in class	Company ABC
Customer-facing metrics — On-time delivery to request (%)			▲ 85.2%		98.3%	69.7%
On-time delivery to commit (%)			▲ 91.4%		98.4%	87.1%
Order-fulfillment lead time (days)		▲	7.0		4.2	5.6
Upside flexibility (days)			101.1 ▲		25.0	90.0
Internally facing metrics — Total supply chain management cost (% of revenue)			▲ 7.1%		3.4%	8.1%
COGS (% of revenue)			70.6%		47.8% ▲	46.7%
Inventory days of supply			▲ 70.4		43.0	109.6
Cash-to-cash cycle time (days)		▲	73.3		20.1	160.5
Net asset turns			1.7	▲	3.4	2.2
Return on fixed assets (%)			80.1% ▲		243.4%	98.6%

▲ Sample company performance
Source: PMG

determine how you can close the gaps. Draw on your analyses to craft a compelling business case for making major process changes.

Setting Aggressive but Achievable Targets

No company can excel at every metric, so don't set sky-high targets for all of them. You want aggressive targets that will align the different parts of your organization and encourage healthy competition. To avoid cynicism or deliberate manipulation of the data, you should make sure that targets will be seen as achievable.

Acknowledging trade-offs is one way to strike a balance. To reach a target in one big area, you may have to accept lower performance in another. Consider a company that competes on speed of order delivery. Managers set a target: 100 percent of orders delivered within 48 hours. To achieve the target, the company may have to keep high levels of inventory on hand or be willing to pay a premium for overnight shipping. Therefore, setting aggressive inventory and freight-cost-reduction targets in parallel may not be realistic. Healthy tension based on competing metrics can be an effective management tool. But goals that are completely out of reach can encourage employees to fudge performance or can lead to greatly diminished morale.

You can also develop specific percentage-improvement goals on the basis of historical and baseline performance. With this method, you simply measure performance in a specific area over a certain time period, determine the baseline, and set a target for improvement. But again, be sure to link the target to your strategy. In too many cases, managers base targets on the assumption that because a certain level of performance may be possible, it should be a goal for their company. That performance level, however, may not make sense—and, in fact, may be entirely unrealistic.

Consider a telecommunications equipment company that embarked on a program to improve supplier on-time delivery. The procurement team measured the performance of its 25 largest suppliers over a three-month period and found that on-time delivery ranged from 70 to 80 percent, far below what was acceptable. So they set an objective of improving performance by 3 to 4 percentage points per month, with the goal of achieving average on-time delivery of 95 percent within six months. The assumption, of course, was that that suppliers would improve with some prompting from the telecommunications company (Figure 5.4).

After six months, however, supplier performance hadn't improved noticeably. The reason: the 95 percent target wasn't tied to an action plan with specified deliverables or time frames for achieving them. But there was another reason to consider as well. After benchmarking delivery performance in the telecommunications industry, the company found that even the top performers weren't achieving supplier delivery performance above 90 percent. "We realized how aggressive our goal really was," says the vice president of supply chain.

Figure 5.4 Original On-Time Delivery Goal

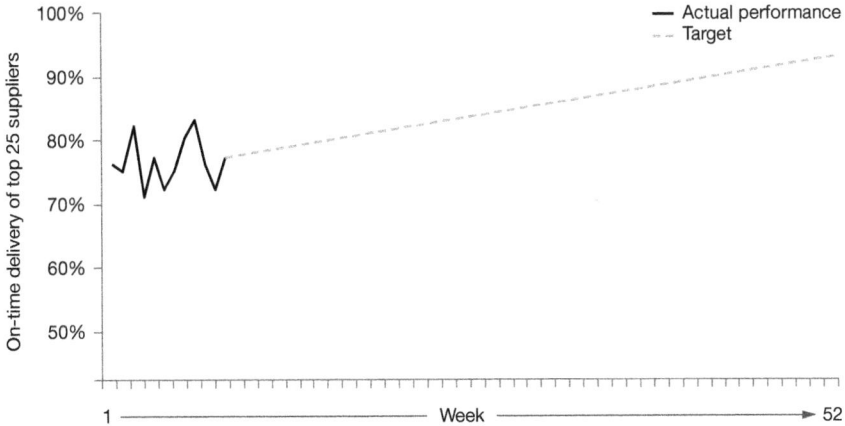

Benchmarking also opened the company's eyes to the importance of understanding specific practices other companies were using. It's not enough to know what level of performance is being achieved by other companies and what is, therefore, theoretically possible. You need to understand what those companies are doing to perform at that level.

The telecommunications company found out that its competitors notified their suppliers of forecast changes every week, whereas it provided updates only once a month. Moreover, competitors invited their key suppliers to product design meetings and established formal programs focused on increasing component commonality. The telecommunications equipment company did neither.

As a result of the benchmarking effort, the company decided to adopt several of the practices it thought would improve delivery performance. It developed formal implementation programs and tied performance improvement goals to a specific timetable (Figure 5.5).

Don't assume that just because you set what you consider to be a feasible target for a particular metric, performance will rise automatically. Employees need to see the target as achievable as well. Providing them with adequate resources, therefore, is essential. Such resources may include

Figure 5.5 Revised On-Time Delivery Goal

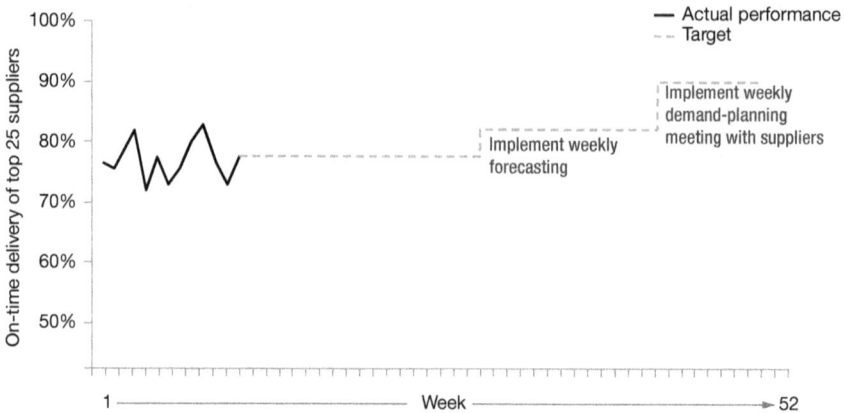

additional training, information systems that increase visibility into performance, and time away from their "day jobs" to focus on required process changes.

SUPPLY CHAIN PERFORMANCE MANAGEMENT: MAKING METRICS MATTER

Selecting metrics and defining targets are only part of the challenge. To advance from supply chain performance measurement to supply chain performance management, you have to deploy your metrics effectively. That means monitoring performance on your metrics regularly and using them to drive continuous improvement.

MONITORING PERFORMANCE REGULARLY

Effective performance monitoring requires selecting a cycle for tracking actual performance on the metrics against targeted performance. It also necessitates metrics that are highly visible, so people can see their goals and know whether they are making progress toward them. And, no less important, it demands a management team committed to addressing performance shortfalls quickly.

Selecting a Tracking Cycle

How often should you monitor your supply chain metrics? That depends on the metric. Monthly reporting is fine for most high-level metrics, such as those related to cost or asset management. On this schedule, you can spot trends before they become problems and avoid over-reporting that yields little value.

A lower-level metric, however, should be monitored as often as you expect it to change. You may want to monitor metrics such as fill rate, inventory, and on-time delivery weekly or even daily, whereas you'd want to track invoiced costs, such as warehousing and transportation, on a monthly basis.

It doesn't make sense to measure something once a week if you have no reason to think it could change—for example, the price you're paying for a component that is covered by a contract. A metric such as head count also doesn't need frequent monitoring, because it's very unlikely that anyone is going to be a surprise addition to the payroll. See Figure 5.6 for frequencies for tracking selected metrics.

Making Metrics Visible

If metrics—and performance data—are highly visible to managers throughout your organization, managers will be able to track their progress toward their goals. This immediate feedback can help them spot performance shortfalls and take corrective action quickly.

Figure 5.6 Frequencies for Tracking Select Metrics

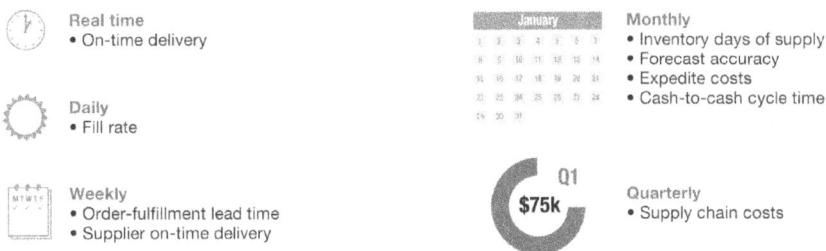

Real time
• On-time delivery

Daily
• Fill rate

Weekly
• Order-fulfillment lead time
• Supplier on-time delivery

Monthly
• Inventory days of supply
• Forecast accuracy
• Expedite costs
• Cash-to-cash cycle time

Quarterly
• Supply chain costs

A data storage system provider was having problems with its order-fulfillment process. At the time, the process took an average of 25 days, whereas benchmarking had suggested that most companies in the industry averaged 2 or 3 days. Members of the sales force complained that they were forced to spend more than 25 percent of their time chasing orders and, as a result, they were losing sales to competitors that could deliver more reliably. Customers, meanwhile, were complaining about how long they had to wait for their orders to arrive.

The source of the problem: too many functional handoffs. The key issues were pricing customer orders, getting them through the contract negotiation cycle, and configuring orders for delivery.

The company launched an initiative to reduce the time of the order fulfillment process from 25 days to 2. Informing employees of this goal, the company developed a plan to track orders as they moved through the process. Convinced that e-mail updates and website postings on performance against targets wouldn't exert the necessary impact, the CFO placed huge "scoreboards" in high-visibility areas—near the executive offices, in the local sales office, in the shipping area—and manually updated the cycle time scores each week. Since the cycle time metric included data from every function involved in order fulfillment, many employees took part in collecting it.

The metrics let the project team look at each activity in the order fulfillment process and eliminate many of the handoffs between functions. But because so many people were involved and because each cause of delay was tracked manually, the initiative actually slowed the process.

In fact, not long after the new tracking system was up and running, the project was in danger of being derailed. "It's going the wrong way," was a frequent comment of project team members. Despite concerns that the highly visible data would discourage people and make them resistant to change, the CFO insisted on continuing to update the scoreboards. To smooth the results and reduce the perception that a onetime backslide was

Figure 5.7 Order-Fulfillment Cycle Time

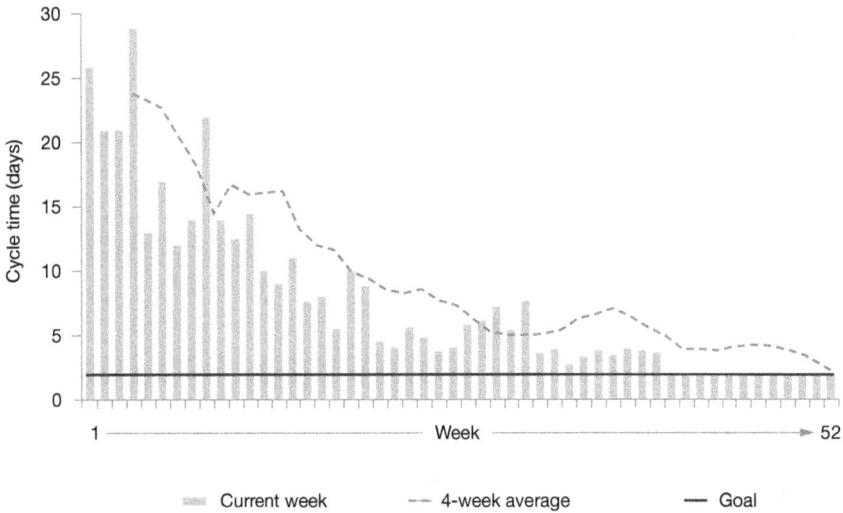

the sign of a negative trend, he added a second metric, a rolling average of the most recent four-week period.

It didn't take long to see significant improvement. After only 8 weeks, average cycle time had been cut by nearly 10 days; after 40 weeks, the stretch goal of 2 days was within striking distance (Figure 5.7). Not only did the scorecard help the company improve a critical area of performance, it also became a powerful sales tool, providing real-life proof of the company's focus on customer service.

Managing Performance Proactively

Whereas a scorecard is a snapshot that shows KPIs at a particular moment in time relative to a competitive benchmark, a metrics dashboard is dynamic and provides customized views that can track specific metrics over time (Figure 5.8). Creation of a metrics dashboard can also be a forcing mechanism: It can prompt the company to automate the processes for recording performance data and for alerting managers of

Figure 5.8 Example of a Metrics Dashboard

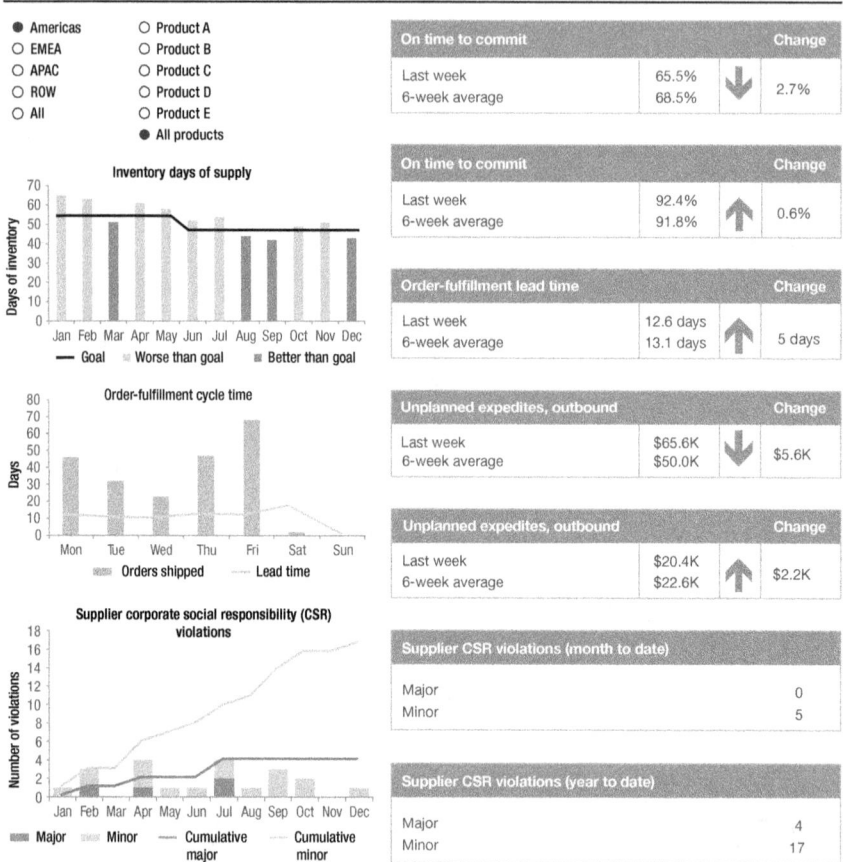

On time to commit		Change
Last week	65.5%	2.7%
6-week average	68.5%	

On time to commit		Change
Last week	92.4%	0.6%
6-week average	91.8%	

Order-fulfillment lead time		Change
Last week	12.6 days	5 days
6-week average	13.1 days	

Unplanned expedites, outbound		Change
Last week	$65.6K	$5.6K
6-week average	$50.0K	

Unplanned expedites, outbound		Change
Last week	$20.4K	$2.2K
6-week average	$22.6K	

Supplier CSR violations (month to date)	
Major	0
Minor	5

Supplier CSR violations (year to date)	
Major	4
Minor	17

problems. A dashboard can also serve as an early warning system, if the metrics chosen provide a predictive view of performance trends.

Ensuring Clean Data

Almost every performance-improvement initiative requires systems support. You may choose to design and build an in-house system for implementing initiatives. Alternatively, you may decide to buy a data warehouse, an Enterprise Resource Planning (ERP) module, or a stand-alone solution that offloads data from your ERP system.

To choose the right system, you'll need to know where various kinds of performance data will be coming from. You'll also have to understand how your management approach will link to improvement programs and metrics used in other core functions. Take time to understand available performance-management tools across several categories. These include reporting, business intelligence, advanced planning and scheduling analytics, supply chain event management, and supply chain performance management.

Identify all the types and sources of data required to monitor the results of an initiative that has been implemented, and make the data accessible. For example, if you want to monitor the percentage of orders delivered on time according to the customer's request, you will need to capture the date received, the date the customer specified, the anticipated lead time, the date to which you committed, and the actual date shipped. Many companies have large volumes of data buried within numerous disparate systems. If that is true of your company, you'll need applications and infrastructure that can pull data from different sources and enable timely decision making. To simplify both data gathering and reporting, design the data capture and reporting infrastructure using standard data and metric definitions.

Today's information systems are capable of collecting and analyzing vast quantities of data, but the data must be converted into useful information before the information can be leveraged. Populate the dashboard with only the data required to calculate the metrics you are tracking. As needed, you can use the detailed data to delve deeper into problem areas.

Above all else, make sure that the data within the systems used for performance measurement are "clean." In order to be effective, the underlying database must be accurate and up-to-date. Without clean data, you risk failing to recognize a problem before it becomes unwieldy or misrepresenting your performance to important constituents, including shareholders.

TAKING A HOLISTIC APPROACH

A major advancement during the past decade has been the embedding of industry-standard supply chain metrics, including SCOR metrics, within the business intelligence functionality of many leading ERP systems. In many cases, supply chain performance management systems purchased as modules that overlay the business intelligence platform allow companies to calculate these standard metrics using data already contained within the company's database, thereby eliminating the need for manual data collection and calculation.

Many organizations are making supply chain performance management an integral part of an overall performance-management strategy through the holistic approach of corporate performance management (CPM), which is also known as enterprise performance management or business performance management.

CPM describes the processes, methodologies, metrics, and systems used to monitor and manage an organization's overall business performance. It's more than software: CPM includes the processes for managing corporate performance, the methodology for choosing the right process metrics, and the processes for managing those metrics. In addition, CPM links disparate points of internal operations because it blends data from ERP, supply chain management, customer relationship management, product life-cycle management, human resources management, and business intelligence systems. CPM solutions usually display KPIs so that employees can track individual and group performance relative to corporate goals and strategy.

Until recently, data used for management reporting was somewhat subjective and dependent on the way it was displayed. Many management reports—for example, the ubiquitous "monthly ops report"—relied heavily on spreadsheets. Data manually entered on spreadsheets then had to be collected, checked, collated, and integrated in order to be included in reports. Only then could the data be analyzed and acted on. Because this approach relied on intensive data entry and manipulation, it was generally cumbersome, prone to error, and difficult to use for comparing performance across different parts of the company.

But CPM solutions are evolving quickly, thanks to the advent of cloud computing. Today's version of CPM combines traditional performance management with business intelligence functionality, so that it enables operational, financial, and executive reporting, as well as ad hoc analysis, all supported by consistent data and definitions. In addition, cloud-based CPM systems have the advantage of being largely hardware independent and configurable from the perspective of each user.

Automated CPM tools that use industry standard definitions can pull data from anywhere and calculate metrics that are based on these definitions. This capability allows companies to conduct longitudinal comparisons and streamline internal and external benchmarking. With reports automated and customized in this way, managers throughout your company can focus on the metrics most relevant to your company's strategic direction.

GETTING THE CALCULATIONS RIGHT

A performance measurement system may have everything going for it: metrics tied to the business strategy, industry standard definitions, and a logical hierarchy. But if the metrics aren't presented in a way that reflects what's really going on, they can be misleading. A company that we will call Executronix Data provides an apt example.

A manufacturer of data storage equipment, Executronix Data sells both off-the-shelf and custom solutions used in data centers around the world. Recently, the company began to get complaints from customers who said that order deliveries were taking too long and delivery dates were consistently inaccurate. This was a serious problem. The customers' data centers had to have numerous engineers and service specialists on hand to ensure equipment installation went smoothly. Every day that an order was delayed meant a day those employees were unavailable for other work.

Customers were not the only ones voicing complaints. Executronix salespeople said that they were having a difficult time getting orders through the fulfillment process and getting updates on the status of orders. The head of sales operations, however, disagreed. Order management data collected weekly, he said, demonstrated that the company consistently met its commitment to ship off-the-shelf products within two days of receiving an order. Indeed, the weekly report showed that that during the previous 52 weeks, order-fulfillment cycle time had averaged 1.74 days—well below the target service level of two days. There were a few spikes, but they were easily explained by temporary material shortages (Figure 5.9).

To get to the bottom of the problem, the CFO suggested reviewing not only the average cycle time for a given week but also the associated variability. The results were somewhat startling. The new charts showed clearly that the process was highly variable, with a standard deviation of more than 3.2 days (Figure 5.10).

Figure 5.9 Executronix Order-Fulfillment Cycle Time

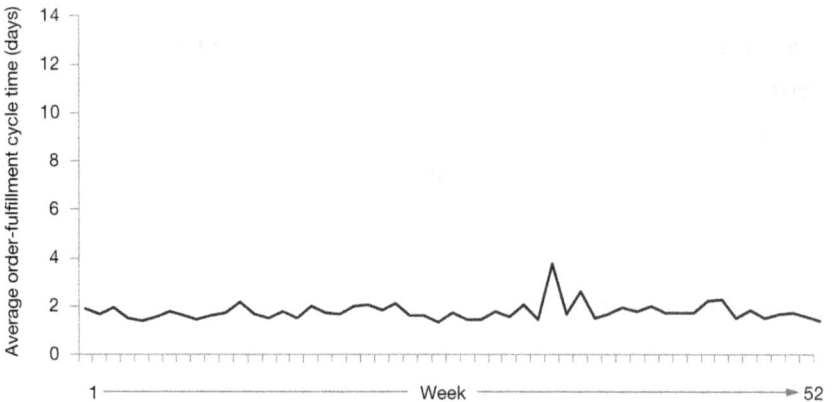

Figure 5.10 Executronix Variability of Order-Fulfillment Cycle Time

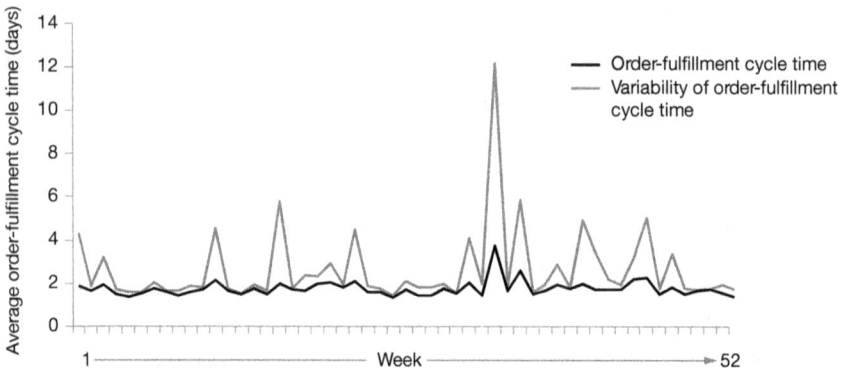

Figure 5.11 Executronix Distribution of Order-Fulfillment Cycle Time

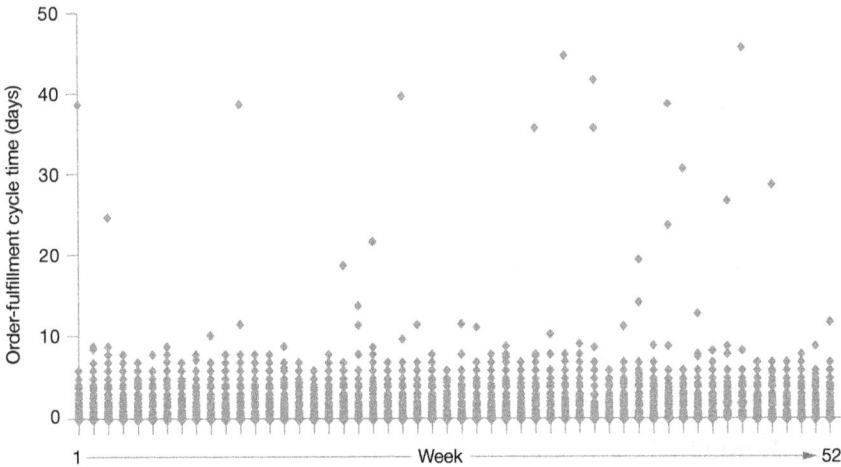

This new perspective compelled the management team to take an even closer look at the data. It turned out that most orders shipped on time. Many of the orders that did not, however, were lost in the queue and could be delayed for weeks (Figure 5.11).

It was this view of the data that alerted the sales order-management team to the need to take a closer look at the process. It turned out that each department measured how long orders sat in their functional areas and tracked the reasons for delays. The order entry group noted how often orders arrived from the field with incomplete or erroneous information and how often customer orders referenced products that had been phased out or were not yet available. Incomplete or incorrect orders were redirected to the function deemed best suited to resolve the issue. As a result, orders that had more than one problem often had to make multiple loops through the process before each problem was addressed. Clearly, no one was tracking these loops or was aware of how much time was elapsing.

The company established a cross-functional team to investigate what was causing orders to stall. It also began measuring lead time variability and lead time distribution as part of the weekly metrics review, easily identifying outliers and working quickly to resolve the problems.

On the surface, Executronix Data was doing everything right. It had a good handle on what was important to customers and a solid understanding of where performance needed to be along key dimensions. It used industry standard definitions in collecting data and monitoring performance. But it made the mistake of using averages to extrapolate performance for a larger process. When your metrics report contradicts feedback from employees and customers, it's time to examine not just what you are measuring but also how you present it.

ENSURING AN EFFECTIVE METRICS PROGRAM

To be an effective management tool, your supply chain metrics program needs to include certain practices.

Integrating Quantitative Targets into Plans and Budgets

If reducing distribution costs is a priority, for instance, adjust budget assumptions to include the specific cost-reduction targets. But also make sure to include any costs and resources needed to restructure the distribution network and to bring a new logistics-services provider on board.

Setting Meaningful Targets

Targets should be established at the individual and departmental (for example, product line, business unit, and region) levels, and they should be linked to overall corporate objectives. For example, if you plan to offer low- or no-cost delivery, a distribution center's targets might aim for a lower percentage of express than standard deliveries. To track process changes, you might measure actual carrier charges and the adoption rate of new practices that drive lower premium-freight costs, such as adherence to order lead times.

Tracking Progress

In order to effectively track progress, you will need to ensure that well-defined mechanisms and processes are in place. We started this chapter by saying "if you can't measure it, you can't manage it." If you plan to monitor how long it takes to fulfill customer orders, make sure your systems capture each of the major process steps. And be sure that your definition of elapsed time to fill an order is the same definition your customers use.

Identifying Performance Exceptions

Understand the level of granularity needed for detection of a process that is out of control and make sure you measure at that level. The way you present your data greatly affects your ability to see what's going on. To understand whether lead times are where they need to be, make sure you can drill down to see individual orders rather than being limited to seeing only the process as a whole.

KEY TAKEAWAYS

- Your metrics should be linked to your company's business strategy. If the business strategy requires the company to excel at innovation, for example, you need to measure how good you are at innovation.

- To ensure you get a complete picture of performance, choose a balanced and comprehensive set of metrics. Make sure they are unambiguous so that everyone measures things the same way.

- Use metrics to encourage continuous improvement. Set aggressive, but achievable, improvement targets for specific performance-improvement initiatives.

- Deploy benchmarking to understand the level of performance possible and the practices that will allow you to achieve it.

- Make metrics visible to the organization and monitor them on a regular basis.

LENOVO:
MOVING FULL-SPEED AHEAD

"As Lenovo expands globally, we are establishing even deeper roots in major markets around the world, as part of a comprehensive 'global-local' strategy. In addition to localizing sales and marketing teams, we're also establishing an even stronger manufacturing footprint, investing in R&D, and ensuring that top local talent helps us build a competitive advantage and a winning business. This global reach with local excellence positions us to more deeply implement our business strategy. We can be faster and more efficient while at the same time driving the best innovation, quality, and customer experience. This is a powerful point of differentiation that helps us better understand and serve our customers around the world."

—YANG YUANQING, CHAIRMAN AND CEO, LENOVO

In 2012, Lenovo announced plans to build a manufacturing facility in Whitsett, North Carolina. The new plant, which is the Chinese PC giant's first in the United States, will manufacture Think computers, Lenovo's commercial product line.

The announcement has received much attention from industry experts, and for good reason. Over the past few decades, most computer companies have done their production in low-cost regions like Asia and Mexico.

What appears to be an anomaly, however, is perfectly consistent with Lenovo's goal of providing faster and more reliable delivery to customers.

"The conventional wisdom is that it's challenging to manufacture in the U.S.," explains John Egan, vice president of global manufacturing. "But we're driving for responsiveness and flexibility as much as profitability. Putting a plant close to our customers ensures the supply chain supports that strategy."

Indeed, unconventional supply chain management has helped Lenovo become the fastest-growing and one of the largest PC makers worldwide. Best known for its laptop and desktop systems, the Chinese company has 29,000 employees in 160 countries. Moreover, it is number one in China, where it has 34 percent of the PC market and more than 15,000 retail stores. Total revenue in the fiscal year ending March 31, 2012, was $29.6 billion.

FROM STARTUP TO UPSTART

It's only in the past decade that Lenovo became well known outside China. Founded in 1984 by Liu Chuanzhi and ten others, "New Technology Developer Inc.," as it was originally called, was a distributor of imported computers.

Led by Liu, the company, which soon changed its name to Legend Holdings, struggled in its early years. Shifting gears, Legend moved into manufacturing circuit boards, or "Han-cards," which allowed IBM PCs to process Chinese characters. Introduced at a time when Chinese demand for computers was on the rise, Han-cards proved a great success.

Legend seized the momentum to try its hand at manufacturing computers for the Chinese market. In the early 1990s, when foreign competitors were beginning to make inroads in China, the company introduced its first branded computer. Legend quickly gained market share for its value-priced, innovative products. It was, for example, the first Chinese company to sell a computer with a Pentium chip—and at a lower price than the slower computers sold by competitors at the time. Legend soon became the biggest computer company in China, deriving more than 90 percent of its revenue there.

Building on its strong position in the China market, Legend turned its sights to global expansion. With Yang Yuanqing now CEO, the company changed its name to Lenovo—"Le" from Legend combined with "novo," the Latin for "from new"—to mark the new start.

Eschewing the option of growing gradually, in 2005 Lenovo took the bold step of acquiring IBM's Personal Computing Division, which had invented the PC back in 1981. Overnight, the acquisition made Lenovo the world's third-largest PC company, with a global footprint and product lines—the Think brand notebook (ThinkPad) and desktop (ThinkCentre) PCs—that were used primarily by large enterprises, governments, and educational institutions worldwide.

But the acquisition also introduced some daunting challenges. Not only did Lenovo have to integrate two distinct supply chains, it also had to improve overall supply chain visibility. Supply-and-demand planning had proven particularly challenging, as evidenced by a chronic problem with inventory obsolescence. Lenovo needed to address these concerns without sacrificing its reputation for innovation or the ability to grow rapidly. That was a tall order in an industry where new products are introduced frequently and life cycles can be as short as six months.

STABILIZE AND TRANSFORM

The first order of business for the newly merged company was to stabilize the international business without stopping the production of ThinkPads. That meant quickly expanding the depth and breadth of operations—and the expertise needed to drive and manage those operations. Losing little time, Lenovo recruited senior executives away from various competitors to leverage what they knew about best practices.

AN INTEGRATED SUPPLY CHAIN ORGANIZATION
One of those recruits, Gerry Smith, who is now president of the North America region, led the transformation initiative. Key to the effort was integrating the major supply chain functions into a central global

organization. "We needed an end-to-end global supply chain, with all functions fully integrated under a single management structure from order to collection, to make rapid progress in improving our operation," explains Smith. "This brought major benefits in terms of execution speed, agility, cost, and quality."

METRICS MAKEOVER

In this initial phase, the supply chain organization launched a major process and metrics reevaluation. At the time of the acquisition, there were so many metrics in place—129 in all—that it was impossible to measure anything significant. "Everyone measured things differently," Smith notes. "Every little area had its own key performance indicator. Everyone was measuring themselves and saying, 'I'm meeting my targets, so why do I need to improve?'"

After two years of intense process reevaluation, the organization whittled down the number to five key metrics: product delivery performance, cash conversion cycle, quality, cost of materials, and end-to-end supply chain costs. These metrics helped provide a clear line of sight on how the end-to-end supply chain was performing.

In conjunction with the metrics makeover, the supply chain organization overhauled its supply-and-demand management processes, implementing a coordinated calendar of supply-and-demand analysis and a consistent set of responsibilities and accountabilities. The recent adoption of a global integrated business-planning system has further enhanced Lenovo's ability to address unanticipated fluctuations in demand.

PROTECT AND ATTACK

The advent of senior executives from the outside brought a fresh perspective and deep industry experience. But it also led to a clash of three distinct management approaches—legacy Lenovo, IBM, and the industry competitor from which most of the new talent was drawn. The differences became even more pronounced with the Great Recession, when revenue, particularly from ThinkPad products, dropped precipitously.

CEO Yang Yuanqing proposed a strategy to position the company for rapid growth while promoting integration. Called "Protect and Attack," the strategy aimed to protect the company's core: the enterprise customers in mature markets inherited from IBM, as well as legacy Lenovo customers in China. At the same time, the strategy aimed to attack new growth opportunities: retail and consumers in mature markets, as well as expansion in emerging markets outside of China.

RELATIONSHIP CUSTOMERS

One of Lenovo's immediate goals was to protect and strengthen the legacy IBM side of the business, focused on commercial customers globally, while returning it to profitability and positioning it for growth. These "relationship customers" are primarily large-scale enterprises and public-sector clients in locations where Think products enjoy a strong following. They tend to make large-volume purchases of specialized or customized hardware bundled with software solutions.

To serve its relationship customers, the company primarily relies on a direct sales force, which consists of inside reps who call customers on the phone, outside reps who call on them in person, and technical specialists. Electronic ordering and configuration ensure that customer requirements are easily converted into production orders and that nothing is lost in the process

Often, relationship customers fulfill their orders through distributors and business partners (i.e., value-added resellers) to optimize responsiveness and delivery times. The reseller initiates the sale, providing its own services that it supplements with Lenovo services where necessary. The resellers are compensated for selling Lenovo services, as well as products.

CHINA

Lenovo also decided to expand its broad market-leadership position in China while improving profitability in that segment. The primary strategy: the retail store, which has proved a great success.

Today, Lenovo is a brand icon in China, owing in no small part to the more than 15,000 branded retail outlets located throughout the country. Ranging in size from megastores to tiny shops, the stores provide consumers with the opportunity to acquaint themselves with the wide range of Lenovo products: notebook PCs, desktop computers, and all-in-ones, as well as mobile devices such as smartphones and tablets. Lenovo plans to open many more stores in rural areas, which are still largely underserved.

TRANSACTIONAL CUSTOMERS IN MATURE AND EMERGING MARKETS

Consumers and small and midsize businesses in mature markets, as well as all segments in emerging markets, also offered great potential for growth. These "transactional customers" typically purchase computers in discrete, low-volume transactions (often one unit at a time), on the basis of value and availability. They usually make these purchases at certain times of the year.

Encouraged by the success of its Chinese retail model, Lenovo is following a similar approach in India. The company is rapidly expanding the number of Lenovo-exclusive stores (LES) and LES Lite stores; the latter offer a smaller selection of products and occupy only 150 or 200 square feet. In 2011, the number of stores in India reached the 1,000 mark.

DUAL OPERATING MODEL

In order to provide innovative, value-priced products to its range of customers, Lenovo created two different operating models. "We developed relationship-based and transactional-based supply chains," notes Smith. "They're both focused on rapid innovation and customer service. But they are structured differently, with different processes, to meet the specific requirements of customers in these distinct segments."

THE RELATIONSHIP SUPPLY CHAIN

The initial asset footprint and process architecture for the relationship supply chain, also known as the "responsive model," came primarily from the acquisition of IBM's Personal Computing Division. Computers are what Lenovo calls "mass customized": they are configured to order to meet larger customers' specific requirements and purchased mostly in large quantities per order.

Relationship products are manufactured and assembled in Lenovo-owned factories and by electronics manufacturing services partners. After coming off the production line, the computers are shipped directly to the customer either by air or by sea, depending on how quickly delivery is needed.

Lenovo has made its processes flexible in order to address unique customer requirements while still turning out large product volumes through the end-to-end supply chain. For customers who want customized software, Lenovo's Imaging Technology Center helps develop that software configuration and ensure compatibility with the systems being purchased, and then streams the software images to in-house and original design manufacturer (ODM) factories around the world for installation on computer hard drives. For customers interested in a standard system with add-ons, such as more memory or specific peripherals, Lenovo has second-stage centers such as the one in Whitsett. At these locations, software, peripherals, and customized asset tags are packaged with the computers before they're shipped to customers. In both cases, the customer sees only the final product, not the multiple steps behind it.

The responsive operating model offers a number of distinct advantages. Having a large percentage of manufacturing capacity in-house makes it easier to meet stringent quality standards and specific customer requirements. Moreover, it's easier to react quickly to unanticipated spikes in demand for a particular product, since there's no need to wait in line to schedule capacity. In-house manufacturing also avoids the risks of errors that can occur when a design is handed off to another company. And intellectual property—a key asset in an increasingly commoditized industry—can be better safeguarded.

It's also easier to respond to the kind of supply disruptions created by the massive flooding in Thailand in 2011. "We couldn't get the hard drives that had the required storage capacity for some of our commercial products, so we needed to quickly update the product configuration to accommodate lower-capacity drives," recalls Egan. "Having manufacturing in-house allowed us to make changes faster."

THE TRANSACTIONAL SUPPLY CHAIN

Computers for transactional customers are produced and delivered by what Lenovo calls its "efficient operating model," in which ODMs and some in-house facilities build PCs in volume according to a plan. The ODMs design and build some computer models to stock on the basis of Lenovo's regional forecasts, which ensure that product is ready for immediate shipment to distributors and retailers. The efficient operating model draws on Lenovo's network of ODMs based primarily in China and Taiwan, as well as some in-house plants located in China.

In the fiercely competitive market for transactional customers, success rests on the ability to build and deliver products at the right volumes and in sync with seasonal market demand. Lenovo's sales account leaders and demand analysts work together closely, leveraging forecasts from retail customers as well as historical data to ensure precise demand forecasts.

POINTS OF CONVERGENCE

While the supply chains run separately, they connect across common areas where Lenovo can leverage economies of scale. This includes the sourcing of raw materials and components as well as the warehousing and distribution of products.

The supply chains also converge in cases where countries have unique customer, cost, importation, and taxation dynamics. In Brazil, Argentina, and India, for example, Lenovo has established in-country facilities that produce a range of commercial, consumer, and small and midsize business products.

When making asset footprint decisions, Lenovo follows the same rules of thumb for both supply chains. A large percentage of the company's total volume is manufactured in China. For products where lead time is critical, Lenovo locates plants close to the customer, so as to shorten delivery time while avoiding high transport and/or import costs. For this reason, Lenovo manufactures in Mexico large Think products bound for North and South America, including desktops, engineering workstations, and servers, while a contract manufacturer in Hungary makes the same product sets destined for Europe. "The goal is to deliver customized products in eight days or less," Egan says.

Today, Lenovo owns eight manufacturing facilities and works with manufacturers located at 24 sites in Europe, China, and South America. A joint venture (JV) with Taiwanese ODM Compal Electronics has enhanced manufacturing capacity for desktops, laptops, and all-in-one PCs in China, while a JV with NEC has helped Lenovo become the number-one PC brand in Japan. The recent acquisition of PC, tablet, and handset maker CCE has extended Lenovo's footprint in Brazil.

Lenovo's Hybrid Manufacturing Network

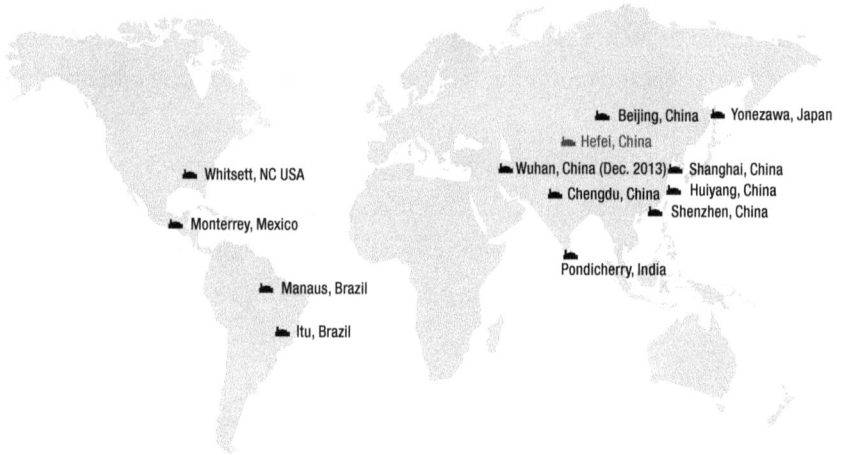

Beijing, China Yonezawa, Japan
Hefei, China
Whitsett, NC USA Wuhan, China (Dec. 2013) Shanghai, China
Chengdu, China Huiyang, China
Monterrey, Mexico Shenzhen, China

Pondicherry, India

Manaus, Brazil

Itu, Brazil

11 in-house plants (12 by end of 2013)
Hefei is a Compal Electronics joint venture and Yonezawa is an NEC joint venture.
Lenovo products are also built at 24 outsourced sites in China, Europe, and South America.

Source: Lenovo

SHAPING FUTURE GROWTH

Lenovo's growth spurt shows no signs of ending soon. While rivals experience sharp declines in PC sales, Lenovo has consistently been gaining market share, largely because of its strong footing in China and in global commercial markets. Reinvesting its profits in growth opportunities, Lenovo is currently focusing on emerging markets and some large growth opportunities in mature markets. The U.S. market is first on the list. Lenovo's goal is to be number one in the U.S. market, and the new North Carolina plant will help support this objective.[1]

The innovative products that fueled Lenovo's ascent will continue to drive its growth strategy. Lenovo plows much of its profits back into product development: The company's R&D investment as a percentage of PC revenue is the highest in the industry. The company has global R&D centers in Beijing, Shenzhen, and Shanghai in China; Yokohama in Japan; and Morrisville, North Carolina, in the United States. Investments are focused on concepts that can be brought to market in 24 months. At these facilities,

Lenovo designs highly engineered products that can be easily configured to meet the specific requirements of relationship customers. At the same time, the computer company is experimenting with new form factors for the consumer market, such as the Ideapad Yoga, a laptop that converts into a tablet. As consumer demand for mobile computing continues to grow, Lenovo also is expanding into smartphones and tablets, and Smart TVs are next.

R&D is only part of the equation, however. To consistently deliver innovative products to market, it's also critical to have a supply base that understands what that involves. "The Yoga product required new commodities and new suppliers," says Egan. "This demanded extensive collaboration between designers and product teams. We also had to prepare capacity at our Shanghai plant."

Through continual assessment and adaptation, Lenovo has made its supply chain a powerful source of competitive advantage: responsive, flexible, and efficient. The engine behind "Protect and Attack," the supply chain will likely be a key driver of business success in the years ahead.

CHAPTER SIX

BENCHMARKING RESULTS: THE BEST-IN-CLASS PERFORMANCE ADVANTAGE

Benchmarking data demonstrate that companies that exhibit superior supply chain performance also experience superior financial performance. These best-in-class companies have honed certain Plan, Source, Make, and Deliver practices to differentiate themselves from the competition. They also manage supply chain complexity to their advantage. This chapter illuminates these practices as well as the size of the improvement opportunity available to companies aspiring to be best in class.

Most companies know supply chain performance matters. But leading companies know how to use it to drive business success.

PwC's Performance Measurement Group (PMG) studied some of these leading, best-in-class companies (BICCs) specifically for the purposes of this book. (See Sidebar "Benchmarking Supply Chain Performance" on page 226.) PMG found that BICCs frequently achieve greater revenue growth and profitability than their competitors. Survey results and years of work with clients support this claim.[1] (See Sidebar "About PMG" on page 228.)

PMG found that BICCs derive tremendous value from excelling in critical supply chain areas such as cash-to-cash cycle time and total supply chain cost management. These companies' best practices are instructive for any company, regardless of industry.

PMG's research has revealed three key truths about supply chain performance:

- Superior supply chain performance is frequently related to superior financial performance.

- Expertise at specific Plan, Source, Make, and Deliver practices can provide an edge.

- Complexity, when managed well, is a source of significant competitive advantage.

THE RELATIONSHIP BETWEEN SUPPLY CHAIN PERFORMANCE AND FINANCIAL PERFORMANCE

PMG's research reveals a relationship between superior supply chain performance and superior financial performance. Companies with the best-performing supply chains outperform others in their industry on key financial metrics.

According to PMG's survey data,[2] BICCs' average annual sales growth is approximately 50 percent higher than that of other companies in their respective industries, and BICCs' profitability is about 20 percent higher. BICCs also demonstrate better asset turnover, with performance about 50 percent better than the industry average (Figure 6.1).

By definition, BICCs exhibit superior supply chain performance. Just how much better are they? Figure 6.2 provides a snapshot of key performance data on five key metrics.

- *Better delivery performance against customer request date.* BICCs schedule a higher percentage of orders in accordance with the dates requested by customers and deliver the goods on the committed date more often. Superior delivery performance

Figure 6.1 Sales Growth, Profitability, and Net Asset Turns

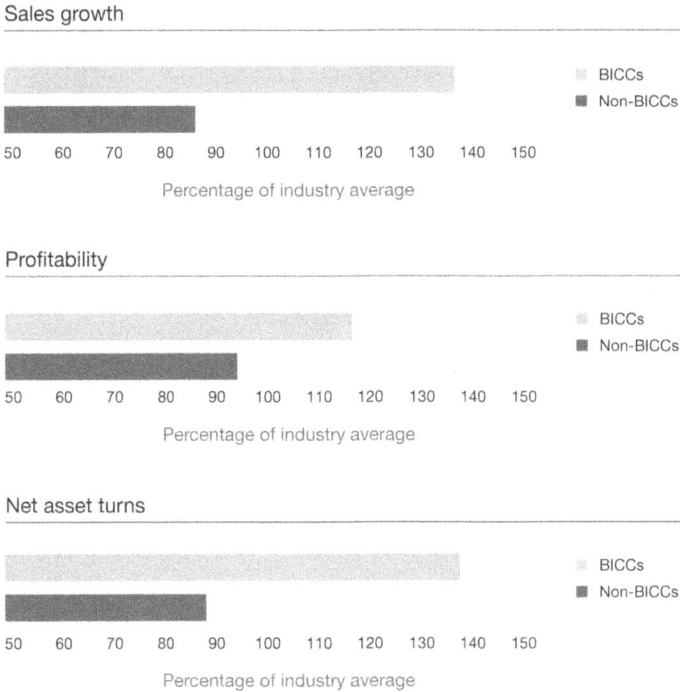

Sales growth

| | | | | | | | | | | | BICCs |
| | | | | | | | | | | | Non-BICCs |

50   60   70   80   90   100   110   120   130   140   150

Percentage of industry average

Profitability

BICCs
Non-BICCs

50   60   70   80   90   100   110   120   130   140   150

Percentage of industry average

Net asset turns

BICCs
Non-BICCs

50   60   70   80   90   100   110   120   130   140   150

Percentage of industry average

© *SC2 Book Analysis*, PMG, 2012

fosters customer satisfaction and loyalty, which help grow revenue and market share.

■ *Greater upside production flexibility.* When demand suddenly jumps, BICCs typically respond faster than the competition, converting increased demand into production more than six times faster. This speaks to BICCs' ability to obtain what's needed—whether labor, materials, or manufacturing capacity— and to ramp up production quickly. In today's increasingly volatile business environment, flexibility is rapidly becoming essential for competing. According to a recent survey, supply chain executives believe flexibility is nearly as important as cost, customer service, and profitability.[3]

Figure 6.2 BICC Index Metrics Performance

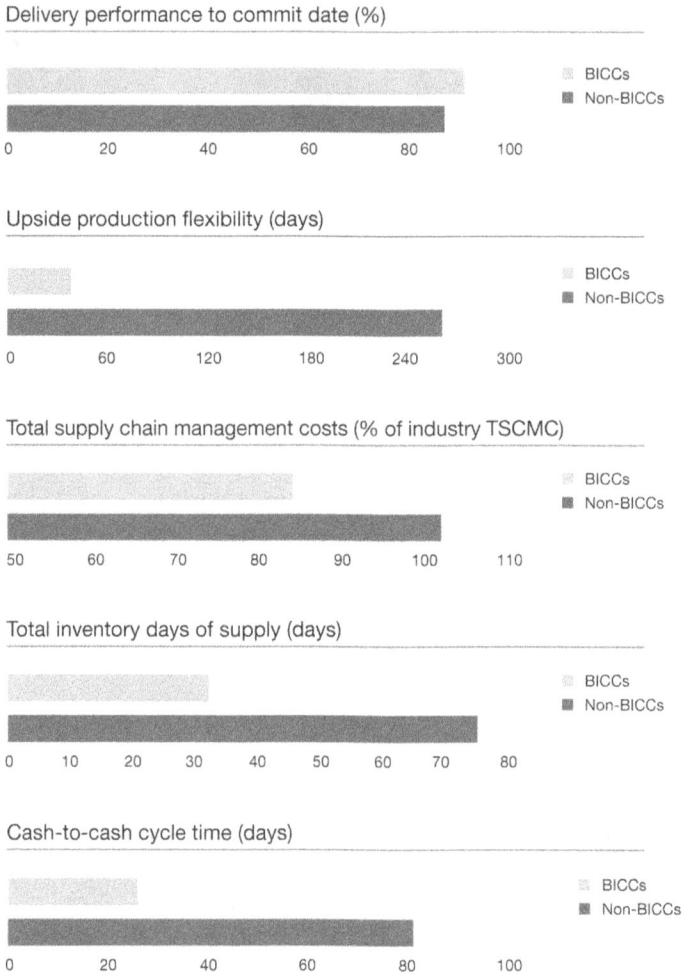

Delivery performance to commit date (%)

BICCs
Non-BICCs

```
0        20        40        60        80        100
```

Upside production flexibility (days)

BICCs
Non-BICCs

```
0        60        120        180        240        300
```

Total supply chain management costs (% of industry TSCMC)

BICCs
Non-BICCs

```
50        60        70        80        90        100        110
```

Total inventory days of supply (days)

BICCs
Non-BICCs

```
0    10    20    30    40    50    60    70    80
```

Cash-to-cash cycle time (days)

BICCs
Non-BICCs

```
0        20        40        60        80        100
```

© *SC2 Book Analysis*, PMG, 2012

- *Lower total supply chain management costs.* When compared with industry averages, BICCs outperform median companies in supply chain management costs by more than 15 percent. By using a balanced and comprehensive collection of metrics to examine BICCs, PMG was able to identify examples of companies that manage assets and costs well without sacrificing flexibility or service levels.

- *Lower total inventory.* BICCs operate with only about one month of inventory, in contrast to other companies, which operate with two to three times as much. Managing with lower inventory levels can dramatically improve cash flow. The ability to do so without sacrificing delivery performance is a testament to superior supply chain practices.

- *Shorter cash-to-cash cycle time.* Significantly lower inventory days of supply is highly correlated with lower cash-to-cash cycle time. Defined as the time it takes to turn a dollar of spending into a dollar of revenue, cash-to-cash cycle time is calculated as days of inventory plus days of receivables net days of payables. BICCs exhibit a cash-to-cash cycle time of approximately three weeks, whereas median companies require more than triple that amount of time.

The size of the gap between BICCs and their industry peers varies across these different metrics. BICCs outperform their competitors far more on inventory management than on cost, for example. Overall, however, the gap is substantial. This is important because it reflects the size of the opportunity available to companies that aspire to be among the best in class.

DRIVING SUPPLY CHAIN PERFORMANCE

BICCs consistently outperform their peers across supply chain metrics because they have finely honed the practices most critical for getting products and services to customers.

PMG's Supply Chain Maturity Model provides a high-level perspective on the supply chain practices that BICCs and other companies deploy.

The framework details dozens of practices within the Plan, Source, Make, and Deliver processes and describes the different phases of maturity for each (Figure 6.3).[4] In PMG's benchmarking surveys, participants typically indicate which supply chain practices are most similar to those employed at their organizations. These responses allow PMG to assess the maturity of each organization's practices and to examine the relationship between specific practices and performance.

PMG's analysis in this area focused on the practices that are more prevalent among companies with superior supply chain performance. Stages Three and Four were of particular interest because they represent relatively mature practices. BICCs have adopted a number of Stage Three and Four practices to a far greater degree than the balance of the population. For the purposes of discussion, this chapter refers to these more mature practices

Figure 6.3 Supply Chain Maturity Model

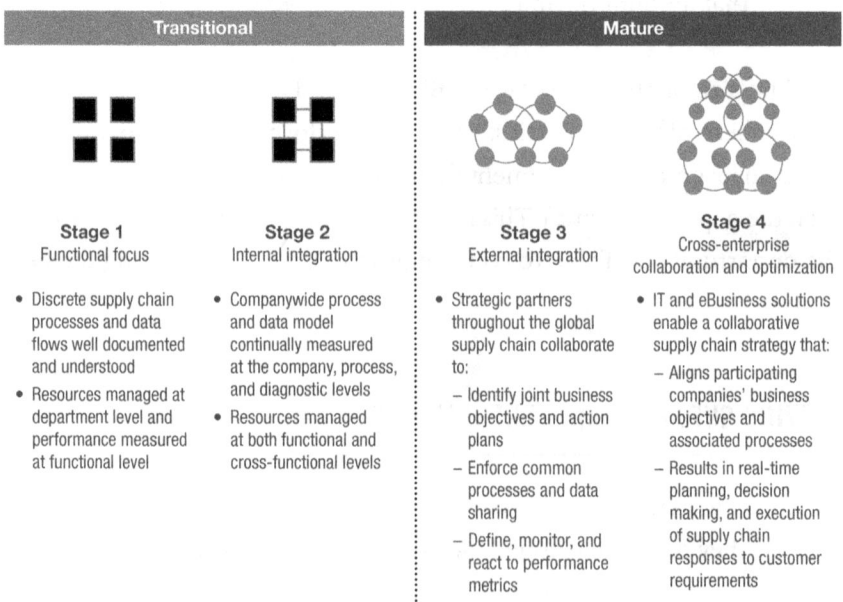

Transitional		Mature	
Stage 1 Functional focus	**Stage 2** Internal integration	**Stage 3** External integration	**Stage 4** Cross-enterprise collaboration and optimization
• Discrete supply chain processes and data flows well documented and understood • Resources managed at department level and performance measured at functional level	• Companywide process and data model continually measured at the company, process, and diagnostic levels • Resources managed at both functional and cross-functional levels	• Strategic partners throughout the global supply chain collaborate to: – Identify joint business objectives and action plans – Enforce common processes and data sharing – Define, monitor, and react to performance metrics	• IT and eBusiness solutions enable a collaborative supply chain strategy that: – Aligns participating companies' business objectives and associated processes – Results in real-time planning, decision making, and execution of supply chain responses to customer requirements

as "differentiators." PMG's data suggest these differentiating practices help drive significant improvements in performance. By contrast, practices used by more than 65 percent of the companies in PMG's study are described as "widely implemented"—basic practices all companies need to embrace to compete in their industries.

The following discussion focuses primarily on the differentiators because they offer the most learning and the biggest opportunities for non-BICCs. The omission of some important supply chain practices by no means suggests their irrelevance; rather, it reflects the absence of a relationship identified with PMG's particular sample and criteria.

PLAN

Of all the major supply chain processes, Plan shows the greatest number of differentiating processes. BICCs are clearly focusing to a higher degree on developing more-mature planning processes and systems so as to better forecast demand and coordinate activities across their customer and supplier networks. A detailed review of the specific differentiating Plan practices shows that BICCs:

- Collaborate more with customers and suppliers in the development of long-range strategic plans
- Integrate key suppliers into the supply-planning process
- Develop clear rules and requirements with customers and suppliers for managing demand-and-supply exceptions
- Address demand-and-supply exceptions from a cross-functional perspective

These findings are especially interesting in light of another finding of the survey: BICCs outperformed non-BICCs on unit-based forecast accuracy by 18 percent. Clearly, the Plan practices that differentiate BICCs are instrumental for better demand forecasting.

Planning is the conductor that orchestrates the performance of the entire supply chain. BICCs focus on planning to gain access to better information from their extended supply chains, and—as importantly—process that information into faster and better decisions. When translated into execution, faster and better decision making is the differentiated capability that allows BICCs to provide better service, with greater flexibility and lower costs.

SOURCE

While Plan provides the greatest opportunities for improvement, Source is the most evolved: nearly all of the Source practices listed in the survey have been implemented by at least 15 percent of the survey population. Additionally, several Source practices are what PMG categorizes as widely implemented practices; these include the use of cross-functional sourcing teams, the development of sourcing strategies to achieve the lowest total cost, and the integration of suppliers into the sourcing process.

However, there are still some Source practices where BICCs stand out from competitors. BICCs show a higher degree of collaborative interaction with their suppliers, as they do in Plan. In Source, BICCs do this by:

- Using electronic data exchange to get real-time data
- Sharing with suppliers a richer set of data, including forecasts, inventory levels, production schedules, engineering changes, and their own performance scorecards
- Collaborating on joint process improvements to reduce costs instead of just applying price reduction pressure

The BICC lesson is clear. In an environment where most companies have adopted many of the best Source practices, BICCs have gone one step further, sharing more of their own data with suppliers in exchange for greater access to real-time data and increased participation in cost reduction efforts. These efforts add up to deeper, more effective supplier relationships.

MAKE

The Make process has a long history of process improvement "inside the four walls"; accordingly, many of the Make practices are widely implemented across the survey population. Nearly all of the companies employ systematic methods for cycle time and in-plant inventory reduction, and are able to rapidly identify disruptions, reprioritize and reschedule production, and communicate implications to customers and suppliers.

BICCs, by contrast, make more extensive use of pull-based mechanisms to drive production activity. The largest differentiating practice for BICCs, though, lies in the engagement of the Make function in product design and life cycle management. BICCs make greater use of design-for-manufacturing (DFM) practices and related mass customization and late-stage postponement. As a result, they are able to get new products into mass production faster, more reliably, and less expensively than the competition.

DELIVER

The heightened focus on delivery reliability and customer service over the past decade has led to the wide implementation of many of the core Deliver practices. These center on order processing and include automating basic transaction information, order status reporting, and delivery date commitment.

BICCs take a broader perspective of the Deliver process because they incorporate customer, supplier, and benchmark information into supply chain footprint decisions. These top-performing companies are also three times more likely to employ differentiated supply chain service levels and policies for different customer segments. Furthermore, they are more likely to tailor specific supply chains to different customer segment needs for speed, flexibility, product variety, cost, or new product introduction. As the 2013 PwC global supply chain study demonstrates, BICCs operate 40 percent more supply chain configurations or operating models than average companies.[5]

Such tailoring, deployed in conjunction with superior planning processes, is the key to BICCs' success. Breaking through the classic trade-off
barriers, these companies have achieved superior service, flexibility, cost,
and working-capital performance.

SUPPLY CHAIN STRATEGY, ORGANIZATION, AND PERFORMANCE MANAGEMENT

BICCs also employ practices that cut across the major supply chain
processes. Consistent with PMG's general experience, BICCs more frequently exhibit key practices that align to the core disciplines of strategy,
process, organization, collaboration, and performance measurement. In
particular, they:

- Develop an integrated process architecture across Plan,
  Source, Make, Deliver, and Return and explicitly define the
  links to product development, sales, marketing, and finance
  functions
- Establish end-to-end performance metrics and targets, including
  key measures such as cash-to-cash cycle time and total supply
  chain management cost
- Measure and include supply chain complexity drivers in their
  key performance indicators
- Define and incorporate supply chain competency requirements
  into recruiting, staffing, and training plans

Having elevated supply chain performance to a business priority, BICCs
more explicitly define and manage their supply chain performance. These
companies use specific Plan, Source, Make, and Deliver practices to drive
better execution across the end-to-end supply chain. At the same time,
they use the five core disciplines to maintain that level of performance on
an ongoing basis.

MASTERING COMPLEXITY FOR SUPERIOR PERFORMANCE

Employing mature practices is a critical step toward stronger supply chain performance. Yet there are other considerations that companies need to keep in mind if they want to become best-in-class. One that has become extremely important in today's global business environment is complexity.

COMPLEXITY DEFINED

There are three major types of supply chain complexity (Table 6.1). Which sources of complexity matter the most? More than 75 percent of the group surveyed named the number of products or the number of direct materials as the biggest drivers of complexity.[6]

COMPLEXITY LEVERS THAT DIFFERENTIATE BICCS

BICCs manage standard complexity factors differently from the competition. Their goal is not necessarily to achieve the lowest level of complexity but to manage complexity with their business strategies in mind.

Products

PMG's research indicates that the number of products and services has a profound impact on supply chain performance. There is a pronounced difference between the BICCs and the non-BICCs with regard to the total number of stock-keeping units (SKUs) offered (Figure 6.4).

Table 6.1 Defining Supply Chain Complexity

Products and services	Represented by the number of finished product-line item codes and can also include new product introductions, seasonal variations, and distinct packaging materials
Supply chain configuration and structure	Refers to the number of nodes or structural components of any given sort along the supply chain; examples include number of manufacturing plants, distribution centers, orders, or customers
Supply chain management processes and systems	Refers to the number of unique IT systems employed throughout the supply chain; this number would include order-processing systems, operations control systems, warehouse management systems, and so on

Figure 6.4 Number of Finished Product Item Codes (SKUs)

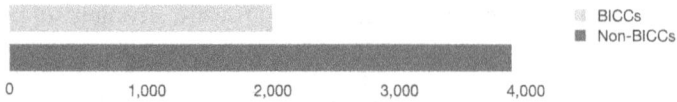

© *SC2 Book Analysis*, PMG, 2012

Figure 6.5 Number of New Product Introductions

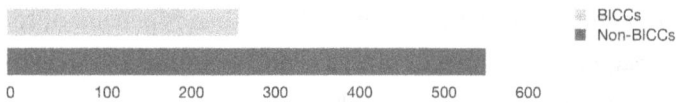

© *SC2 Book Analysis*, PMG, 2012

When it comes to the number of new product introductions each year—said by survey participants to be the most important factor affecting product proliferation—the difference between BICCs and their peers is considerable.[7] According to PMG's benchmark, BICCs introduce less than half as many new products as non-BICC competitors (Figure 6.5).

Companies need to rationalize existing product portfolios to reduce the number of SKUs that provide low returns. Equally important, they need to manage the new product introduction process to ensure that newly launched SKUs will be top performers.

Supply Chain Configurations

BICCs do not reduce every type of complexity. They, in fact, have significantly more manufacturing sites, distribution centers, and customers than does the balance of the population (Figure 6.6).

Information Technology Systems

BICCs use far fewer systems and applications than their peers (Figure 6.7). Ten may seem like a fairly large number of unique systems, but not when

Figure 6.6 Supply Chain Configuration and Structure

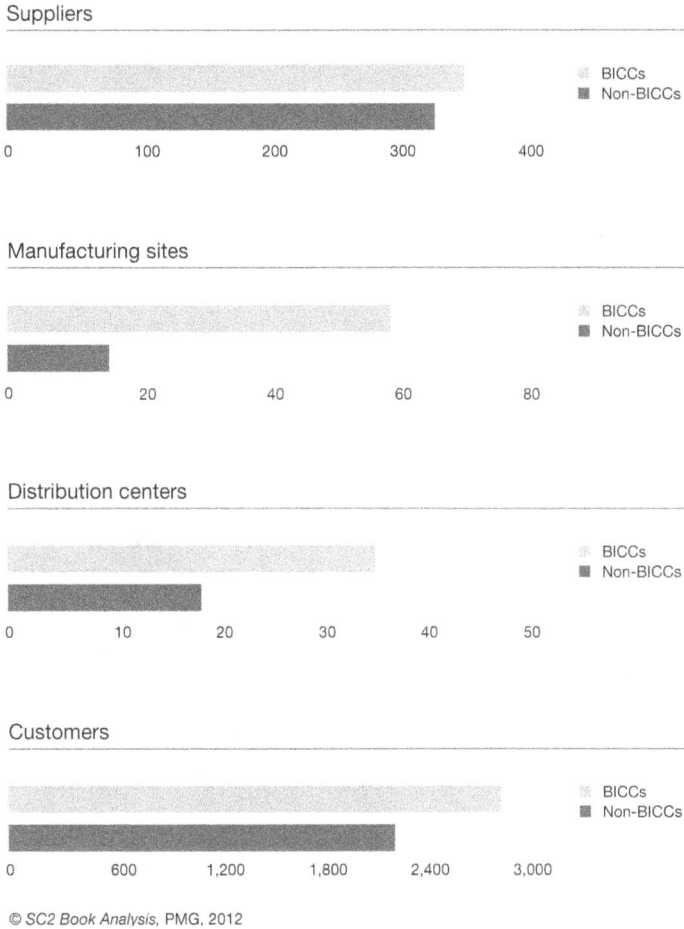

Suppliers

Manufacturing sites

Distribution centers

Customers

© SC2 Book Analysis, PMG, 2012

Figure 6.7 Number of Unique Systems and Applications

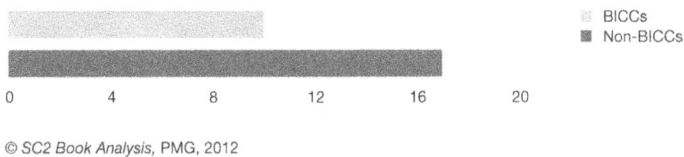

© SC2 Book Analysis, PMG, 2012

compared with the 17 deployed by the non-BICC group. Therefore, reducing the number of systems used across the supply chain can potentially contribute to improved performance.

In sum, BICCs manage overall complexity in three ways. They introduce fewer new products than the non-BICC competition, which helps suppress the number of SKUs in the portfolio. Moreover, they streamline the number of systems in use to improve management reporting and control.

At the same time, BICCS configure their supply chains in accordance with the needs of the customer base. They use better practices to manage the attendant complexity in the realization that it is necessary for competitiveness.

The benchmark data presented here make a compelling case for the importance of supply chain performance. Companies with superior performance enjoy superior financial results. Understanding the supply chain's strategic potential, they have honed the practices most critical for getting their products and services to customers. For any company aspiring to become best in class, these practices point the way forward.

BENCHMARKING SUPPLY CHAIN PERFORMANCE

Quality benchmarks are rooted in the age-old phrase "an apples-to-apples comparison." To be effective, a benchmark must be defined in a way that allows it to be applied consistently across companies. Benchmarks can be quantitative (metrics) or qualitative (practice measures). A metric requires a clear description of the formula and the data sources; a practice measure requires a detailed characterization of the practice and an assessment of how consistently it is used in the organization.

The BICC Index

To distinguish companies with top-performing supply chains, PMG developed the "BICC Index," which consists of five metrics: delivery performance to commit date, upside production flexibility, total supply chain management cost, inventory days of supply, and cash-to-cash cycle time. These metrics are defined and calculated in the same way as those used in PMG's ongoing supply chain benchmarking survey, which are based on those in the Supply Chain Operations Reference (SCOR®) model framework.

BICC Index Metrics Overview

Metric	Definition	Rationale for selection
Delivery performance to commit date	A customer-facing metric that captures the percentage of orders delivered on time to the customer commit date	Companies have more control over performance that they commit to than they do over delivery performance to request, which can vary considerably
Upside production flexibility	The number of days required to achieve an unplanned sustainable 20 percent increase in quantity delivered with the assumption of no other constraints	Companies with more-flexible manufacturing capacity are better able to rapidly respond to changes in market conditions
Total supply chain management cost	Total cost to manage order processing, acquire materials, manage inventory, and manage supply chain finance, planning, and IT costs; it is inclusive of salary, benefits, space and facilities, and general and administrative allocations	This is the best way to measure costs across the end-to-end supply chain
Cash-to-cash cycle time	The length of time, in days, that it takes for cash to flow back into a company after it has been spent for raw materials	This metric has a comprehensive view of payables, receivables, and inventory levels
Inventory days of supply	The number of days that inventories would satisfy demand; it includes only inventory that is on the books and currently owned by the business entity	This metric is used across industries and reflects an efficient use of assets and streamlined supply chain throughout

The metrics that make up the BICC Index are SCOR Level 1 measurements. They are high-level metrics calculated from companies' responses to detailed SCOR Level 2 and 3 questions. For example, delivery performance to commit is calculated from the number of orders delivered on the date requested by the customer, divided by the total number of orders delivered.

The quantitative part of the survey also includes questions that provide further insight into supply chain operations—for example, the number of weeks of firm forecast needed in advance of a ship date window.

Normalization

To remove industry bias, every company's performance on each of the five BICC Index metrics was normalized according to the company's industry. In other words, the performance of the individual company was divided by the industry average for that particular metric. For example, if a specific consumer-goods company's delivery performance is 99 percent and the consumer goods industry average for delivery performance is 90 percent, then the company's normalized delivery performance value is calculated as 99/90, or 1.1. The BICC Index represents the score derived from the sum of the five normalized values.

Of course, the metrics in the BICC Index are not the only measures appropriate for measuring overall supply chain performance. The net-asset-turns metric, for example, is still widely used, but it was not included in the BICC Index because it is affected by capital structure (i.e., short- and long-term debt-to-asset ratio). Similarly, order fulfillment lead time was not included because it can vary widely as a result of the primary operating model in use.

ABOUT PMG

The benchmarking data and analysis presented in this book are drawn from the studies conducted by the Performance Measurement Group (PMG), an internal PwC organization. Experts in the design and management of supply chain performance metrics, the people who constitute today's PMG played a key role in the development of the SCOR model in the 1990s.

PMG conducts an ongoing benchmarking of companies worldwide to determine median and best-in-class supply chain performance levels, dominant and emerging supply chain practices, and related complexity levels. These data are maintained in a repository; companies that wish to assess their supply chain performance against an appropriate comparison population are given access to aggregate metric data in exchange for completing an extensive questionnaire regarding their own performance and practices.

To ensure data integrity, PMG provides support and logical estimation techniques to participants during data collection and validates all survey submissions. Only companies that provide a certain minimum number of data points are included; extreme outliers are screened out. PMG updates its benchmarks on a regular basis with the latest survey submissions. To ensure confidentiality, only aggregate benchmarks—no company-specific data—are disclosed.

KEY TAKEAWAYS

- Companies with the best-performing supply chains also outperform their competitors on key financial metrics.
- Best-in-class companies consistently—and significantly—do better than the competition across a range of supply chain metrics because they have honed the Plan, Source, Make, and Deliver practices most critical for getting products and services to customers.
- Managing the number of SKUs through the new product introduction process is the single most effective technique for reducing supply chain complexity.

SCHLUMBERGER: INTEGRATING PEOPLE AND TECHNOLOGY FOR SERVICE EXCELLENCE

Imagine that you have built a "smart" house on the coast of California. In building this house, you have hired the best experts you can find. They've figured out exactly where the foundation should be placed. They've even perfectly wired everything in the kitchen, bedrooms, and media room.

After months of nail-biting, you move into this dream house to find that this team has perfectly installed all your plumbing, heating, fuel, and electrical systems. The team has tested everything to make sure it all works. They even stick around long after moving day, checking in by remote control to make sure everything is working in top condition.

Multiply the complexity of that undertaking by 100 or even 1,000 times, and on a far larger and riskier scale, in oil and gas fields around the world.

Founded in 1926, Schlumberger, the world's leading oil-field services company, performs such logistical feats for its oil and gas customers every day, whether in the tundra of western Siberia or in the deep waters off the coast of Brazil. With headquarters offices in Paris, Houston, and The Hague, Schlumberger is also the first truly global company in its industry. With 115,000-plus employees, the company provides services at the wellsite thousands of times a year in some 85 countries the world over. Schlumberger employees and equipment operate anywhere energy sources are found. Revenue in 2011 was $39.54 billion.

Schlumberger provides a full range of exploration, development, and production services for its customers, which include international operators like ExxonMobil, national oil companies such as Saudi Aramco, and independent producers like Chesapeake. Schlumberger supplies the intellectual know-how, technology, information solutions, and integrated project management needed not just to extract energy from the earth but also to cover the entire life cycle of its customers' oil and gas reservoirs.

Schlumberger Services Throughout an Oil-Field Life Cycle

Schlumberger services cover the three phases of an oil-field life cycle: exploration, development, and production.

Exploration—Oil company scientists identify locations that contain subsurface oil or gas reservoirs and contract companies like Schlumberger to perform various geophysical and geological surveys to build a model of the subsurface. Schlumberger refers to this phase as "reservoir characterization." The goal is to understand where and how much oil or gas is present and whether it is economical to produce it. One or more exploration wells are needed to confirm reservoir potential.

Development—Oil company engineers design how they are going to develop the field and drill it to produce oil or gas. The goal is to place the wells in the reservoir as effectively and efficiently as possible to meet production goals.

Production—Schlumberger provides different services and products to ensure that the well continues to produce throughout its life cycle. The goal is to maximize reservoir recovery.

Source: Schlumberger

Simply stated, Schlumberger is number one because, thanks to its people and technology, it provides the widest range of services, the broadest geographical reach, and the strongest focus on execution.

GETTING TO FIRST OIL

Because most of the earth's easily accessible oil and gas supply has been discovered and much is already in production, exploration increasingly occurs in remote places. The challenge in finding and tapping such reserves is huge, and the mobilization of people, equipment, technology, and raw materials to service these operations is a massively complex undertaking.

If drilling can't start on the scheduled date, the delay drives extra costs for the oil company of between $0.5 million and $1 million per day for each deepwater oil rig it deploys in an offshore environment, not to mention one fewer day of revenue. So Schlumberger must do everything right the first time. This challenge is especially daunting in remote locations, where the risks are that much higher.

In a typical offshore project, the oil and gas company hires a mobile offshore-drilling unit from a drilling contractor. Offshore rigs vary in type from platforms that "jack up" on legs standing on the sea bottom, to drillships or semi-submersible structures for deeper waters. Schlumberger provides almost all the products and services needed to drill and complete the well.

After the drilling unit is positioned above the selected location, which in this case is located beneath the sea floor, drilling begins, using a drill-string made up of 30-foot sections of drillpipe that are screwed together and that convey the drill bit and its measurement equipment into the well. As the drill advances, the drill bit cuts the rock, and the cuttings are conveyed up to the surface, where they can be analyzed. From time to time, drilling stops and measurements are made of the physical parameters of the rock formations through which the well has been drilled. Once the reservoir has been reached, the drill is removed from the hole, and steel tubes known as casings are run into the well to provide a permanent protective sheath once cemented in place. With this done, the well can be completed with the valves and gauges needed for production.

THE MOBILIZATION CHALLENGE

That's the way a typical offshore well is drilled. Now imagine starting a well site from scratch in a country with a developing oil and gas industry, like Mozambique in East Africa. In this situation, Schlumberger has to get the right people, equipment, and infrastructure in place so that preparation of the well site can start without delay and, even more important, so that drilling can start without a glitch.

Successful execution requires comprehensive planning. For one site off the coast of Mozambique, planning was begun an additional six months in advance to allow for the extra time it would take to get resources to a location with limited infrastructure. By conducting a readiness assessment, Schlumberger employees identify areas of concern and develop an action plan to address them. This approach covers areas such as procurement, logistics, human resources, and facilities. "The readiness assessment builds on years of Schlumberger experience," says the company's global head of procurement, Phil Teijeira. "It's critical for ensuring on-time execution."

Schlumberger's Mobilization Challenge

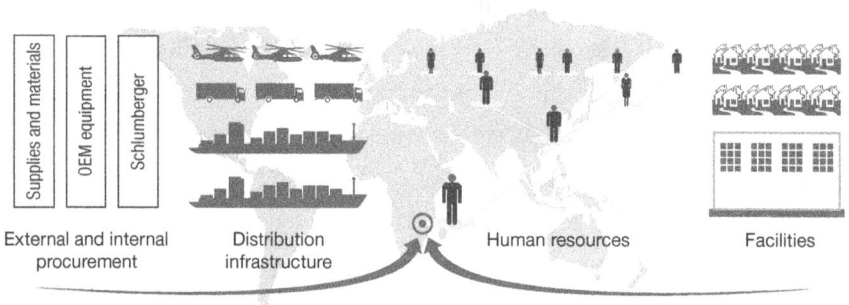

Source: Schlumberger

PROCUREMENT

Various activities will be conducted at any well site once operations begin—among them drilling, casing, data acquisition, and pressure monitoring—and numerous types of technology and materials will be needed for these activities. Some equipment will come from Schlumberger product centers and other equipment from external suppliers; it will need to be ordered months in advance. Some things won't require much lead time because they can be sourced locally (like the barite needed for the drilling operation); they will, however, require a scrupulous qualification process to ensure well integrity.

LOGISTICS

For drilling locations in well-established areas such as the U.S. Gulf of Mexico or the Scottish North Sea, all the necessary infrastructure is in place. It's not difficult to find third-party logistics providers to haul in the equipment and materials.

Few logistics companies, however, are set up to go to places as remote as a location in Mozambique. So, Schlumberger has to do its own logistics, deploying trucks, charter planes, and commercial air so that everything—containers, piping, testing equipment, and so on—arrives at Pemba, the northern Mozambique capital of Cabo Delgado Province, in time to begin operations on the date set by the customer. Schlumberger may use its own trucks and, in some cases, even contract civil-engineering companies to build the roads if the infrastructure is not in place.

HUMAN RESOURCES

Getting the people in place to staff operations at the well site can pose even greater challenges. For a typical customer project, employees are brought in from a local or regional base of operations. In certain countries, recruiting and training can be much more arduous. The pool of talent is limited simply because there is no oil and gas industry or perhaps no educational infrastructure. So Schlumberger brings in employees from other regions, organizing all aspects of their relocation such as visas and work permits. The day-to-day management of more than 10,000 "mobile" employees worldwide is a logistical challenge in itself.

FACILITIES

Each oil well operation is supported by a Schlumberger base, where engineers maintain and repair equipment used by Schlumberger and its customers at the well site. A large base, which consists of offices, warehouses, and workshops, can accommodate as many as 700 trained staff.

Schlumberger sets up a base in any region where there is a critical mass of oil or gas companies involved in drilling operations. In a region where hydrocarbons have not yet been discovered in substantial quantities, Schlumberger provides support from a remote base. In the case of Mozambique, Schlumberger used the base in Angola and set up containers to serve as temporary quarters. Later, when large gas discoveries were made, Schlumberger built a more permanent location. The company has amassed a solid network of bases over the years. All told, more than 1,000 are currently in operation worldwide.

While offshore rigs are self-contained and provide sleeping and dining for all crew members, land-based staff also need a place to live. Schlumberger therefore often has to rent houses and apartments in advance. In some cases, remote locations lack even such accommodations, so Schlumberger may need to have housing built.

MAKING THE SERVICE SUPPLY CHAIN WORK

Each step in the oil-field development is a complex operation involving multiple Schlumberger product lines that work in tight coordination with the customer-facing "GeoMarket" organization that provides core management, human resources (HR), finance, and infrastructure support. There are more than 30 GeoMarkets in all. Some consist of just one country, like Angola, while others, like Continental Europe, cover many countries.

GLOBAL SHARED SERVICES

Orchestrating these resources across the company is critical for creating value for the customer. That's where Global Shared Services comes in. The "functional backbone" of Schlumberger, this 12,000-person umbrella organization includes the functions of procurement, logistics, materials, facilities, information technology (IT), contract management, finance back-office, and HR administration.

By providing these services to all the product lines in all the GeoMarkets across Schlumberger, Global Shared Services is able to standardize ways of working and leverage best practices. The organization aims to improve the quality and cost-effectiveness of the support that the various functions provide to the field operation—support that in turn helps improve the quality of the services Schlumberger provides its customers.

"ONE FIRM"

The shared services model is a good example of how Schlumberger's "one firm" way of operating drives organizational agility. "Other companies talk about subsidiaries and internal board meetings, whereas for us, it's all about making it happen for the customer," head of Global Shared Services Stéphane Biguet notes. "There are no barriers. We just pick up the phone and call. When we go into a new country, it's the same structure as on the other side of the world, so communication is much easier and we can quickly implement our standard processes."

CUTTING-EDGE TECHNOLOGY AND THE EQUIPMENT SUPPLY CHAIN

Behind the services that take place at customer sites is an array of tools and equipment, made possible by the Schlumberger technology-development organization. This organization runs the gamut: fundamental research, proprietary technology development, original equipment manufacturer (OEM) integration, and product testing. The technology it develops provides a critical source of differentiation for Schlumberger.

Providing cutting-edge technology is under the purview of Research, Engineering, Manufacturing, and Sustaining (REMS), an organization of about 10,000 people that is designed to support the technology needs of all the company's different product lines. REMS includes manufacturing and engineering centers, which are often located near each other.

PRODUCT DEVELOPMENT

Schlumberger designs and produces its equipment, both internally and externally. Internally, the company has R&D centers in Brazil, the United Kingdom, Saudi Arabia, Russia, Norway, the United States, Canada, Japan, Singapore, and France, where it designs and develops proprietary tools and equipment. Notably, Schlumberger spends more on R&D than its two closest competitors combined.

Consider, for example, a wireline logging tool, a technology used for acquiring reservoir characterization data from the bottom of an oil well via an electric cable. A tube measuring only 3⅜ inches in diameter, this logging tool contains ten times the electronics of a laptop computer. Moreover, it is able to withstand intense pressure, extreme vibration, and temperatures of up to 150 degrees centigrade. "It's as if I took my computer and dropped it 1,000 times on the concrete floor and then put it in the oven," notes Magali Anderson, vice president of Shared Services for Europe and Africa. "Those are the kinds of extreme conditions our technology has to deal with."

Schlumberger also uses equipment produced by OEMs. In a process called "external integration," suppliers manufacture products such as engines and transmissions according to Schlumberger's exact specifications. Because reliability and safety are essential, suppliers go through an exhaustive vetting process. They are evaluated on quality, reliability, and safety standards. The oversight doesn't end there. After passing the Schlumberger test, each supplier works with a Schlumberger engineer to ensure equipment is consistently produced to Schlumberger's high standards, with performance reviewed through a quarterly business-review process.

PRODUCT CENTERS

Schlumberger's various "product centers" provide equipment for the company's 17 product lines. Well Services, for example, is supported by product centers in the United States, France, and Singapore. The Well Services product centers provide the equipment—pumps, cementing units, and so on—for well services conducted on trailers and trucks or installed as skids on offshore rigs or floating vessels. They are responsible for managing design, sourcing, and manufacturing.

The product centers always remain accountable for the quality and reliability of what they supply. Each center continuously solicits and gets feedback on product issues from field personnel, which it uses to solve problems as well as to improve product designs for future use.

Take, for example, the internal suction damper (ISD) used in certain types of well site pumps. On the basis of extensive feedback from the field, the product center designed a new ISD that weighed a lot less, cost less, and functioned better.

Having the perspective of internal customers is paramount. "We regularly hire people with field experience for positions in the product center," notes the product group supply chain manager for pressure pumping and chemistry, Tammy Macaluso. "That way people in the product center can understand how the customer feels when the product arrives late or doesn't function correctly. It gives us more integrity as an organization."

PEOPLE: MAKING THE DIFFERENCE

While Schlumberger's services and technologies are important, its people are the key reason for the company's success. To retain its leading edge in service delivery, the company makes an enormous investment in its employees, going to great lengths to find the best and the brightest and then developing them through rigorous training and career management.

HIRING THE BEST

Schlumberger hires a staggering number of engineers and scientists—some 5,000 a year. Finding that many qualified people requires combing top universities for students completing degrees in mechanical, electrical, and industrial engineering as well as physics, chemistry, and geophysical sciences.

Typically, new hires become field engineers, the key entry-level position. Since engineering programs don't generally provide the hands-on knowledge needed in an oil well operation, field engineers go through an intensive training program that lasts six to seven months. The Schlumberger way is to promote from within, so training as well as job rotation play a key role in the development of technical and managerial skills.

Field engineers typically progress toward promotion to operations managers, who are responsible for a particular product line in their location or GeoMarket. They may be in charge of drilling operations in East Africa, for example, or production operations in Australia. The operations manager oversees everything related to that activity. "The ops manager basically runs the business of that segment," Magali Anderson notes. "That's everything—managing the customers, getting the tenders, winning the tenders, and organizing the operations. He is running his or her little company."

DEVELOPING A GLOBAL TALENT POOL

For field engineers, service managers, and operations managers alike, Schlumberger's goal is to develop a global talent pool. The company makes a practice of sending people to other countries where they can learn directly about different field operations, technology development, and more. As these employees gain skills and knowledge, they are given the opportunity to try other locales or to return to their country of origin. Schlumberger provides this opportunity while at the same time developing the diversity among the workforce that only a truly global organization can achieve.

Some operations managers go on to hold senior management positions. Many of the company's senior managers, in fact, started out in the field. "Schlumberger challenges people with high potential to learn the entire business. They'll put a field guy in assignments in human resources, or in procurement," says Phil Teijeira. "By the time they're in a senior management position, these people have been in every role, and understand every region and every operation."

Schlumberger does not limit professional development to engineers. Functional staff, such as sourcing experts, logistics specialists, IT technicians, and accountants, are required to participate in the company's competency-management program.

EXCEEDING CUSTOMER EXPECTATIONS

Despite all of the oil and gas drilling technology currently in use and the new methods in development, a question remains: Will the world have enough energy to meet its needs? The International Energy Agency forecasts the global demand for primary energy to grow by approximately 35 percent from 2011 through 2035 and that oil and gas, along with coal, will still dominate the energy mix.[1]

Meeting this demand requires a wide range of energy resources. When it comes to oil and gas, the majority of new reservoirs are located in unconventional and difficult-to-access places. Doing jobs right the first time in the worst conditions will require Schlumberger to keep doing what it has been doing—maintain its focus on service execution, technology, and people while aspiring to always exceed customer expectations.

CHAPTER SEVEN

TRANSFORM YOUR SUPPLY CHAIN

Transformational change within the supply chain is a tall order. For one thing, these efforts cross many functions within the organization and many geographic locations—not to mention customers, suppliers, or both. They also must take place while the company continues to operate. A structured approach that involves senior executives and line managers alike is critical for delivering truly sustainable results.

We've discussed the five core disciplines of the supply chain—strategy, process architecture, organization, collaboration, and performance measurement and management—in separate chapters. But the supply chain can confer real strategic advantage only when all five are deployed together in support of the business strategy. How, then, do you marshal those disciplines to transform the supply chain into a greater competitive asset?

A great many books have been written on corporate-transformation initiatives. Yet despite all the information out there, many companies that try to improve major aspects of their supply chain—to achieve *transformational change*—miss the mark. And in some cases, such efforts actually end up harming business performance. That's because all too many companies treat these initiatives like any other change effort. In fact, supply chain transformations pose some unique challenges.

To begin with, most supply chain transformation initiatives involve a wide range of functions across the organization, including product management, sales, engineering, and finance. It's not only about improving the performance of a supply chain organization, it's about orchestrating change across the entire enterprise. Even in cases in which the transformation initiative focuses on improving just one function, the upgrade affects multiple sites and teams across the globe.

Consider, for example, a company that wants to implement a standard operating model across 20 production sites. Given the different operational areas (for example, order management, materials management, and maintenance) in each plant, the company can quickly have an initiative that changes the work of 100 operational teams. That's just within one department of the company's own organizational structure. If you factor in the interactions with customers and suppliers, the change effort gets even more complex.

Adding to the challenge, supply chain transformation initiatives must take place while the company continues to operate—without missing a beat. The company still has to process incoming orders, deal with suppliers, and get deliveries to customers on time, even as it adjusts its processes, organization, and metrics. It's like working on a car while you're driving it.

We've found that the best way to deal with these challenges is to approach supply chain transformation in four steps. First, you set improvement priorities on the basis of your strategic objectives. The second step consists of designing the transformation road map, and the third comprises the implementation of the solution and management of the change. The fourth and final step is to operate the supply chain and ensure ongoing performance (Figure 7.1).

These phases may sound fairly standard. But in the context of a complex, cross-functional supply chain transformation, each has specific ingredients for success that need to be taken into account.

Figure 7.1 Making Supply Chain Transformation Happen

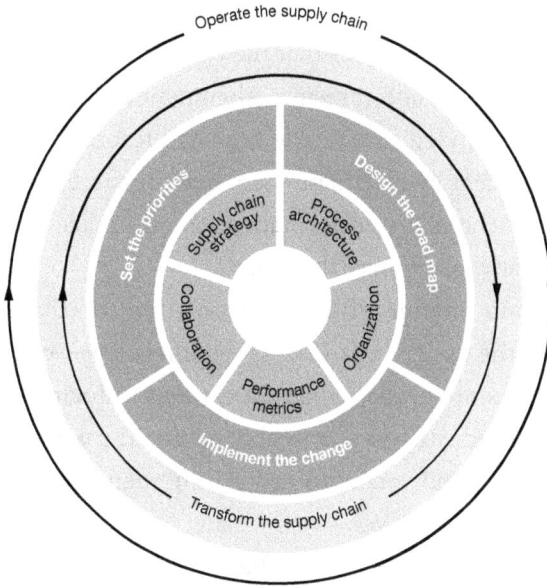

SETTING IMPROVEMENT PRIORITIES

Supply chain transformation can have tremendous impact and can require significant investment, so the first step in any supply chain transformation is to set clear priorities for change. This will require alignment across the senior management team on the magnitude of the transformation, the potential impact on the organization, and the reasons for undertaking the change.

One clarification is in order. Our discussion on making changes to the supply chain assumes that the company's fundamental operations are working. Clearly, if any basic process—for example, production quality assurance—is broken or if a supplier is unable to meet its delivery commitments, you'll need to fix that before you undertake a supply chain transformation.

AGREEING ON THE MAGNITUDE OF THE TRANSFORMATION

The first step in setting the priorities of supply chain transformation is to have the senior management team reach a consensus on the scope and scale of change needed. This ensures that the team is aligned on the required resources, governance, and timeline. Alignment is crucial because companies commonly underestimate the time and resources—as well as the level of management involvement—required for successfully revamping a supply chain. Generally, transformation initiatives take at least a year to execute, and many take longer than that.

Supply chain change efforts fall into one of three categories (Figure 7.2). At the upper end of the spectrum is *supply chain innovation,* which companies undertake when they are introducing practices that are new to their industry—and possibly new to the world. Well-known examples include Dell's make-to-order fulfillment model and Procter & Gamble's consumer-driven supply chain.

It is not surprising that supply chain innovation is a relatively rare phenomenon.[1] It requires significant simultaneous change in multiple core

Figure 7.2 Types of Supply Chain Change

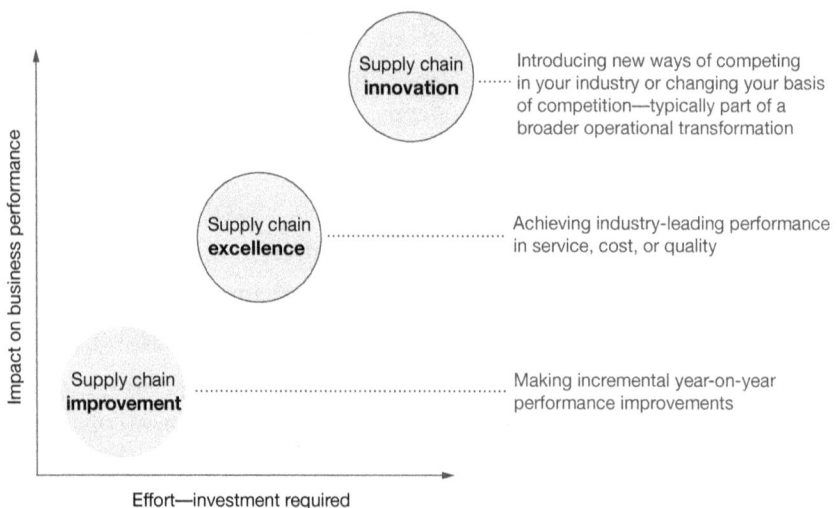

- Supply chain **innovation**: Introducing new ways of competing in your industry or changing your basis of competition—typically part of a broader operational transformation
- Supply chain **excellence**: Achieving industry-leading performance in service, cost, or quality
- Supply chain **improvement**: Making incremental year-on-year performance improvements

Impact on business performance

Effort—investment required

processes, supported by a large investment of resources over several years. Changing the company's basis of competition (for example, repositioning the company from a cost-based to a service-based model) is in the same league of difficulty. Given the extent of change involved, senior management directly oversees innovation initiatives and provides regular progress updates to the board of directors.

At the opposite end of the spectrum is *supply chain improvement*, which consists of smaller, incremental changes. Although not transformative in nature, improvement plays an important part in ensuring sustainable performance. Typically managed by people at lower levels of the management hierarchy, improvement efforts are continuous and ongoing. Furthermore, they do not require dedicated resources or exceptional levels of management attention.

Most supply chain transformation efforts fall in the middle of the spectrum, *supply chain excellence*. Situated between supply chain innovation and supply chain improvement, these initiatives involve making changes across the end-to-end supply chain to achieve industry-leading supply chain performance with the goal of growing market share, increasing margins, and improving working capital. Examples include redesigning products to make them easier to order, produce, and deliver; deploying a global supply chain planning process; and moving from a global to a regional production and order-fulfillment model. Because supply chain excellence initiatives require considerable resources and time to execute, they are managed as strategic initiatives and sponsored by a member of the senior management team.

In this chapter, we focus on the most common type of transformations— supply chain excellence efforts. Most of the lessons here can be applied to supply chain innovation as well.

BUILDING A SOLID CASE FOR CHANGE

To build a compelling case for change, you should set specific performance targets for your supply chain and the individual processes that are most critical to your supply chain strategy. You will need to start by determining how supply chain performance can contribute to market share, margins, and working-capital performance.

As part of the process of building a case for change, companies typically conduct an assessment and benchmarking exercise. Take, for example, a fictional company that we'll call "Consumer Electronics Company (CEC)," a manufacturer of flat-screen televisions. CEC has three sales regions—Asia-Pacific; the Americas; and Europe, the Middle East, and Africa—and conducts sales in more than 25 countries. The company serves two major customer segments in each region: distributors and small specialty retailers. Most of the production facilities are located in Asia, but a plant in Eastern Europe services the European Union. Regional distribution centers are located in each of the major markets to promote fast deliveries.

CEC competes primarily on customer experience, so delivery is a critical factor. Nevertheless, the company's delivery performance in developed markets—where margins are higher than in other markets—has been substandard, resulting in eroding market share and a longer cash-to-cash cycle. External benchmarking data show that CEC is operating with an order fulfillment cycle time of 20 days and 75 percent on-time delivery to commit, while its major competitors are operating with an order fulfillment cycle time of 10 days and 95 percent on-time delivery to commit.

To reach benchmark performance levels, CEC needs to set quantitative, time-phased targets for supply chain metrics. A target might be "improve on-time delivery to commit performance by 5 percent every six months." Moreover, CEC needs to link such goals to specific objectives for market share and working-capital improvement in order to demonstrate the potential return on investment from the transformation (Figure 7.3).

ENSURING THAT SOLUTIONS ARE SCALABLE

In traditional change management, after a solution has been designed, it is piloted in a small area of the company. The company pays little attention to defining the implementation approach for the entire initiative (including

Figure 7.3 Aligning Supply Chain Targets and Business Goals

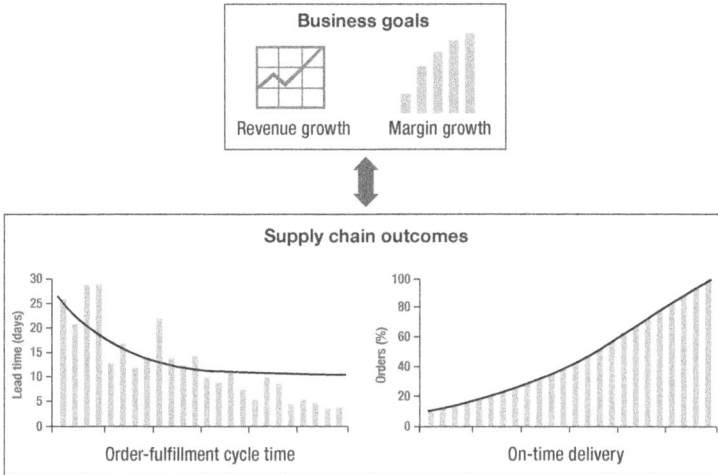

all applicable locations, departments, teams, and individuals) until it can first confirm that the proposed design actually works.

This approach has significant drawbacks, however. The major risk is that the solution won't scale because sites differ in their skill levels, information systems, work profiles, and work volumes. As a result, a prohibitive amount of effort and time are needed to reach the targeted performance level.

We recommend instead that companies develop the solution and implementation approach *at the same time*. This will help ensure that the proposed changes are scalable across the organization. Given that today's global supply chains involve so many sites and employees in far-flung places, an implementation approach defined for scalability is a prerequisite for meeting the target implementation schedule and budget.

Organizational Mapping

In order to ensure scalability, you will need a clear and comprehensive line of sight on the full impact of the change initiative, including every location, department, team, and individual that the new solutions will

Figure 7.4 Organizational Mapping for Change

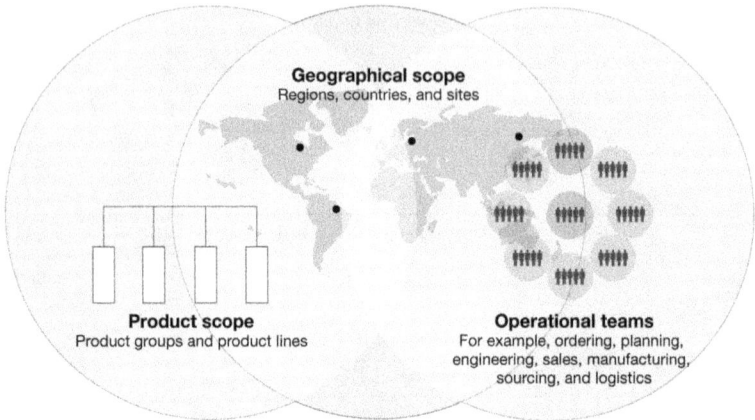

affect. This will require a specific effort, such as an organizational mapping (Figure 7.4). You should start the mapping effort as early as possible, although you won't be able to finalize it until later after developing a view of your detailed actions. (See the section "Designing the Transformation Road Map.")

To develop an organizational mapping for change, first look at each action to identify the relevant product scope (such as product lines and divisions) and geographic scope (regions, countries, and sites). Then identify the specific operational teams and the positions in each team that will be affected by the change and that, therefore, must be involved in designing, testing, and deploying the solution. These teams typically reflect the existing organization entities in functions within the company, such as sales, purchasing, order management, manufacturing, product management, and engineering.

Lessons from Mapping

In many cases, the mapping activity reveals that the change effort will affect considerably more people than management initially imagined. A change effort around the planning process, for example, typically involves teams not only from planning but also from manufacturing, sourcing, and logistics, along with finance, product management, sales, and engineering. When you take into account the multiplier effect of different product lines, regions, and countries, you may find that so many people will be affected that it will be necessary to adjust the solution—or divide it into more manageable chunks to be deployed over a longer time period.

For example, a capital-equipment manufacturer decided to implement a new sales and operations planning (S&OP) process over a 12-month time frame, understanding that this would entail major changes to sales forecasting, manufacturing planning, and supplier planning. Analysis soon revealed, however, that the problem stemmed not from the S&OP process per se but from poor management of the sales pipeline. Many of the company's 20 sales territories had gotten into the habit of not updating their sales opportunities in the customer-relationship-management system until the leads had turned into actual orders. This meant that the information available for planning was largely out of date, and the resulting inaccuracies rippled through the S&OP process. When the company realized that the required scale of change was far greater than it had originally thought, management restructured its approach. Before making improvements to planning for production and suppliers, the company would first focus on several hundred sales managers to stabilize sales forecasting.

DESIGNING THE TRANSFORMATION ROAD MAP

Once you agree on the scope of the change and have alignment on the case for change, it's time to identify the specific actions needed to hit the new performance targets and define the approach for implementing those changes. The transformation road map spells out all of this.

In contrast to a project plan, which covers only one project or action, a transformation road map covers all of the actions needed to achieve a company's business objectives, showing what will be executed, in which order, and in what time frame. The road map communicates the major blocks of change required and identifies clear milestones and deadlines that help ensure that the company achieves specific performance improvements within the necessary time frame. Critically important, a road map also determines the sequence of actions, ensuring that prerequisite actions have been taken where needed. In short, the road map is a powerful tool that makes the overall journey understandable for everyone.

DEFINING THE PREREQUISITES FOR A ROBUST ROAD MAP

Before building a transformation road map, a company must have a good understanding of its current performance, capabilities, and capacity to absorb change. In other words, it must have a good handle on its current operations before it plans for the future. Companies should conduct two actions to assess their current performance levels:

- Identify the drivers of current performance
- Understand the relationships between actions

Identify the Drivers of Current Performance

In order to design the right solution, you'll need to identify the root causes of current performance—not only where gaps and pain points exist but also how the supply chain operates. This is no easy task, given the many interactions among supply chain processes. Gathering data is a starting point, but it's not enough: you also need to drill down to see how people are really working so that you understand why they work as they do.

In Chapter 5, we discussed the importance of supply chain performance measurements and the usefulness of benchmarking. Data, reports, and scorecards provide a starting point, but you will also need to understand how your processes are operating.

Since the supply chain exists to satisfy customer needs, the experience of customers should drive the analysis. How do customers use your product or service, and how does this shape their expectations of your supply chain? Are they happy with your performance and, if not, why not? Do they find it easy to do business with your company in terms of planning, ordering, delivery, and invoicing?

The classic article "Staple Yourself to an Order" makes this point emphatically. Every customer's experience with a company, the article argues, is determined by the company's order-management cycle. From the customer's perspective, order fulfillment starts when he or she places an order and ends when the product is received. Every interaction—from order creation to delivery—represents a customer interaction and the possibility of creating a good or bad customer experience.[2]

Let's go back to the case of the fictional CEC. The company already has a good idea of how its performance compares with that of its competitors. CEC knows that it's falling short in order fulfillment cycle time and on-time delivery levels and that this is affecting market share and working-capital performance. Now it needs to dig deeper to understand the root causes of the delays and missed commitments. To do so, the company needs to understand the path that orders take once they're placed.

That means determining where and why an order gets "stuck," and whether the supply chain includes any areas of rework, backtracking, or duplicated activities. How much time does each activity add to the process? There is one critical question: Why is the activity performed the way it is? If you continue drilling down and asking this question again and again, you'll likely find that the real answer is, "This is how we've always done it." CEC will also need to investigate the root causes of all other delays and problems, including internal policies that trap orders in an extensive credit-verification process, lack of clear ordering rules with customers (such as order cutoff times), orders arriving at the plant with incomplete information from order desks, and skill gaps inside the organization that limit overall effectiveness.

This root-cause analysis will likely uncover issues that the company may have believed were only marginally related to delivery performance. As a result, this process will broaden the scope far beyond the initial focus on the order fulfillment process. For example, if product availability issues are causing a large percentage of problems, the company needs to look more deeply to find the root cause of the stock-outs. In some cases, suppliers may not be delivering on time. In other cases, the factory could be having yield issues. In still others, there could be a problem with the forecasting or demand-management process. Are the systems that are supposed to balance demand and supply working properly? Is the company interpreting the information systems output correctly and taking the right actions in response?

Such considerations will allow you to identify the major areas or work streams that you'll need to address in your transformation effort. In the case of CEC, those areas are order management, procurement, supply chain planning, and enablers (specifically, organization and performance measurement). Together, these four areas will form the basis of the road map for CEC, in which key actions occur across three phases (Figure 7.5).

To make sure that the road map is effective for them, companies should develop and manage it as an iterative and ongoing activity. The lessons you

Figure 7.5 Consumer Electronics Company's Transformation Road Map

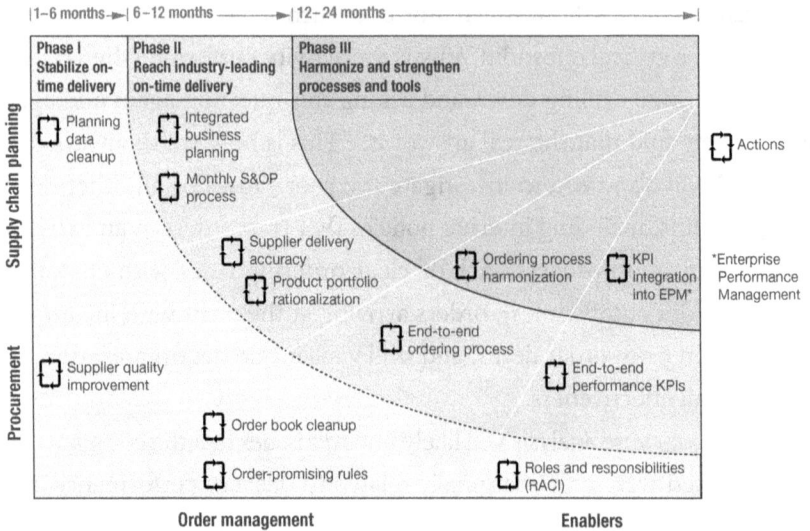

learn from deploying one action may change your view of how to proceed in future phases, and possibly in some actions already under way. You will need to update the road map to reflect these changes, and such updating must happen throughout the transformation.

Understand the Relationships Between Actions

Because the supply chain has many interacting parts, it's important to ensure that the right prerequisites are in place for each action. In that context, you'll need to determine which actions should happen concurrently and which should happen sequentially. As we discussed in Chapter 2, planning processes can't function when execution processes such as order management, production, and logistics are not robust, or when the company hasn't first defined enablers such as business rules.

Consider again the case of CEC and its goal of improving delivery performance. To address execution, planning, and enabling processes, the company will have to develop a clear understanding of interdependencies among the improvement actions. A redesign of the planning process may not have the desired impact if practices related to new product introductions are not in place. Do people in key roles have the experience and skills to define and execute the required process changes? Do the new processes depend on new information systems?

Identifying these interdependencies may reveal that actions previously thought to lack great importance are, in fact, critical to the success of the overall effort. CEC may also find that a proposed action is likely to impact the return on investment for one or more existing projects, which may lead to reprioritizing or even canceling an improvement effort that is already under way.

With this understanding, CEC can determine which phase of deployment it belongs in. CEC's transformation road map has three phases. The goal of Phase 1 is to stabilize on-time delivery and regain market share. This involves actions such as improving the accuracy of inventory information. The objective of Phase 2 is to reach industry-leading levels of on-time delivery and grow market share with the specialist retailers (one of CEC's two most important distribution channels). This phase includes actions on redefining the end-to-end ordering process, implementing a monthly planning process, and clarifying roles and responsibilities. The purpose of Phase 3 is to ensure robust and sustainable operations. It focuses on harmonizing the ordering process between the two market segments (in CEC's case, distributor and retailer), and deploying new information systems for planning and performance measurement.

DEPLOYING THE FIVE DISCIPLINES IN THE RIGHT ORDER

To build a successful road map, a company must focus on the core disciplines in the right order. Even though all five play important roles in any supply chain transformation, and will factor in iteratively throughout, some disciplines are more important than others, especially at the outset. Specifically, strategy and organization deserve special attention from the earliest stages of the change effort. Companies that lack a well-defined supply chain strategy often find themselves making improvements that don't support the business strategy. And many companies that are hazy on organization—without clear accountabilities for supply chain activities—see their transformation efforts fizzle before the finishing line.

Strategy

The first discipline to focus on is supply chain strategy. This discipline dictates key performance objectives and how the supply chain needs to be organized to support the business strategy. It therefore effectively governs and influences decisions concerning the other disciplines: process architecture, organization, collaboration, and performance measurement and management. It's the foundation that underlies the entire transformation.

Through the lens of your supply chain strategy, you can identify the changes that are required to reach the major supply chain performance objectives. Say, for example, your supply chain strategy indicates that, in order to support market-share growth targets, you need to deploy a regional production and delivery model that will reduce order delivery times by 50 percent. You will look at the impact these changes will have on the other four disciplines. This analysis is likely to identify a need to modify your planning processes and supporting information systems, as well as accountabilities between global, regional, and country organizations.

Organization
Talent acquisition and development are also important considerations. New ways of working may require new skills, so it's important to identify any skill gaps as early as possible. This will allow you to use the transformation as an opportunity to ramp up new hiring and develop existing talent.

Supply chain transformation also requires strong line-organization leadership across many functions including sales, product management, and product development. In that context, organizational roles and responsibilities should be the next area of focus. To develop that leadership you need to clarify who's going to be responsible and accountable for each major supply chain activity after the transformation initiative is completed. (See the RACI discussion in Chapter 3.) Those decisions will help ensure that the right functions and individuals are involved from the start.

ALIGNING INFORMATION SYSTEMS WITH THE FIVE DISCIPLINES
A high-performance supply chain depends on integrating processes and data both inside the enterprise and outside, with customers and suppliers. But many companies cannot fully leverage the information systems that enable integration, because their strategy is unclear, their processes are weak, their organization lacks the required skills and capabilities, or the companies they want to partner with aren't ready to do so.

To understand the appropriate role of IT systems in creating your road map, think of a ladder that leads from your current level of performance to your target level. The five supply chain disciplines form the sides of the ladder, and the information systems are the rungs you step on. Although it's possible to ascend a ladder with no rungs—that is, with the five disciplines but no information systems—this would require great effort. Now imagine the rungs (the IT systems) without any supporting sides (no disciplines). In this case, there's no way to climb at all. This is what happens when companies attempt to implement information systems without simultaneously addressing issues within each of the core disciplines. IT is not a separate entity; it is embedded within each discipline.

Research backs this up. Companies that implement information systems without paying the same level of attention to their processes and organization actually perform worse than companies that make no use of information systems at all. This was demonstrated in a 2002 study that focused on advanced planning systems, and it still applies today, particularly to information systems that provide decision-making support.[3] Technology is a tool, not a substitute for clear thinking regarding operational processes. Although cloud computing will increase access to supply chain applications, companies still won't be able to take advantage of these systems without a solid foundation of process and capability.

IMPLEMENTING THE CHANGE

Given that the company must make changes to the supply chain while continuing to operate and fill customer orders, the way it approaches implementation can have a major impact on revenue. A structured deployment approach, therefore, is essential for delivering the transformation while managing the inherent risks and still meeting agreed-upon budgets and timelines.

ADOPTING THE DEFINE-TEST-DEPLOY METHOD

In our work with companies, we've found that define-test-deploy is a robust method for implementing transformational change in the supply chain (Figure 7.6). Here's how it works.

Figure 7.6 A Structured Approach to Implementation

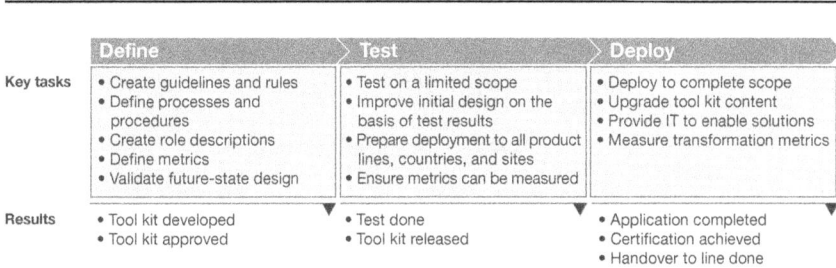

	Define	Test	Deploy
Key tasks	• Create guidelines and rules • Define processes and procedures • Create role descriptions • Define metrics • Validate future-state design	• Test on a limited scope • Improve initial design on the basis of test results • Prepare deployment to all product lines, countries, and sites • Ensure metrics can be measured	• Deploy to complete scope • Upgrade tool kit content • Provide IT to enable solutions • Measure transformation metrics
Results	• Tool kit developed • Tool kit approved	• Test done • Tool kit released	• Application completed • Certification achieved • Handover to line done

In the *define* phase, the expert team defines the specific solutions needed to address the root causes of current performance gaps. The team bundles these solutions into tool kits for every action or project on the road map. If the change is to stick, the new ways of working must be described at a level of detail that's relevant to each operational team. This means that the capabilities that the operational teams and employees need in order to execute their required activities must be made abundantly clear. For that reason, each tool kit must contain detailed process descriptions, metrics, rules, and responsibilities that are documented with examples and imparted through training.

During the *test* phase, the expert team tests each tool kit to ensure that it is technically adequate, feasible, and robust. The technical test confirms that the tool kit provides the expected results and that the supply chain is able to function normally and at the targeted level of quality. The feasibility test confirms how much effort will be required to apply the new way of working (detailing, for example, how much time it will take to process each customer order). The robustness test confirms that the tool kit is clear enough for operational teams to use for making changes to a given activity. Together, the results of the feasibility and robustness tests provide the feedback needed to ensure that the solution is scalable.

Finally, during the *deploy* phase, the operational teams make the change happen. All of the teams that need to deploy a given change follow a

Figure 7.7 Deployment: From Beginning to End

Step 1	Step 2	Step 3	Step 4	Step 5
Mobilization session	**Application start**	**Application complete**	**Certification**	**Hand over to line**
Affected teams are clear on needed changes and required resources.	Resources are in place and ready to work.	Needed changes have been made and consistent performance is demonstrated.	Changes and performance are validated.	Additional improvements are the responsibility of line management; project mode stops.

prescribed set of steps. As Figure 7.7 illustrates, these steps include mobilization (organizing to making the change happen), application (applying the tool kit content), certification (validating the capability to a published standard), and handover to the line (transferring the change leadership from the project organization to the line organization to provide for ongoing performance improvement). The goal of the deploy phase is not so much to implement the complete solution as it is to reach just enough capability to reach the performance target established for the transformation initiative.

USING A COMBINED BOTTOM-UP AND TOP-DOWN APPROACH

Successful supply chain transformations require input from all levels. A project team of 10 or even 100 cannot be effective at changing the way all the people in the supply chain work just by pushing them. Companies that have had the greatest success in supply chain transformation have found that a mix of top-down guidance from management and bottom-up contributions from employees—a push–pull approach—yields the best results.[4]

In a typical push-only implementation approach, senior management dictates timelines and new ways of working, often without taking into account the actual situation on the ground. By contrast, the push–pull approach puts frontline managers in the driver's seat. While management sets the major deadlines and targets, frontline managers develop a deployment timeline, pulling any support they need from the overall organization. Additionally, while expert teams are developing solutions, frontline managers are providing feedback on the design before it is released for deployment. Managing the role of expert teams made up of people with deep knowledge of the process is key: although the expert teams may have the best technical grasp of the target way of working, they can all too easily develop solutions that are technically excellent but unnecessarily complex.

The power of push–pull doesn't come just from putting power in the hands of the frontline managers. In today's global supply chains, many of which have grown through acquisition, different locations may very likely be at different starting points in terms of managerial competencies, process capability, and tools. The push–pull approach acknowledges this and allows those teams that can go faster to do so. In addition, it takes into account the likelihood that a lot of the knowledge needed to make the change program successful lies beyond centralized teams of experts. Tapping into that knowledge base helps the overall organization learn and improve faster.

Making all of this work requires some guidelines or design rules. Without them, you risk generating a vast number of different processes and supporting information systems, with the associated costs and complexity. (See Chapter 2.)

Take the example of Alstom, a France-based company focused on transportation, power generation, and the electrical grid. Alstom Transport, the company's transport division, develops and markets a range of systems, equipment, and services in the railway sector. Known for its innovative TGV (Train à Grande Vitesse) and AGV (Automotrice à Grande Vitesse), it is number one in the high-speed and very-high-speed train categories. Alstom Transport is also a leading producer of urban transit solutions, such as metro and tramway systems; its products are used by millions in cities around the world, including Shanghai, São Paulo, New York, and London.

Because many of Alstom Transport's customers have unique requirements, it provides customized solutions through an engineer-to-order operating model. Its trains, metros, and trams often include customized specifications for interior and exterior design.

From 2004 through 2007, Alstom Transport conducted a major transformation initiative to improve customer project delivery and time to market for new products, with the ultimate goal of improving margins and market share. The effort involved some 800 operational teams located across 60 sites worldwide. "We needed to define standard processes in product development and customer project delivery to achieve industry leadership," notes Bernard Gonnet, Alstom Transport senior vice president and project champion. "This required keeping a tight link between the target standards and the needs of the operational teams—that is, the design, sourcing, manufacturing, and project teams."

Gonnet oversaw the transformation effort firsthand. "I visited all the sites where our operational teams are located to find out what issues they were dealing with and then discussed these issues with the expert teams designing our processes," he explains. "This loop ensured that the changes that were proposed were acceptable to our operational teams."

The initiative had impressive results. Not only did it introduce new practices into the rail industry, including product platforms and standard subsystems, it also allowed Alstom to reduce delivery cycle times and engineering costs, enhance its ability to share designs across products for multiple customers, improve quality, and significantly increase its operating income.

MEASURING TRANSFORMATION

In measuring the results of supply chain transformations, many companies tend to focus only on outcomes—the business or operations metrics —because these are the concrete numbers. This seems like an intuitive approach, but in fact it's insufficient. You also need to determine whether the change is taking root and whether your people are acquiring the new capabilities needed to ensure sustainable performance over time.

Figure 7.8 Transformation Performance Perspectives

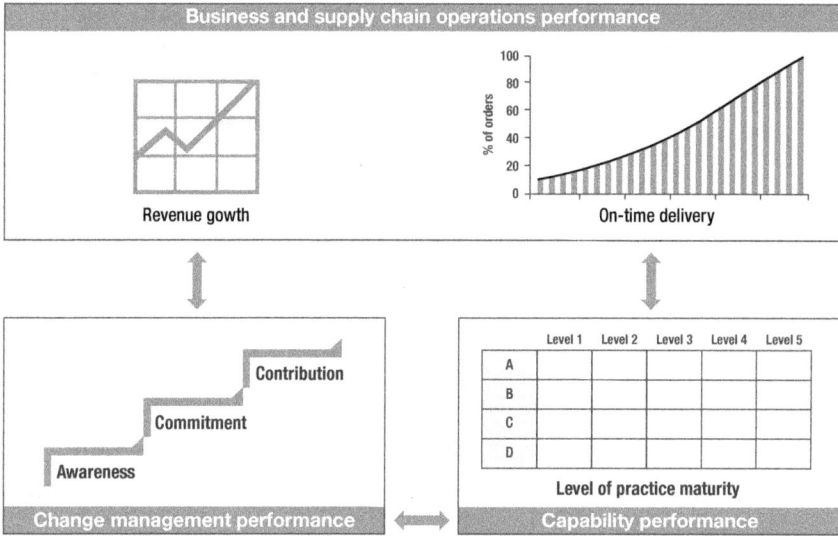

The key is to consider four performance perspectives: business performance, supply chain operations performance, change management performance, and capability performance. Together, they provide a complete picture of transformation performance (Figure 7.8).

Transformation Performance Perspectives

Each of the four transformation-performance perspectives comes with its own distinct set of metrics (Table 7.1).

Business metrics represent the key business outcomes driven by supply chain performance. They include working capital improvement as well as P&L-related outcomes such as revenue growth and margin levels. Business metrics should also cover nonfinancial outcomes, such as those related to corporate social responsibility.

Operations metrics reflect the levels of supply chain performance required to achieve the outcomes set by the business metrics. Firmly

Table 7.1 Supply Chain Transformation Metrics

Metric types	Areas covered	Examples
Business	P&L, balance sheet, and overall corporate outcomes	Revenue, market share, margins, working capital, corporate social-responsibility score
Operations	End-to-end supply chain KPIs	Order-fulfillment cycle time, on-time delivery, cash-to-cash cycle time
	Select supply chain performance indicators for priority process areas	Order quality, forecast accuracy, bill of materials, on-time release
Change management	Achievement of main milestones by location, department, and team	Kickoff done, deployment complete, certification achieved
Capability	Process maturity at target level	Department or team at maturity level 3 on a scale of 1 to 5

linking the supply chain to business targets, operations metrics include such measurements as on-time delivery, order fulfillment cycle time, total inventory days of supply, supply chain management costs, cost of goods sold, and net asset turns. (See Chapter 5.)

Change management metrics demonstrate the progress of the organization against clearly defined goals at every step of the transformation. These metrics are used to set the pace of change, establish milestones, and indicate where teams are struggling and may need support. Metrics most often indicate the achievement of a milestone: "gap analysis completed," "action plan defined," and "deployment complete" are three such examples. Measurement in this case requires checking specific deliverables before checking the box "done."

Capability metrics indicate whether the organization has acquired the process capabilities needed for sustainable performance over the long term. Metrics, such as the demonstrated maturity level of a process or the adoption (or lack of adoption) of a best practice, measure each operational team's progress in acquiring the needed capabilities and indicate how much further each team has to go. These kinds of metrics can also bring to light specific areas in which a number of teams are struggling to make progress and, hence, where additional training would be beneficial.

Defining the metrics is only the first step; assigning direct account-ability for the results is also important. While the management team will collectively own the overall, end-to-end operational metrics, individual managers in specific areas will be responsible for the underlying performance indicators. For example, the head of sourcing may be tasked with developing efforts, in conjunction with the head of engineering, to reduce the reliance on single suppliers, while the head of each plant would be responsible for ensuring sufficient labor is available for plants to meet the agreed-upon supply plan. This exercise is painful—especially for those on the receiving end—but is essential for reaching the business performance goals outlined in the case for change.

Change at Alstom Transport began with the conviction that such clarity was critical. "We put the whole organization under pressure by setting capability certification as an objective for all locations with a fixed end date," Gonnet notes. "This focused people's minds and forced the operational units to make real changes in the way they were working. We maintained the pressure by setting objectives for the management team and making sure those objectives cascaded throughout the organization." At Alstom, capability certification was a top objective for both site managers and their operational teams. Sites received certification only when they had reached the minimum required level of 3 on a scale of 1 to 5. A team led by the quality organization, acting as an objective third party, made the call as to whether the level had been reached.

Creation of Visibility

One of the most powerful ways to accelerate change is to make progress visible to all affected sites and teams throughout the enterprise. A chart can be especially effective (Figure 7.9). This kind of visibility allows teams that are further along to share their best practices with other teams. It also generates a spirit of healthy competition that adds to the motivation for

Figure 7.9 Visibility on Change Management and Capability: Progress by Team

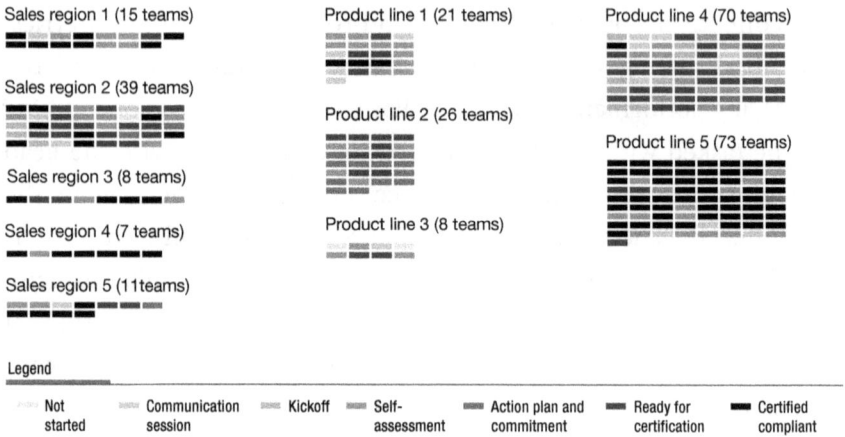

Sales region 1 (15 teams)

Sales region 2 (39 teams)

Sales region 3 (8 teams)

Sales region 4 (7 teams)

Sales region 5 (11teams)

Product line 1 (21 teams)

Product line 2 (26 teams)

Product line 3 (8 teams)

Product line 4 (70 teams)

Product line 5 (73 teams)

Legend

| Not started | Communication session | Kickoff | Self-assessment | Action plan and commitment | Ready for certification | Certified compliant |

change. No less important, it helps the organization focus its resources on the teams most in need of support.

Alstom Transport created visibility by tracking and sharing progress on the four transformation-performance perspectives. Operational metrics were established for each customer project, including a metric on the actual cost of engineering versus the targeted cost at major customer-project milestones. Change management and capabilities were also closely tracked; the level of adoption of new practices was rated on a scale of 1 to 5, with 3 being the minimum acceptable level.

As Alstom Transport demonstrates, well-designed supply chain transformation initiatives have the potential to dramatically improve business performance in far-reaching ways. A structured approach, along with the right set of tools, can ensure that the necessary steps happen in the right sequence, with minimal disruption to operations. With the right level of planning and with the full engagement of the organization, the transformation effort can yield the targeted value and a real competitive advantage.

KEY TAKEAWAYS

- Many supply chain transformation efforts miss the mark because companies treat them as if they were no different from any other change effort. In fact, they're far more complicated because they cross multiple functions across the organization and because you can't stop operations while you're trying to make changes.

- The most successful transformation initiatives break the effort into four distinct phases. They set performance improvement goals that everyone agrees on; they design the transformation road map; they implement the change; finally, they operate the supply chain and ensure ongoing performance.

- Many companies underestimate the time, resources, and management attention required for a successful supply chain transformation effort. Such efforts usually take at least one year.

- While all five disciplines factor into the transformation, strategy and organization are the two most crucial at the early stages.

- In assessing results, many companies look only at the operations metrics—that is, the concrete numbers. You also need to track whether the change is taking root and whether your people are acquiring the new capabilities needed to ensure sustainable performance over time.

NOTES

CHAPTER 1

1. Andrew Sentence, "Time for West to Adjust to 'New Normal,'" FT.com, July 30, 2012. Accessed November 1, 2012. http://www.ft.com/intl/cms/s/0/9213d8a4-d4d4-11e1-b476-00144feabdc0.html#axzz2Ay16urJX.

2. Bob Bruning, Matt Kaness, and Kevin Lewis, "Close Encounters," *PRTM Insight*, 2007.

3. Inditex Annual Report, 2011; "Fashion Forward," *Economist*, March 24, 2012.

4. PwC Performance Measurement Group.

5. Mithun Samani and Brett Cayot, *The Best of Both Worlds: Strategies for a High-Service, Low-Cost Supply Chain*, PwC, 2011.

6. Ian Mount, "Men's Clothing Firm Wants to Expand into Online Sales," *New York Times*, November 2, 2011.

7. Tropicana company website, http://www.tropicana.com/#/trop_grovetoglass/grovetoglass.swf.

8. Pamela Cheema, "The Right Prescription: Dr Reddy's Laboratories Discusses Their Complex Supply Chain," *LogisticsWeek*, July 5, 2011.

9. Michael Porter, *Competitive Advantage*, New York: Free Press, 1998.

10. Stephanie Clifford, "Nordstrom Links Online Inventories to Real World," *New York Times*, August 23, 2010.

11. Porter, op. cit.

12. Peter Vickers and Charles Thomas, "Reducing Exposure," *PRTM Insight*, 2009.

13. Shoshanah Cohen and Joseph Roussel, *Strategic Supply Chain Management*, New York: McGraw-Hill, 2004, 16.

14. Takahiro Tamino, *Nissan Production Way and Build-to-Order Systems: Comparative Study to Toyota System*, July 3, 2010.

15. "3D Printing: The Shape of Things to Come," *Economist*, December 10, 2011.

16. *Next-Generation Supply Chains: Efficient, Fast, and Tailored*, Global Supply Chain Survey 2013, PwC, 2012, 12–13.

17. Scott Constance, Tavor White, Alex Blanter, and Jim Snyder, "Pot of Gold," *PRTM Insight*, 2010.

18. PwC Performance Measurement Group.

19. Dirk De Waart, "Be SMART About Risk Management," *Supply Chain Management Review*, 2007; Mark Crone, Jeff Holmes, and Kyle Hill, "Ounce of Prevention," *PRTM Insight*, 2009; "10Minutes on Business Continuity Management," PwC, 2012.

20. Reinhard Geissbauer and Shoshanah Cohen, "Globalization in Uncertain Times," *PRTM Insight*, 2009; Reinhard Geissbauer and Michael D'Heur, *Global Supply Chain Trends 2011: Achieving Flexibility in a Volatile World*, PRTM, 2011.

21. David J. Doorey, "The Transparent Supply Chain: From Resistance to Implementation at Nike and Levi-Strauss," *Journal of Business Ethics*, May 19, 2011, 103, 587–603.

22. Jean-Léon Vandoorne, "Danone Bounces Out of the Slump," *Danone 09 Economic and Social Report*, 2009, 43–51.

23. *Insights from the Boardroom 2012: PwC's 2012 Annual Corporate Directors Survey*, PwC, 2012, 23.

BASF

1. Erich-Christian Oerke, "Crop Losses to Pests," *The Journal of Agricultural Science*, Vol. 144, Issue 01, February 2006, 31–43.

CHAPTER 2

1. PwC Performance Measurement Group, SC2 Book Analysis, 2012.

2. Suzanne VanGilder, "Manufacturing IKEA Style," *Surface and Panel*. http://www.surfaceandpanel.com/articles/cool/manufacturing-ikea-style.

3. *Supply Chain Operations Reference Model,* Revision 11.0, Supply Chain Council, October 2012.

4. Michael Giguere and Glen Goldbach, "Segment Your Suppliers to Reduce Risk," *CSCMP's Supply Chain Quarterly,* Quarter 3, 2012. http://www.supplychainquarterly.com/topics/Global/20121001-segment-your-suppliers-to-reduce-risk/. Accessed November 2, 2012.

5. Sanjiv Sharma, "How to Manage and Mitigate Risk Using S&OP," Institute of Business Forecasting and Planning, May 10, 2011. http://www.demand-planning.com/2011/05/10/how-to-manage-and-mitigate-risk-using-sop/.

6. Angharad H. Porteous, Sonali V. Rammohan, Shoshanah Cohen, and Hau L. Lee, "Maturity in Responsible Supply Chain Management" (working paper, Stanford Global Supply Chain Management Forum), Stanford University, October 10, 2012.

7. Shoshanah Cohen and Mark Hermans, "A Blueprint for Green," *PRTM Insight,* Third Quarter 2008.

8. Xerox Green World Alliance, "Managing supplies responsibly," Xerox Corporation, 2010. http://www.xerox.com/digital-printing/latest/GWA-FL-01UA.pdf.

9. Nathaniel Rowe, *The State of Master Data Management 2012,* Aberdeen Group, May 2012.

10. Marcus Messerschmidt and Jan Stüben, "Hidden Treasure, A Global Study on Master Data Management," PwC, November 2011.

ESSILOR

1. "Supply Chain: L'Atout Cache D'Essilor," *Essilook,* June 2010.

CHAPTER 3

1. Russell Goodman, "IBM's Integrated Supply Chain Creates Strategic Value Throughout the Enterprise," *Global Logistics & Supply Chain Strategies,* December 1, 2006.

2. Johnson & Johnson, About J&J, Our Company, http://www.jnj.com. Accessed December 6, 2012.

3. Pier Luigi Sigismondi, "Winning Through Continuous Improvement," presented at the Unilever Investor Relations Conference, November 2012.

4. Nick Martindale, "Scrubbing Up Well: An Interview with Marc Engel," *CPO Agenda*, Spring 2010.

5. http://www.unileverusa.com/mediacenter/pressreleases/2012/Unilever-SupplyChainBreaksintoWorldTop10.aspx

6. *Next-Generation Supply Chains: Efficient, Fast, and Tailored*, Global Supply Chain Survey PwC, 2012.

7. Based on an interview conducted by Shoshanah Cohen with Carlos Garcia, May 15, 2012.

8. *Delivering Results: Growth and Value in a Volatile World*, 15th Annual Global CEO Survey, PwC, 2012.

9. Dan Gilmore, "The Integrated Supply Chain Organization," *Supply Chain Digest*, June 5, 2008.

10. Shoshanah Cohen and Joseph Roussel, *Strategic Supply Chain Management: The Five Disciplines for Top Performance*, New York: McGraw-Hill, 2004, 120.

11. *Next-Generation Supply Chains: Efficient, Fast, and Tailored*, Global Supply Chain Survey 2013, PwC, 2012.

HAIER

1. Haier press release, December 16, 2011, http://www.prnewswire.com/news-releases/haier-ranked-the-1-global-major-appliances-brand-for-3rd-consecutive-year--euromonitor-135722313.html. Accessed March 11, 2013.

2. Tarun Khanna, Krishna Palupu, and Philip Andrews, "Haier: Taking a Chinese Company Global in 2011," *Harvard Business Review*, 2011.

CHAPTER 4

1. Kevin O'Marah, "Collaborative Execution: Speed, Innovation, and Profitability," *SCM World*, March 2012.

2. Shoshanah Cohen and Joseph Roussel, *Strategic Supply Chain Management: The Five Disciplines for Top Performance,* First ed., New York: McGraw-Hill, 2004, 39–48.

3. Shoshanah Cohen and Joseph Roussel, *Strategic Supply Chain Management: The Five Disciplines for Top Performance,* First ed., New York: McGraw-Hill, 2004, 151–152.

4. Michael Giguere and Glen Goldbach, "Segment Your Suppliers to Reduce Risk," *Supply Chain Quarterly,* CSCMP, Q3 2012.

5. Based on an interview conducted by Shoshanah Cohen with Jose Luis Bretones, June 27, 2012.

6. *Creating a Collaborative Enterprise: A Guide to Accelerating Business Value with a Collaboration Framework,* Cisco Systems, 2009, 20.

7. Kevin O'Marah, "Collaborative Execution: Speed, Innovation, and Profitability," *SCM World,* March 2012, 10.

8. Michael Riley and Ashlee Vance, "Inside the Chinese Boom in Corporate Espionage," *Bloomberg BusinessWeek,* March 15, 2012.

9. "The Wheels of Change: Questions & Answers with Ed Melching," *Inbound Logistics,* January 2011.

10. "The Wheels of Change: Questions & Answers with Ed Melching," *Inbound Logistics,* January 2011.

11. http://www.shutl.co.uk/feedback, accessed January 3, 2013.

12. "Supply-Chain Management: Growing Global Complexity Drives Companies into the 'Cloud,'" Knowledge@Wharton, January 12, 2011.

KAISER PERMANENTE

1. "The 2012 Long-Term Budget Outlook," The Congressional Budget Office, June 2012.

2. "Another American Way," *Economist,* April 29, 2010; see www.economist.com/node/16009176.

3. "Kaiser Permanente Leads Nation in Cost Effectiveness Measures," Kaiser Permanente, October 10, 2011.

4. Michael Darling and Sandy Wise, "Not Your Father's Supply Chain," *Materials Management in Health Care,* April 2010.

5. GS1 US, a member of GS1, is an information standards organization that provides unique numbering and identification systems, bar codes, Electronic Product Code-based RFID, data synchronization, and electronic information exchange. The GS1 family of standards includes the GS1 Global Trade Item Number (GTIN) for identifying products, the GS1 Global Location Number (GLN) for identifying locations, and the GS1 Global Data Synchronization Network (GDSN) for sharing standardized product information.

6. Jeff Ferenc, "How Are Your Nurses Spending Their Time?" *Hospitals and Health Networks Magazine,* May 2010.

CHAPTER 5

1. *Supply Chain Operations Reference Model,* Revision 11.0, Supply Chain Council, October 2012, p. i.5.

2. Robert S. Kaplan and David P. Norton, "Using the Balanced Scorecard as a Strategic Management System," *Best of HBR,* Harvard Business School Publishing Corporation, July 2007, p. 2.

3. Supply Chain Council, p. i.5.

LENOVO

1. Shara Tibken, "Lenovo Exec: We Didn't Realize How Big Touch Would Be," CNET, December 5, 2012. http://news.cnet.com/8301-1001_3-57557355-92/ lenovo-exec-we-didnt-realize-how-big-touch-would-be/

CHAPTER 6

1. See also *Next-Generation Supply Chains: Efficient, Fast, and Tailored,* Global Supply Chain Survey 2013, PwC, 2012.

2. PMG selected the 48 companies from a database of hundreds with the broadest and deepest data in various industries for use in this study. PMG chose only those submissions that contained complete quantitative, qualitative, and complexity data. Additionally, PMG included only those submissions that met all data validation screens for submission quality. Twelve of the 48 were considered BICCs.

3. *Next-Generation Supply Chains: Efficient, Fast, and Tailored,* Global Supply Chain Survey 2013, PwC, 2012.

4. Return and Enable, the fifth and sixth of the six major processes, are not included in the PMG benchmarking analysis.

5. *Next-Generation Supply Chains: Efficient, Fast, and Tailored,* Global Supply Chain Survey 2013, PwC, 2012.

6. To facilitate the comparison of complexity management across different companies, PMG normalized the data, dividing each factor by billions of dollars of cost of goods sold (COGS). The number of manufacturing sites, for instance, represents not the actual number of sites but the number of sites per billions of dollars in COGS. PMG used COGS instead of revenue to eliminate the variability connected with margin.

7. For the purposes of this discussion, new product introductions are defined as the number of new finished-product item codes added during the previous fiscal year.

SCHLUMBERGER

1. *World Energy Outlook 2012,* International Energy Agency, November 12, 2012, 51.

CHAPTER 7

1. "Operational Innovation: Fortune Favours the Brave," *Economist Intelligence Unit,* 2007.

2. Benson P. Shapiro, V. Kasturi Rangan, and John J. Sviokla, "Staple Yourself to an Order," *Harvard Business Review,* July 2004.

3. Jakub Wawszczak and Mark Hermans, "Gaining a Competitive Edge with Supply Chain Planning," *Signals of Performance: Supply Chain*, PwC Performance Measurement Group, 2002.

4. Joseph Roussel and Peter Vickers, *Capability Driven Operational Transformation: A New Approach to Large-Scale Change Management*, PRTM, 2008.

BIBLIOGRAPHY

BOOKS, ARTICLES, SURVEY REPORTS, AND REFERENCE WORKS

_____. "3D Printing: The Shape of Things to Come." *Economist*, December 10, 2011.

Bruning, Bob, Kaness, Matt, and Lewis, Kevin. "Close Encounters." *PRTM Insight* (First Quarter 2007): 1–9.

Cheema, Pamela. "The Right Prescription: Dr Reddy's Laboratories Discusses Their Complex Supply Chain." *Logistics Week*, July 5, 2011. http://logisticsweek.com/feature/2011/07/the-right-prescription-dr-reddy%E2%80%99s-laboratories-discusses-their-complex-supply-chain/

Clifford, Stephanie. "Nordstrom Links Online Inventories to Real World." *New York Times*, August 23, 2010. http://www.nytimes.com/2010/08/24/business/24shop.html?_r=0

Cohen, Shoshanah and Roussel, Joseph. *Strategic Supply Chain Management.* New York: McGraw-Hill, 2004.

Cohen, Shoshanah and Hermans, Mark. "A Blueprint for Green." *PRTM Insight* (Third Quarter 2008): 2–8.

Constance, Scott, White, Tavor, Blanter, Alex, and Snyder, Jim. "Pot of Gold." *PRTM Insight* (First Quarter 2010): 1–5.

_____. *Creating a Collaborative Enterprise: A Guide to Accelerating Business Value with a Collaboration Framework.* Cisco Systems, 2009.

Crone, Mark, Holmes, Jeff, and Hill, Kyle. "Ounce of Prevention." *PRTM Insight,* 2009.

_____. *Delivering Results: Growth and Value in a Volatile World.* 15th Annual Global CEO Survey. PwC, 2012.

De Waart, Dirk. "Be SMART About Risk Management." *Supply Chain Management Review,* 2007.

Doorey, Dick. "The Transparent Supply Chain: from Resistance to Implementation at Nike and Levi-Strauss." *Journal of Business Ethics* 103 (May 19, 2011): 587–603.

_____. *Global Supply Chain Trends 2011: Achieving Flexibility in a Volatile World.* PRTM, 2011.

Geissbauer, Reinhard and Cohen, Shoshanah. "Globalization in Uncertain Times." *PRTM Insight* (Fourth Quarter 2008): 2–7.

Giguere, Michael and Goldbach, Glen. "Segment Your Suppliers to Reduce Risk." *CSCMP's Supply Chain Quarterly* (Quarter 3, 2012). Accessed November 2, 2012. http://www.supplychainquarterly.com/topics/Global/20121001-segment-your-suppliers-to-reduce-risk/.

Gilmore, Dan. "The Integrated Supply Chain Organization." *Supply Chain Digest,* June 5, 2008.

Goodman, Russell. "IBM's Integrated Supply Chain Creates Strategic Value Throughout the Enterprise." *Global Logistics & Supply Chain Strategies,* December 1, 2006.

Haier press release, December 16, 2011, http://www.prnewswire.com/news-releases/haier-ranked-the-1-global-major-appliances-brand-for-3rd-consecutive-year--euromonitor-135722313.html. Accessed March 11, 2013.

Gouillart, Francis and Deck, Mark. "The Craft of Co-Creation: Taking B2B Collaboration to a Whole New Level." *PRTM Insight* (Second Quarter 2011): 1–6.

_____. "Inditex Annual Report, 2011; Fashion Forward." *Economist,* March 24, 2012.

_____. *Insights from the Boardroom 2012: PwC's 2012 Annual Corporate Directors Survey.* PwC, 2012.

Jacka, J. Mike and Keller, Paulette. *Business Process Mapping: Improving Customer Satisfaction*, 2nd ed. Hoboken: John Wiley and Sons, 2009.

Kaplan, Robert S. and Norton, David P. "Using the Balanced Scorecard as a Strategic Management System." *Harvard Business Review*, July 2007. http://hbr.org/2007/07/using-the-balanced-scorecard-as-a-strategic-management-system/ar/1

Martindale, Nick. "Scrubbing Up Well: An Interview with Marc Engel." *CPO Agenda*, Spring 2010. http://www.supplybusiness.com/previous-articles/spring–2010/features/interview-scrubbing-up-well/?locale=en

Messerschmidt, Marcus and Stüben, Jan. "Hidden Treasure: A Global Study on Master Data Management." PwC, November 2011.

Mount, Ian. "Men's Clothing Firm Wants to Expand into Online Sales." *New York Times*, November 2, 2011.

_____. *Next-Generation Supply Chains: Efficient, Fast, and Tailored.* Global Supply Chain Survey 2013, PwC, 2012.

Oerke, Erich-Christian. "Crop Losses to Pests." *The Journal of Agricultural Science*. Vol. 144 Issue 01 (February 2006): 31–43.

O'Marah, Kevin. "Collaborative Execution: Speed, Innovation, and Profitability." *SCM World*, March 2012.

_____. Our Company, Johnson & Johnson. Accessed December 6, 2012, http://www.jnj.com/connect/about-jnj/.

_____. "Operational Innovation: Fortune Favours the Brave." *Economist Intelligence Unit*, 2007.

Porteous, Angharad H., Rammohan, Sonali V., Cohen, Shoshanah, and Lee, Hau L. "Maturity in Responsible Supply Chain Management." Working paper. Stanford Global Supply Chain Management Forum, Stanford University, October 10, 2012.

Porter, Michael. *Competitive Advantage*. New York: Free Press, 1998.

Riley, Michael and Vance, Ashlee. "Inside the Chinese Boom in Corporate Espionage." *Bloomberg BusinessWeek*, March 15, 2012. http://www.businessweek.com/articles/2012–03–14/inside-the-chinese-boom-in-corporate-espionage

Roussel, Joseph and Vickers, Peter. "Capability Driven Operational Transformation: A New Approach to Large-Scale Change Management." PRTM, 2008.

Rowe, Nathaniel. "The State of Master Data Management 2012." Aberdeen Group, May 2012.

Samani, Mithun and Cayot, Brett. "The Best of Both Worlds: Strategies for a High-Service, Low-Cost Supply Chain." PwC, 2011.

Sentence, Andrew. "Time for West to Adjust to 'New Normal.'" Accessed November 1, 2012, http://www.ft.com/intl/cms/s/0/9213d8a4-d4d4-11e1-b476-00144feabdco.html#axzz2Ay16urJX.

Shapiro, Benson P., Rangan, V. Kasturi, and Sviokla, John J. "Staple Yourself to an Order." *Harvard Business Review* (July–August 2004): 113–121.

Sharma, Sanjiv. "How to Manage and Mitigate Risk Using S&OP." Institute of Business Forecasting and Planning, May 10, 2011. Accessed January 7, 2013. http://www.demand-planning.com/2011/05/10/how-to-manage-and-mitigate-risk-using-sop/.

_____. Supply Chain Operations Reference Model, Revision 11.0. Supply Chain Council, October 2012.

"Supply-chain Management: Growing Global Complexity Drives Companies into the 'Cloud.'" *Knowledge@Wharton*, January 12, 2011. http://knowledge.wharton.upenn.edu/article.cfm?articleid=2669

Tamino, Takahiro. "Nissan Production Way and Build-to-Order Systems: Comparative Study to Toyota System." July 3, 2010.

_____. "10Minutes on Business Continuity Management." PwC, 2012.

_____. "10Minutes on Supply Chain Flexibility." PwC, 2013.

_____. Tropicana Products, Inc. Accessed January 7, 2013. http://www.tropicana.com/#/trop_grovetoglass/grovetoglass.swf.

_____. Unilever Supply Chain Company, Unilever. Accessed December 6, 2012. http://www.unilever.ch/karriere/einstiegsmoeglichkeiten/supply_chain_company/.

_____. "Unilever supply chain in top 10 wereldwijd." Unilever. Accessed January 7, 2013. http://www.unilever.nl/media/persberichten/2012/Unilever-SupplyChainintop10wereldwijd.aspx.

Vandoorne, Jean-Léon. "Danone Bounces Out of the Slump." *Danone 09 Economic and Social Report* (2009): 43–51.

VanGilder, Suzanne. "Manufacturing IKEA Style." *Surface and Panel*. Accessed January 7, 2012. http://www.surfaceandpanel.com/articles/cool/manufacturing-ikea-style.

Vickers, Peter and Thomas, Charles. "Reducing Exposure." *PRTM Insight* (Fourth Quarter 2009): 24–32.

Wawszczak, Jakub and Hermans, Mark. "Gaining a Competitive Edge with Supply Chain Planning, Signals of Performance: Supply Chain." Performance Measurement Group, 2002.

_____, "The Wheels of Change: Questions & Answers with Ed Melching." *Inbound Logistics*, January 2011. http://www.inboundlogistics.com/cms/article/the-wheels-of-change-questions-and-answers-with-ed-melching/

Xerox Green World Alliance. "Managing supplies responsibly." Xerox Corporation, 2010. Accessed January 7, 2013. http://www.xerox.com/digital-printing/latest/GWAFL–01UA.pdf.

INTERVIEWS

Christine Altimore (Kaiser Permanente), interview with Shoshanah Cohen and Julia Heskel, August 29, 2012.

Magali Anderson (Schlumberger), interview with Joseph Roussel, Marc Waco, and Julia Heskel, September 24, 2012.

Andreas Backhaus (BASF), interview with Joseph Roussel and Julia Heskel, August 8, 2012.

Stéphane Biquet (Schlumberger), interview with Joseph Roussel and Julia Heskel, September 20, 2012.

Jose Luis Bretones (McDonald's), interview with Shoshanah Cohen, June 27, 2012.

Claude Brignon (Essilor), interview with Joseph Roussel and Julia Heskel, August 7, 2012.

Natasha Cherednichenko (Schlumberger), interview with Joseph Roussel and Julia Heskel, October 3, 2012.

Henry Comolet (BASF), interview with Joseph Roussel and Julia Heskel, November 12, 2012.

John Egan (Lenovo), interview with Shoshanah Cohen and Julia Heskel, November 28, 2012.

Brooke Fan (Kaiser Permanente), interview with Shoshanah Cohen and Julia Heskel, August 29, 2012.

Greg Frazier (Avnet), interview with Shoshanah Cohen, June 26, 2012.

Carlos Garcia (Korn/Ferry International), interview with Shoshanah Cohen, May 15, 2012.

Liang Haishan (Haier), interview with Joseph Roussel, Lillian Wang, Craig Kerr, Helen Zhang, and Julia Heskel, October 17, 2012.

Michael Innes (Kaiser Permanente), interview with Shoshanah Cohen and Julia Heskel, August 29, 2012.

Eric Javellaud (Essilor), interview with Joseph Roussel and Julia Heskel, July 16, 2012; September 16, 2012; and September 21, 2012.

Laurel Junk (Kaiser Permanente), interview with Shoshanah Cohen, August 10, 2012; and August 29, 2012.

Lim Chin Chye (Haier), interview with Joseph Roussel, Lillian Wang, Craig Kerr, Helen Zhang, and Julia Heskel, September 3, 2012; and October 16, 2012.

Tammy Macaluso (Schlumberger), interview with Joseph Roussel, Marc Waco, and Julia Heskel, October 25, 2012.

Traci May (BASF), interview with Joseph Roussel and Julia Heskel, November 23, 2012.

Geoff Meinken (Stanford University), interview with Shoshanah Cohen, September 30, 2012.

Carl Mount (Yum! Restaurants International), interview with Shoshanah Cohen, June 29, 2012.

Temara Peet (Schlumberger), interview with Joseph Roussel, Marc Waco, and Julia Heskel, October 4, 2012.

Robert Schlaefli (Exalt Communications), interview with Shoshanah Cohen, July 2, 2012.

Gerry Smith (Lenovo), interview with Shoshanah Cohen and Julia Heskel, September 4, 2012.

Phil Teijeira (Schlumberger), interview with Joseph Roussel and Julia Heskel, September 24, 2012.

Gérard Tourencq (Essilor), interview with Joseph Roussel and Julia Heskel, September 21, 2012.

Xiao Hui (Haier), interview with Joseph Roussel, Lillian Wang, Craig Kerr, Helen Zhang, and Julia Heskel, October 17, 2012.

Gray Williams (Oclaro), interview with Shoshanah Cohen, June 28, 2012.

Yang Qiaoshan (Haier), interview with Joseph Roussel, Lillian Wang, Craig Kerr, Helen Zhang, and Julia Heskel, October 17, 2012.

Zou Xiwen (Haier), interview with Joseph Roussel, Lillian Wang, Craig Kerr, Helen Zhang, and Julia Heskel, October 17, 2012.

INDEX

ABOUT THE AUTHORS

Shoshanah Cohen is director of the Global Supply Chain Management Forum, an academic / industry partnership at Stanford University's Graduate School of Business. Prior to joining Stanford, she was a senior partner at PRTM Management Consulting, where she led PRTM's Global Supply Chain Innovation practice. She is a frequent writer and speaker on global operations strategy. She holds a BS in Industrial Engineering from Stanford University, an MA in Technology Strategy from Boston University, and an MBA from Harvard University.

Joseph Roussel is a partner in PwC's Strategy and Operations practice. Prior to joining PwC, he was a partner at PRTM Management Consulting, where he helped develop the original SCOR® model. A graduate of Louisiana State University, l'Université Libre de Bruxelles, and The Fletcher School at Tufts University, he regularly leads executive education in operations innovation and transformation.

www.ingramcontent.com/pod-product-compliance
Lightning Source LLC
Chambersburg PA
CBHW060331220326
41598CB00023B/2672